A. P. Herbert

A BIOGRAPHY

To
Gwen; and to Crystal, Jocelyn, Lavender, and John, with memories of happy times at 12 Hammersmith Terrace

Contents

List of Illustrations

Author's Acknowledgments

For facilities, permissions to quote, other forms of help, and for an abundance of goodwill, I thank Lady Herbert, her family, and the late Sir Alan Herbert's executors; the editor of *The Times* for publishing an announcement that brought a splendid response from admirers of APH and his work; Mr Paul Yeats-Edwards, FLA, Fellows' Librarian, Winchester College, for answering questions about APH as a scholar there; Mr Jack Parr, Mr Frank Morley, and Professor L. F. Rushbrook Williams for information about APH at Oxford; Brigadier B. B. Rackham, CBE, MC, DL, President of the Royal Naval Division Association, a fellow officer of APH's in the First World War; Mr H. F. Ellis, a *Punch* colleague of his between the wars and after; Commander S. R. Brown, Lieutenant-Commander L. M. Bates, and Mrs J. M. Patterson, for information, technical and anecdotal, concerning APH's Second World War service on the Thames.

I also acknowledge with thanks the helpful co-operation of The Arts Council of Great Britain; the Society of Authors and Mr Victor Bonham-Carter, the general secretary; the Performing Right Society (Mr Royce Whale and Mr G. M. Neighbour, MA); the British Copyright Council (Mr Reynell Wreford); the Chief Herald, Genealogical Office (Office of Arms), Dublin; Miss Winifred Matthews, Information Officer, Trinity College, Dublin; the Town Clerk & Chief Executive, London Borough of Hammersmith; the staffs of the House of Commons Library and the London Library; the Public Record Office of Ireland; the Ministry of Defence Naval Personnel (Pay Division); the Judge Advocate General's Office (Mr E. Moelwyn Hughes); Mr William Roberts, The Bancroft Library, University of California; Mr Brooke Whiting, Department of Special Collections, Research Library, University of California; Mr Gordon Phillips, archivist, *The Times*; Mr Malcolm

Muggeridge and Mr Bernard Hollowood, successive editors of *Punch*; Mr R. G. G. Price, historian of *Punch*; the General Committee of the Savage Club and Mr Alan Wykes, honorary secretary; Mr John Russell, owner of the Pearsall Smith copyrights; Mr Michael Horniman (Messrs A. P. Watt & Son); Sir Arthur Bryant, CH, CBE; Mr T. C. Foley, OBE (The Pedestrians' Association for Road Safety); Mr T. A. Ende; Mr Vivian Ellis; Mr Anthony Rubinstein (Messrs Rubinstein Nash & Co); the late Mrs Audrey Scott, and the late Lieutenant-General Sir James Gammell, KCB, DSO, MC.

As APH himself would have it, I salute also Mr Robert Aickman, founder of the Inland Waterways Association; Mr Stanley Atkins, crew member of HMS *Water Gipsy*; Sir Max Aitken, Bt; Mr Alan Dent; Lieutenant-Commander G. A. Jones (East Coast Sail Trust); His Honour Commander L. K. A. Block; Mr E. J. Beaven (Quicksilver Switchgear Ltd); Mr E. J. S. Brisland, *Daily Express* library; Miss Angela Baddeley; Mr Gerard Bryant; Mr Vernon Bartlett; Miss Elizabeth Barber, CBE; Mr George Baker CBE, FRCM; Mrs Malcolm Begg; Sir Rupert De la Bere, BT, KCVO; Major W. H. Carter, MA; Mr Ian Campbell; Mr Frank Carr, CB; Mrs Caroleen Conquest; Mr John Dodwell; Mr Tom Driberg; Mr Brian Davidson, CBE; Sir Trevor Evans; Mrs P. Ward Freeman; Mr Trevor Fenwick; Miss Diana Gardner; Miss Ena Gladwell, Epsom Reference Library; Mr Anthony Hern; Mr Sam Heppner; Mr Lionel Hale; Mr Richard Hughes; Sir Geoffrey Harmsworth, Bt.; the Revd H. S. Holden; Mr Laurence Irving, OBE; Sir Geoffrey Jackson, KCMG; Miss Susan Jeffreys, *Punch* Librarian; Mr Frederic Lloyd, Savoy Theatre Ltd; Dr C. G. Lawson; Sir Martin Lindsay of Dowhill, Bt, CBE, DSO; Prebendary G. A. Lewis Lloyd; Mr Robert H. Land, Reference Department, Library of Congress, Washington, DC; Captain John Litchfield, RN; Mr Philip Larkin, MA; Mr John G. Milner; Lord Marchwood; Sir John Masterman, OBE; Mr M. Morton-Evans; Mr Raymond Moss; Mr Augustus Muir; Mrs E. D. Man; Mr Derek McCullough; Mr Frank Muir; Mr E. E. A. Norris; Mr Beverley Nichols; Editor, the *National Westminster*; Major and Mrs W. O'Bryen; Mr Roy Plomley, OBE; Mr Martin Parr, CBE; Mr Victor Pasmore; Mr Peter Pound; Dr F. R. Philps; Miss Julie Phillips, The Oxford House, Bethnal Green; Miss Winifred Phillips, Programme Correspondence Section, BBC; Mr John Pudney; Dr Magnus Pyke, FRSE; Mr

J. P. Roberts; Miss Edith Reynolds; Miss Margaret Rawlings (Lady Barlow); Mr John Russell (Logan Pearsall Smith papers); Mr F. A. Rhoden; Mr Gerry Stewart; Mr A. L. Stampa; Commander I. A. Scrymgeour-Wedderburn, RN (Retd); Mr Peter Saunders; Mr Raglan Squire, FRIBA; Sir Charles Taylor, TD; Mr Eric Udale; Mr Michael Venner; Mr H. L. Withrington; Mr Ian Watt; Mrs Giles Hunt.

For invaluable help of a specialist kind I record my thanks to Mrs J. St G. Saunders (Writer's & Speaker's Research); and to Miss Helen Rogers for keeping a keen eye open for literals and punctuation errors and omissions while producing an impeccable typescript.

TENTERDEN   R. P.

The following pictures are reprinted by permission of *Radio Times* Picture Library.

APH in 1918; Rehearsing for *Big Ben* 1946; Sunday Night Broadcasts for the BBC in 1941.

An Heirloom Nose

'You know he changed his name from Hertzog?' Evidently I showed disbelief, for A. G. Macdonell transposed his question into an assertion that A. P. Herbert was not of Anglo-Irish descent, as I had long understood.

Macdonell's intelligence and wit had been displayed to the reading public of the thirties in his lauded book, *England, Their England*.[1] Those social attributes suffused his personality. His military bearing, his clipped incisive speech, suggested the *beau sabreur*. Naïvely, perhaps, I was made uncomfortable by that revelation of his susceptibility to vulgar prejudice, for there could be no doubting the implication of his remark. It was provoked by my mentioning that I had been asked by the then editor of *The Strand Magazine* to write a 'profile' of A. P. Herbert, whose name was becoming familiar to a public that never read *Punch*.

My attempted rebuttal had no effect. Like A. P. Herbert, 'Archie' Macdonell was an Old Wykehamist. His perverse notion derived from his Winchester years. 'You'll find I am right,' he said. 'His name used to be Hertzog,' on which slightly discordant note we went our respective ways after a companionable lunch at Oddenino's. It was my last encounter with him, except through the post, his last letter to me subscribed: '*Yrs till death doe us pt*'. It parted him from his friends with shattering suddenness a few months later.

Reviewing the incident now, I reflect that no such *idée fixe* would have found lodgement in the mind of APH (as I shall hereinafter refer to him, in deference to the majority who knew him only by his initials). He was remarkably free from the crude responses to race, class, creed. If sometimes his prejudices seemed quixotic, they were never morbidly self-centred or mean. Mostly, they had the sanction of common sense, as when he made play with the more ponderous fatuities of the law. Only occasionally did emotion hold sway; for example, in his scorn for the 'disgusting ecstasies' of modern professional footballers.

His nose and his wit inevitably induced the speculation that he was of Jewish origin. A speaker at Hyde Park Corner, declaiming from the rostrum of the Catholic Truth Society against APH's Matrimonial Causes Bill (1937), made the disparaging remark: 'Look at his nose! That will tell you what kind of a man it is who is trying to tear up the institution of marriage by the roots!' Travelling shortly afterwards to Manchester, APH sat in the train opposite a priest, who turned out to be the misguided spokesman for the Catholic Truth Society. By journey's end, APH had heard the priest's confession of error. 'Like the Catholic Truth Society,' he subsequently wrote, 'I prefer the truth'; and the truth about his ancestry is that his father was 'full-blooded Irish' (his phrase), his mother English.

He was born on 24 September 1890, the eldest of the three sons of Patrick Herbert, and a grandson of William Herbert, merchant, so-called in the records of Trinity College, Dublin, where Patrick Herbert completed his education after leaving Clongowes College, Co. Kildare, then the leading Catholic boarding-school for boys. Patrick Herbert gained a junior clerkship at the India Office in 1872, and thereafter made his home in England. His official career did not take him far up the ladder of promotion. He became a Resident Clerk in 1885. He edited the India Office List, and was said to have devised the Office cipher code.

APH wrote only sketchily about his paternal forebears; he 'was not so clear' about that side of the family. He stated in print that his father was 'the last of a long line of Irish Catholics',[2] descended from the Herberts of Muckross, which he did not bother to discover, until late in his life, was in Co. Kerry. Nor was he aware that the Muckross Herberts were allegedly a Protestant line. He remembered that his father wore a signet-ring bearing the crest of the Pembroke earls, 'who are Herberts too but I have never gone into that'. Had he done so presumably he would have encountered the same obstacles as the researchers of the Genealogical Office at Dublin Castle, who reported in 1974 that no trace of William Herbert, APH's grandfather, is to be found in the available records. William Herbert, who clearly was able to give his son a good education, remains obstinately in the shadows, whether as 'merchant' – *vide* the Trinity College records – or as 'esquire' as shown on his son's marriage certificate.

Patrick Herbert, APH's father, was 40 when on 7 December 1889 he married Beatrice Eugenie Selwyn, 24, daughter of Sir Charles Jasper Selwyn, deceased (1815–1869) a Lord Justice of Appeal. Presumably the Selwyns, whose family lustre warranted them six entries in *The Dictionary of National Biography*, were sufficiently assured of the Herbert social standing. A Selwyn bishop officiated at the wedding at St George's, Hanover Square, London W. – Sir Charles's brother John, Bishop of Melanesia. Their father, George Augustus Selwyn, was sometime Primate of New Zealand and the ninety-first bishop of Lichfield, Staffordshire. Bishop John Selwyn had volunteered to serve in his Pacific diocese in succession to the martyred Bishop Patteson. Those devoted overseas labours shortened John Selwyn's life. He returned to England to pass his few remaining years in the relatively easeful post of Master of Selwyn College, Cambridge, founded in memory of his father.

The bridegroom signed the register at St George's as Patrick Herbert. For what reason he later equipped himself with two additional forenames, to be known thereafter 'by adoption and presumption' (according to his will made in 1914) as Patrick Herbert Coghlan Herbert, is now beyond explanation. If there was social satisfaction in signing himself with three initials he seldom indulged it. At the India Office, and among his friends, he was known as P. H. Herbert.

His deceased father-in-law was the youngest son of William Selwyn, an eminent nineteenth-century lawyer who, as Treasurer of Lincoln's Inn, tutored the Prince Consort in British constitutional history. The Prince recalled him as 'old, baldheaded, lame, with staring eyes, skin like parchment, and a voice like a lion'.[3] Sir Charles, his son, represented Cambridge University in Parliament – one of his distinctions that went unnoted and probably unnoticed by APH, who was to enter the House of Commons as member for 'the other place'. Sir Charles was Solicitor-General in the Derby administration of 1867. Disraeli, who nominated him for office, also made him a privy councillor. Although he lacked forensic brilliance, he was 'listened to with great attention by the court' (*DNB*). Consistently making a good impression, he also made one of the Bar fortunes of his time, leaving £110,000.

APH inherited the Selwyn family nose; what else genetically is speculation that might take into account the consanguinity of George Augustus Selwyn, an eighteenth-century 'wit and politician' whose mother was a woman of the Bedchamber to Queen Caroline, wife of George the Second. A scuffle in her house in Cleveland Court, St James's, inspired a celebrated scene in *The Beggar's Opera*, notably revived in the Hammersmith of APH in the 1930s.

The ancestral nose impelled APH's naval brother Sidney to exclaim, on approaching a Selwyn tomb with its recumbent figure: 'Why, there's Alan!' APH commemorated it in lines called *The Heirloom*:

> This is the nose that, age by age,
>   Adorns our precious line.
> Full many a Prelate, Prince and Sage
>   In carven stone recline.
> All, all distinguished, more or less,
> By this peculiar nosiness,
> Though few of them, I must confess,
>   Were quite as large as mine.

Lineage did not greatly interest him. The indifference implied in verses he wrote on an anthropological theme, *I don't seem to care, What my origins were*,[4] was carried over into the domestic realm. He was confused about ancestral names and status; his great-grandfather was not a bishop, as he once claimed in a speech, but a bishop's brother; his grandfather's Christian name was not George, as he wrote, but Charles. He would have been unlikely to show more than casual interest in his youthful resemblance to one of the few notable Herberts of the Wilton line, namely Sidney, who was Peel's Secretary of State for War. Nor would he have been more than mildly struck by the coincidence that the signature of a contemporary member of that line uncannily resembled his own.[5]

The best-known Herbert of our time was not given to self-aggrandisement. Every honour, testimonial, tribute, that came his way was 'surprising but gratifying', his stock reply to congratulations on those occasions. None who knew him doubted that he spoke truly.

He referred to Ireland as his 'near native land' but he was a stranger to it, except by repute. He went once to Dublin to lecture; an over-night stay. The only other time that he set foot on Irish soil was when landing briefly at Shannon airport in 1943. One cannot imagine him flourishing his Irish paternity as a card of introduction. He had little use for the freemasonries of nationality or class; much for the human comity.

His father is recalled as having no marked Irish accent. Although he was a cradle Catholic whose two sisters had taken the veil, he seems to have had no difficulty in adjusting himself to the formidable Anglican bias of the Selwyns. His right to determine his children's religion apparently went into abeyance. All three boys were christened in the Anglican communion. As the châtelaine of Ashtead Lodge near Leatherhead, Surrey, where they were born, their mother was content to see that they were regular in their church-going; otherwise, her eldest son said, 'she dealt gently' with them in matters of religion. In his adult years, APH considered himself 'a foul weather worshipper, an inferior religious species', while retaining his respect for the liturgy of the Church of England, with nostalgic feelings for certain hymns A & M, especially *The day Thou gavest . . .*

Ashtead Lodge is included in the 'List of Antiquities in the administrative county of Surrey', 1965. According to the *Proceedings of the Leatherhead and District Local History Society*, Vol. 2, No. 4, 'it is very lamentable that such a fine building has been allowed to fall into decay and ruin'. As Patrick Herbert's name does not appear in a list of Ashtead Lodge owners between 1882 and 1909, it is assumed that he held the property on lease.

In one of his rare lapses into sentimental reminiscence, APH wrote that he had 'every reason to suppose' that he had a happy childhood. 'We had a nice big garden with a shrubbery for adventure, and a capital wood not far away. My father and mother gave every satisfaction. I was a good boy on the whole; but was beaten now and then with a wide strap, as a rule for refusing to finish my tapioca or sago pudding. I remember this without resentment; indeed, since I now know that tapioca and sago are quite devoid of vitamins or virtue, it is pleasant to think how early I formed the habit of being right.'[6]

He put dental treatment first among the crises of his childhood. 'One expected to be hurt, and if you had teeth like mine you generally were hurt.' He remembered having a newly stopped tooth mechanically polished. 'The dentist was a keen rose grower and was complaining about greenfly. His hand slipped – or perhaps he was making a gesture descriptive of appropriate action against that pest. The whirling little disc plunged into my tongue and tore a nasty furrow in it.'[7]

Still more vividly he remembered when and how his five-year-old innocence was shattered. He was taken daily to an infants' school in

Epsom by dogcart. It was driven by Pat, an Irishman from Cork. There was a morning when traffic was held up in the main street. The dogcart came to a standstill outside a baker's shop. Prominent in the window was a pile of shining brown buns. 'I climbed down, went into the shop, and said to the first lady I saw: "Can I have a bun, please!"' He was given one, with the polite enquiry: 'And how is your dear mother today?' Inspired by the pervading good nature, he asked: 'Can I have a bun for Pat, please?' A young girl assistant, Rose, also from Cork, escorted him into the street. She and Pat talked about Ireland, while the young APH munched his penny bun. 'This, I suppose, was my first contact with the great world, my first solo flight, as it were. It struck me as a friendly and enjoyable world. You had only to ask politely for what you wanted and you got it.'

Driving back from school that afternoon, Pat asked him: 'Would you be liking another penny bun?' The morning's 'pleasant cere- mony' was repeated, except that Pat and Rose 'talked longer than before' having, it appeared, 'fallen instantly in love'. (They married, 'and opened a cake shop in Leatherhead'.) Thereafter, 'twice a day, five days a week, for many weeks', he was set down at the baker's shop to ask for penny buns. 'It came to be part of the natural order of things.' Then the blow fell, 'terribly'. His father studied the household bills. 'I heard him ask my mother about a bill from the bun shop. "Here, I say, what's this? Two hundred and fifty-nine penny buns?"' APH remembered 'very well the sense of shock' that followed his discovery that this was not after all a world of free penny buns.

He associated that disturbing realization with a mishap that marked him for life. An India Office colleague of his father named Frederic Welles Newmarch lunched one Sunday at Ashtead Lodge. He was delighted by the bun story. 'You'll go to the top, my boy!' he said and, with symbolic exuberance, swung the young APH aloft to his shoulder. It was an ill-judged gesture. 'I went straight over and fell head first on to the nursery fender behind him.'

There were fears of spinal injury. He was made to lie on a 'back board' sloped at fifty degrees, two hours a day, for weeks after. Whether or not a later diagnosis of cervical spondylosis was the right one, he said that he felt ever after that his head was 'stuck on in the wrong place'. He developed a tendency to stoop and with it a curious involuntary upward jerk of the head that in schooldays

gained him the nickname Peck. It remained a personal mannerism
for the rest of his life. In moments of argumentative stress he was
given to nervous blinking accompanied by a certain hesitancy in
pronunciation; for instance, as a public speaker he would never risk
the word 'illegitimate'.

Writing his autobiography, he made more of his nursery accident
than of the death of his mother, which occurred when he was eight,
shortly before he was 'packed off' to his preparatory school, The
Grange, Folkestone. His memories of her were crystallized in his
remark that she was 'a well-named Beatrice'. She was thirty-three, a
victim of tuberculosis, then commonly known as consumption.
That early bereavement may have accounted for his singular
freedom from envy and jealousy. Intuition might also see in it the
source of the peculiar private reticence that baffled those who most
closely shared his life and affections, and was liable to disconcert
those who did not. Emotionally, he always seemed to be on his guard.

The chronic invalidism of the mistress of Ashtead Lodge led to the
ascendancy of the family nanny, Millicent Deakin, still affectionately
remembered as Deakie, a small-framed, sturdy spinster who became
the strongest influence in the Herbert boys' upbringing, giving her
best years to playing the maternal role in their lives. She managed
the household, and in all that related to it domestically her decisions
were mostly final. One of her foibles was an inflexible faith in the
remedial power of brandy in almost every ill. Parental chastisement,
the resort to the wide strap, was more often than not applied at her
request. Deakie surely merited more than the glancing reference to
her as 'our faithful nanny' in APH's memoirs. Her concern for his
personal well-being remained active up to her death at over eighty,
when he was well on in years.

Patrick Herbert's salary as an India Office clerk was £470 a
year. His wife had inherited £15,000 from her father's estate at
her coming-of-age, having previously received from it an allowance
of £300 a year. At her death in 1898 she left £905. That Patrick
Herbert sought extra-mural earnings was confirmed by his election
to the Savage Club in 1892 as a 'Literary Journalist'. No evidence
of his work has been traced. His chief sponsor for the club was Dr
Phineas Abraham of 66 Harley Street, a founder-member of the Der-
matological Society of Great Britain and Ireland, which suggests that
the candidate's literary qualification was not powerfully endorsed.

The young APH's growing pains, physical and mental, were those of the next boy and the next, having no exceptional significance as personal history. Two years earlier, Harold Nicolson had been 'so unhappy' at The Grange, Folkestone.[8] With APH it was quite otherwise. 'If I was not happy at The Grange I must have been hard to please.'

He learned 'a lot of Latin and English', won prizes that amounted to 'a row of bound volumes', and acquired a taste for the piano that later added to the pleasure in life of himself and his friends. In spite of hay fever, an increasing plague of his youth, he shone on The Grange playing-fields too, winning more prizes.

Adolescence and Winchester College changed the pattern. Sterner competition brought set-backs. The emphasis, anyhow, was on success at work rather than at play, so much so that slackers were likely to be asked to leave — 'superjammed', in the Wykehamist vocabulary. He graced the Winchester tradition of serious study by winning the King's Medal for English Verse. Prosody was said to be 'in the air' at Winchester, and a prefect named Heseltine[9] who put the collected works of C. S. Calverley in his hands bestowed on him a particular boon. 'That fixed my fate', he wrote. Had he known, he could have stood by Calverley's grave in the cemetery at Folkestone; not that the *memento mori* mood was ever strongly upon him.

At Winchester he was a willing apprentice to the art of platform speaking, active in his membership of the college debating society, proposing more often than opposing: for example, 'That this House disapproves of vivisection' (October 1908); 'That it is desirable to extend the suffrage in some form to women '(December 1908); or speaking in favour of public schools' reform (February 1909); supporting the motion 'that this House views with extreme disfavour the approaching conquest of the air' (November 1909). When, at a meeting of the college Shakespeare Society, he read the part of the Bishop of Carlisle in *Richard II*, readers of *The Wykehamist* were informed that he was 'entirely wanting in dramatic quality' and 'made no impression at all' (November 1909). The same year, he won the King's Medal for English Speech, reciting a passage from Macaulay. 'A very spirited oration,' said Mr Asquith, the Prime Minister, handing him the medal.

Next, he won the King's Medal for English Verse with his dramatic poem, *Messina*, its fifty stanzas reflecting the dismay caused by the Sicilian earthquake of 1908. Like the similar great disaster at San Francisco two years before, it shook civilized nerves; and there were many who believed it to be a renewed demonstration of divine wrath.

> Once have we heard, and once again,
>   That clarion messenger of God,
> Twice heard the earth cry out in pain,
>   At the Almighty's nod.
>
> Twice this our age hath bowed its head
>   'Neath Thine inevitable doom,
> Twice rendered up its toll of dead
>   To the embracing tomb.

Messina was subsequently discarded by its author as 'an odious composition – 200 lines of tosh'. Meanwhile, as the holder of two King's Medals, he could walk proudly among his fellows. In Wykehamist parlance, he was a 'tug', a clever chap, whose achievement was held worthier than any playing-field victory. Calverley and W. S. Gilbert – the last-named discovered through the melodies of Sullivan – infected him with 'the itch to write in rhyme' (his words). His *Song of a Socialist*, written while he was still at Winchester, was prompted by the Labour Party's formal adoption of Socialist doctrine at its annual conference:

> Woe to the owner of titles and palaces,
>   Nothing for you in the Socialist plan.
> Projects in which not a shadow of malice is,
>   Nought but a fervent affection for Man;
> Law, and religion, and order must tarry, at
>   Least till he's finished dividing the pelf,
> Croesus disgorging to 'Arry and 'Arriet;
>   Everything else can look after itself.
>
> All will be Comrades and Brothers (for Mr he
>   Thinks should be changed into Comrade, you know),
> All will be equally rich, though a mystery
>   Seems to encircle the when and the how.
> That is sufficient to baffle the cleverest,
>   But we shall all have the deuce of a time,
> Money, perhaps, will be wafted from Everest:
>   Possibly, anything does for a rhyme.

Light verse had contributed to the reputation, if not precisely to the circulation, of *Punch*. From Winchester, APH sent verses to the offices in Bouverie Street. Instead of rejection slips, he received marginal notes of encouragement and suggestion from the editor, Sir Owen Seaman (1861–1936); for example: 'Verse three, logically, conflicts with verse one'. Or: 'I don't like the rhyme'. Against the couplet:

> Full dress (with decorations) will be worn
> When General Officers are shot at dawn,

Seaman wrote: 'Do you say *dorn*?' It was rare and exemplary editorial behaviour, and APH never ceased to appreciate it. Sixty years after, he wrote: 'I still marvel at the trouble he took.'

APH's facile versifying did not inhibit him from giving a sympathetic ear to the loftier poetic aims of an unhappy college contemporary named Robert Nichols, whose work he encouraged 'even if I did not understand or like it'. He claimed to have led the way 'in perceiving a superior talent' – acknowledged since in many anthologies, including *The Oxford Book of Modern Verse* (1936).

Home no longer meant the freedom of Ashtead Lodge and its private acres, surrounded by the Surrey countryside of conifer and heather. Patrick Herbert had transferred the household, its retainers and appurtenances, to the 'shamelessly middle class'[10] inner suburb of Kensington, where he had rented a high-roomed mid-Victorian house in Argyll Road. His eldest son, looking back to that change in their lives, referred to the family's 'modest circumstances', blandly recalling that a cook, a housemaid, and a parlourmaid worked and gossiped in the 'enormous basement'. The cook had a saying that went with him down the years: 'I laughed enough to kill a military horse.'

Possibly obeying an Hibernian instinct, Patrick Herbert desired that his sons should learn horsemanship, and enrolled them at a Kensington riding school. Unpublished notes of APH survive in which he remembered one morning when 'after a lot of tedious trotting, the horses were walking round and round the ring, while the instructor was telling us how to make our mounts walk sideways. I had no ambition of that sort and was not paying much attention.

Suddenly my horse sank to the ground and rolled over on its side, with most of me underneath it. It turned out that he had been brought up in the yeomanry and trained to lie down so that his rider could fire over him. As I had been given no notice of this accomplishment, the episode set up a nervous barrier between me and the species'.

Argyll Road led straight down to the arterial Kensington High Street where there were constantly flowing traffic tides to bear the young Herberts to the museums, the Drury Lane pantomimes, the new cinemas (some of them already emblazoned 'de Luxe'), to roller-skating at Olympia, exhibitions at Earl's Court and the White City, and to the great railway termini that were portals to summer holiday enchantments at the seaside. For APH, Bognor (not yet Regis), Colwyn Bay, Frinton, Tenby, were more than holiday resorts. They were havens of blessed relief from the misery of hay fever. The guide books were still referring to Hastings, Eastbourne, Brighton, Bournemouth, Torquay, as 'watering places'. An air of spa town invalidism still pervaded them. At St Leonards-on-Sea, APH was driven to write in 'a frenzy':

> Here every house is a Home or a Hospital,
> Here every creature's a crock with the gout;
> As when you tread on the nest of a wasp, it'll
> Gather a host of its comrades about,
> So when old Phoebus appears in the firmament,
> Out come the crocks for a bask in a swarm–
> Heroes who know what a bask out in Burma meant,
> Colonels with tempers and only one arm . . .

A Winchester contemporary, Jack Parr, recalls him from that time as 'a bit of a hypochrondriac – he had a tendency to think that he wasn't well'. Not that he shirked the exertions and risks of the playing fields. He was Captain of Houses, one of the three college football divisions. The Wykehamist version of the game was singular and tough. Undoubtedly it schooled APH in the tenacity that was a hall-mark of his character. Ruefully, he was out of the side in his last term because of injuries received: both ankles sprained, water on both knees. Those disabilities may not have influenced his leaving the college before his time, though he had gained his Exhibition to New College, Oxford, and may have seen no point in

staying on. Saving two months' fees may also have been a consideration. His father was about to retire from the India Office on a
pension of two-thirds of his salary of £470.

'Grateful for many blessings', APH departed from that venerable
scene at Short Half (Christmas) 1909, sincere in his belief that the
good in the English public schools' system outweighed the bad, and
always instantly ready to give battle to those who argued otherwise.
Its great virtue, he would say, was its nurture of the team spirit,
which he considered the best possible expression of the slavishly
invoked 'social conscience'. Wykehamist training inculcated 'a
sharp sense of duty to one's neighbour', and it would be a mean
intellect that interpreted it in terms of 'the old boy network' concept.
Egotism was deplored. 'It was a bad thing to be selfish or superior.'
Opportunism disgraced manners as well as morals.

One of the 'blessings' that he did not acknowledge, and may not
have realized, was the odd Winchester institution called 'toys'. A
large hall, the Toy Room, was divided into 'small spaces, each about
three feet wide and deep. Here, 'APH recalled, 'you kept your books
and photographs and treasures; it was your own tiny citadel and,
if you wished, you could draw a curtain against the world'. The
advantage of that amenity was somewhat diminished by the fact that
each space or 'toy' was open at the top; 'you could not shut out the
noise'. The extra effort of concentration imposed on the scholar
during the evening preparation period may have been of particular
significance in APH's case. 'Toys' at Winchester probably generated
the formidable capacity for 'shutting out the noise' that was a
feature of his working life.

He was nearing his final six feet; lithe of form, easy in bearing
and manner, and retaining the slightly bewildered, blinking look
of one whose innocence is somehow intact in a wicked world. Some
of his schoolfellows thought him touched by piety, and he was
conscious of attempts to shield him from 'smutty talk'. He was also
aware of being classed with the college 'tarts', and of harmless
sentimental attachments, 'as in a girls' school'. That, he avowed,
was as far as 'the sex thing' went with him at Winchester, adding
the jaunty disclaimer: 'In my time no boy ever became a father.'

The emotional wrench for him of leaving Winchester was from
place rather than from persons: 'the beauties of Winchester abide
with a Wykehamist for ever'. He wrote valedictory lines with an
unexpectedly sardonic twist:

The sunset glimmers faintly o'er the plain,
(Likewise upon the hill), and plants a kiss
On faces that I ne'er shall see again,
And faces that I shall not greatly miss.

Academically, he pronounced himself 'a lover of Greek and Latin', with reservations about the classical emphasis in his education. 'I spent years upon the grammar of Latin, Greek and French, but never an hour upon the rules of English grammar', criticism that included the syllabus at his preparatory school at Folkestone. He would have preferred 'more mathematics, especially those fascinating logarithms', self-taught later. He would have liked more history too, while never doubting that 'whatever was taught was finely taught'. The Sixth Book (Wykehamist for Senior Sixth), when at last he came to it, proved to be 'a forum rather than a class'. Masters and pupils 'discussed the wide world together', an heuristic climax that he warmly approved.

NOTES ON CHAPTER 1

1 He also wrote *Napoleon and his Marshals* (1934), made a reputation as a broadcaster in the Overseas Service of the BBC and stood twice as a Liberal candidate in parliamentary elections; potentially, a formidable back bencher.
2 A. P. Herbert: *The Ayes Have It* (1937).
3 Martin: *The Life of the Prince Consort* (1876).
4 A. P. Herbert: *A Book of Ballads* (1931).
5 See *Second Son* by David Herbert (1972), signature to pencil portrait of Tallulah Bankhead.
6 *APH, His Life and Times* (1971).
7 Sir Alan Herbert: unpublished article.
8 Harold Nicolson: *Diaries and Letters 1930–39* (1966).
9 Michael Heseltine, CB (1886–1952). Assistant Secretary, Ministry of Health; and Registrar, General Medical Council.
10 H. J. Massingham: *London Scene* (1933).

2

Before and After 1914

By family report, soon after leaving Winchester APH had a nervous breakdown. The reality, one suspects, was less critical, a warning against the mental exhaustion that became his main health liability of the future. A pocket diary that he kept throughout 1910, a year that nominally marked the close of the Edwardian era in which he came to manhood, gives many indications of lassitude, few of symptomatic depression, and none whatever of melancholic despair. Its prosaic daily entries, every one prefaced by a weather report, show him exercising a normal young man's response to his circumstances, especially to those that bored him.

From the personal memoranda page in the diary one learns that 4 Argyll Road, Kensington, was not yet on the telephone; that he was a member of Habitation 2037 of the Primrose League;[1] that he was still taking the schoolboy collar size of 14½; that his height 'in socks and pumps' was 5 ft. 11 in. In spaces left for glove, hat and footwear sizes he wrote respectively: 'Can't remember', 'Don't care', 'Don't know'.

On New Year's Day 1910 he awoke 'full of good resolutions', one of which took him that afternoon – 'icy wind, devilish cold' – to the Home of Rest for Horses at Cricklewood, whether from curiosity or compassion one is left to guess. Some of those superannuated horses may have been, probably were, the last in the London omnibus service before the advent of motor traffic. APH returned to Kensington by motorbus, still a novelty in public transport: 'a long and interesting journey'. He had travelled hopefully to Cricklewood and arrived to be 'pretty bored'. 'Didn't stay long' (*Diary*).

The bicycle was not yet driven off the streets. He calculated that in the first months of 1910 he pedalled 'more than 500 miles' in and about central London on his Rudge-Whitworth machine, which he frequently had to take to Tottenham Court Road for readjustments or repairs. In the Haymarket, 'dust and petrol appalling'. He rode to a suffragette meeting at Caxton Hall, Westminster. 'Most amusing. Refused to sign petition. Escaped whole.' Using a vulgarism despised since the rank and fashion abandoned cycling to the lower orders in the nineties, he 'biked up and down Brompton Road for hours' (*Diary*). He may be entitled to a footnote in transport history as one of the last cyclists to experience the frustrations of a punctured tire in Regent Street (6 October 1910).

He volunteered as a canvasser for Lord Claude Hamilton, 'our candidate', at South Kensington in the Budget election that year. He listened to speeches in the House of Commons. 'Balfour awfully good'; McKenna 'hopelessly squashed'. He was alternately elated and cast down as the poll results came in, his apprehensions centred in Radical fortunes, singling out Victor Grayson, the Socialist, whose later disappearance remains an unsolved mystery, and H. M. Hyndman, founder of the Socialist-Democratic Federation: 'he will have to be shot', that diary note expressing the current middle-class terror of change from below.

Between school and university he passed much of his time at roller-skating rinks, hypnotically popular then as bingo-halls are today. He acquired some of the higher skills, becoming 'quite hot' as a specialist in the 'two-step backwards'. Also, during that inter-regnum, 'played 250 games of backgammon, lost 150'.

He saw 'the new comet very dimly' and, in a lowlier firmament, the rising political star, Winston Churchill: 'awfully good and not a bit violent'. At a meeting of the Kensington branch of the Tariff Reform League, APH made his first public speech. 'Spoke extempore on Home Rule – jolly brave! Great surprise for them!'

He enjoyed the 'living pictures' which were to become 'the movies', and thought *Charley's Aunt* splendid – with three exclamation marks. He saw his brother Sidney 'off to Portsmouth with other majestic "snotties" '. Nowhere in that diary of a year is his military brother Owen mentioned. His father, 'Dada' in those pages, took him to Saturday Night Dinners at the Savage, notable events in London's clubland. 'Heard some awfully good music and some very amusing things.'

With the looks and air of an apprentice faun, he danced badly and played tennis erratically with old Wykehamists' sisters and the daughters of his father's friends, always 'young ladies' in the diary.

Mostly, they are anonymous and do not appear to have had any existence for him beyond that of polite acknowledgment. Taking the diary as evidence, one assumes that he was still immune from the social insinuations of sex. One night he 'dreamed wonderful dreams', the next, 'Dreamt I was being married' (February 1910). Intimate personal disclosure is otherwise not a feature of the diary. The constraint was profoundly temperamental and never resolved.

Making his daily notes he drew freely on the glossary of a generation that was not to know maturity. It gives the impression that life for APH in those years, nostalgically categorized as 'before the war' by the survivors, consisted in the main of a sequence of experiences adjectivally defined as 'ripping', 'hot stuff', 'beastly', 'topping', or 'bally – rhymed with valley – awful'. Recurrent in the same place are the slang nouns 'blighter', 'rotter' and 'silly ass'.

On the day (28 April 1910) that he noted: 'Special editions all over the place about Paulhan getting to Manchester',[2] he left London for Shorwell Vicarage, near Newport, Isle of Wight, to resume his classical studies in readiness for Oxford. His private mentor was the Revd. G. E. Jeans,[3] with whom he began reading the twenty-first book of the *Iliad* the following morning. The day was more memorable for the soup served at lunch. 'I discovered it to be made of slugs, rather good but an awful shock!' (*Diary*).

Mornings with Homer, Aristophanes, Demosthenes and Cicero, were followed by afternoon 'bike' rides, desultory games of golf, 'struggling with verse', or 'walking forlornly over the downs'. He was riveted by 'the wonderful view all across the Island right up to Southampton Water. Lovely seeing England'. The next day: 'Did 400 lines of 23rd Book – 3½ hours. Walked up to the top of down & looked across at England. "England, my England!" Spent a lot of time hiding under bushes', his outing spoilt by 'a rapid succession of bitter, cold, beastly showers racing over the Island'.

On Friday 6 May 1910: 'Feeling rather distracted. See the King has got bronchitis'. After lunch, 'walked more aimlessly than ever on some blooming down'. Returning to the vicarage, 'made a hideous din' at the piano. In the evening, 'to the village dance. Very amusing'. And at the end of the day, written in capitals at the top of the diary page: 'KING EDWARD VIITH DIED. 12.45.'

He was 'sorely afflicted' by hay fever, 'my worst attack. Couldn't get settled or comfortable anywhere. Read poetry, which made it worse'. Another cause for complaint was self-diagnosed as 'gout in the fingers, appalling'. Setting out on another of his walks 'up on the down (I know not its name)', he 'mused sorrowfully upon a gate'.

There were few deeper notes in his emotional scale. His was an equable temperament that assured him relative mental ease if it also denied him poetic insights. Only occasionally did the equanimity desert him. Then it was at the mercy of what he called his 'little volcano', a sudden eruption of temper that he put down to 'the Irish blood'.

His industry as a classics student often flagged. He finished the Third Book of Homer with the verdict that it was 'most boring'. He was 'awfully bored with Diomedes'. Thucydides was 'intensely boring'. After completing 'some Iambics, felt bored to death'. Juvenal provoked him to extremes of impatience: 'most hopeless stuff'; his final epithet for the Roman satirist was 'loathsome'.

His first verse collection, *Poor Poems and Rotten Rhymes*, was brought out in June by Wells, the printer to Winchester College, price one shilling. A reviewer in *The Wykehamist*, June 1910, agreed that he had 'a great capacity for metre, though at times he strains it rather far'. The review bore the initials of a college contemporary, Gilbert Talbot, a name that was to shine in a more sombre context in the years ahead.

APH was reading Winston Churchill's biography of his father, and at the same time a life of Gladstone. He also recorded in the diary the dramatic arrest of Dr Crippen, and the death of Florence Nightingale. At home for the holidays, he bought his first safety-razor; considered tea at Fuller's in Sloane Street 'very dear'; watched Anthony Wilding at the top of his tennis form at Queen's Club; saw Sarah Bernhardt at the Coliseum, Phyllis Neilson Terry at the Haymarket, was 'in part disappointed' by *The Follies*; and 'spent pots of money' on the Scenic Railway, the chief attraction at the White City.

His first contribution to *Punch*, 'a set of verses' with the punning title of *Stones of Venus*, appeared in the issue dated 24 August 1910 and earned him a guinea. He stuck another feather in his cap when the editor accepted his valedictory to adolescence, *The Last Teen*. It appeared just before he went up to New College, and brought him £1 10s. Payments to contributors were referred to in the office then as 'honoraria'.

When I was merely 'M or N',
  I wanted more than peace and plenty,
When I was six, when I was ten,
I thirsted for the moment when
I should achieve the years of men
  And reach the glorious age of twenty.

Nor had my ardour lessened yet
  When I discarded G. A. Henty,
Learned to indulge without regret
The humours of the cigarette,
And, in a word, contrived to get
  Most of the faults that come at twenty.

But be the years approaching lean,
  Or be they fat (*deo volente*),
They will not be as this has been,
This last and most delightful teen;
And I shall make a sad, sad scene
  On Friday next, when I am twenty.

Taking with him the nickname Peck, tacked on to him at Winchester, as Sir James Gammell remembered 'because of the way he moved his head', he 'went down to Oxford by the 10.33'. (*Diary*, 13 October 1910). 'Icy cold wind all day, fearfully draughty'. He arrived at an empty college, 'and an enormous barrack of a room with nothing in it, not even an inkpot', which may explain his subsequent and often tiresome addiction to writing letters, verse, libretti and much else in pencil. Two days after, 'cursed my rooms, which are revolting'. He hired 'an enormous grand piano', chiefly for the base use of 'strumming'.

Tea with the Warden of New College, the obliquely celebrated Revd Dr Spooner (1844–1930), was 'very terrifying'. Occurring in those notes of APH's first weeks at the university are names of the laurelled members of 'the wonderful band of New College scholars' of Professor Gilbert Murray's proud remembrance: Gilbert Talbot, Leslie Hunter, G. L. Cheesman, Douglas Gillespie, Arthur Heath. The name of Ronnie Poulton also appears there, heroic in the annals of Rugby football, with Bobbie Palmer, another of the paragons of that Oxford generation.

True to the Wykehamist equation of work with virtue, APH was not beglamoured by the possibility of success at the Union. 'Terrified of the place', he spoke there for the first time in November 1910, dismissing his speech as 'awful rot', and writing off some of his attendances as 'very boring'. At one time he was talked of as a likely future president. Preferring academic excellence to paltry eminence, he chose to stay close to the studies required of him as an Exhibitioner.

The university clubs, the Chatham and the Canning, provided a kind of relaxation that came naturally to him, sitting on the floor to drink mulled claret and argue with Duff Cooper (New College), Harold Macmillan (Balliol), and Philip Guedalla (Balliol), the last-named recalled by APH as 'a brilliant and biting Liberal'.[4] For more raffish entertainment, he joined The Midwives, remembered by Victor Gollancz as 'a delightful little society', formed for mutual aid in the birth pangs of literary production. One of its chief sponsors was Hubert Phillips (Merton), afterwards 'Dogberry' of *The News Chronicle*, puzzle-master and international bridge expert. Turning up uninvited at one of The Midwives' meetings, Harold Laski was allegedly 'debagged' for his intrusion. The Midwives were patrons of the 'East Ocker', their jargon for the old East Oxford Theatre in Cowley Road, where the programmes bore the injunction: 'No Whistling, Shouting, or Stamping Allowed'. Apart from the melodrama on 'the bill', the theatre had the compelling attraction of being out of bounds to undergraduates. Not that the excitements of the rising curtain were new to APH. Since the family's move to Kensington he had often been taken to the West End theatres by his father, who hoped to convince him that the Irish Players were a superior breed to the Savoyards. Those illicit excursions to the 'East Ocker' may not have made him hunger and thirst after fame behind the footlights. Rather they were an early intimation of his disrespect for the more censorious forms of authority. It was to become an active principle of his public life.

'Did some loathsome Greek elegiacs', the diary recounts. And again: 'Did three beastly Cicero papers.' Compensatory satisfaction was supplied by his little successes as a light verse poet. Apart from *Punch*, his work was appearing in *The Observer*, the *Pall Mall Gazette* and *Vanity Fair*. Mostly it was a distillation of his school and university experience; academic in subject but not in spirit. He was sentimental about Winchester, humorous about Oxford. The best of it was published in a thin shilling volume, *Play Hours with Pegasus*, by

Blackwell at Oxford in 1912, with no adverse effect on the reputation
of Cambridge as the cradle of English poesy.

He secured 'a not very good Second' in Honours Moderations
and, apparently disenchanted with the classics, 'turned eagerly to
the law'. No explanation of the change of direction is given in his
autobiographical record of it.

He went into lodgings at 8 Long Wall with Walter Monckton,
who was reading history and law; with Gilbert Talbot and E. R.
Besley who were reading law; and Jack Parr, who was working for a
First in Greats. 'Augustine, Justinian, Descartes, Disraeli, Lloyd
George and Asquith competed for our attention at the breakfast
table', from which Talbot would push back his chair and 'take a
flying leap downstairs' to be first with the morning paper. 'One of
the lasting pictures in my mind', APH wrote years later of that
impetuous habit of Talbot's.

He summed up his university time as 'vital experience'. He had
easily assimilated the Oxford temper, its broad outlook on the
world, its prime concern for the dignity of the intellect. Oxford
gave him respect for the disciplined mind and will. 'From first to
last I enjoyed Oxford and am grateful for it still', written long years
after and suggesting that he did not necessarily endorse the view of
Cyril Asquith, his contemporary, that 'one's time at Winchester is
one's golden age'.

Assessing his Oxford gains, he gave first place to companionship.
Himself one of the most companionable of men, he could not look
back on his university time and exclaim as Thackeray did: 'What
passions our friendships were!' He had companions and a capacity
for affection, yet he never appeared to need, and did not cultivate,
close friendships. Among the Oxford men he remembered familiarly
were Harry Strauss (afterwards Lord Conesford), classics man of
Christ Church, eminent lawyer, Conservative MP and holder of
various Government posts; Walter Monckton, a foremost figure of
the Abdication crisis of 1937; Christopher Morley, American
journalist, novelist and essayist, whose family roots were in East
Anglia; Robin Barrington-Ward, editor of *The Times*, 1941–48;
Francis ('Cherry') Newbolt, son of Sir Henry, the poet-patriot;
Jack Parr, who returned to Winchester to teach a new generation
at his old college; and Harold Macmillan, Prime Minister, 1957–63.

APH's voice was raised in cheers for the Oxford crew in the Boat
Race of 1913, which he watched from Duke's Meadows below

Barnes Bridge. New College was almost always Head of the River in those years; almost always a New College man stroked the university crew. Walking back along the river path, he 'fell in with a little old man who was the famous F. Anstey', author of *Vice Versa* and *The Brass Bottle*, and a prolific contributor to *Punch*.[5] To APH, Anstey personified shining literary success, and he gladly abandoned his intention of catching a 'bus back to Kensington when Anstey proposed that they walk together along the riverside to Hammersmith.

Coming presently to a row of seventeen tall waterfront houses known as Hammersmith Terrace, 'he stopped and showed me a favourite curiosity of his – Number Thirteen'. It had two front doors, one wider and more ornate than the other. The disparity had been given various romantic explanations. One was that the more impos-ing doorway had been adapted to admit George III in his sedan chair (a) when visiting his mistress, (b) when he went to sit for his portrait by Philip de Loutherbourg, who lived there. The artist also had a reputation as a healer, and a further idea survived that the wider doorway was put in to admit the crowds of invalids who sought his help. 'And now look back', Anstey bade APH as they walked on towards Hammersmith Bridge. 'One of the finest views in London'. The green and graceful curve of the river enticed his gaze to the skyline of Chiswick Mall, where spring-blossoming trees embellished the scene. Parting there, he and Anstey never met again.

APH went down from Oxford in 1914 with regret tempered by his minimal capacity for unhappiness. He had obtained 'a very good First' in Jurisprudence, having written in the diary that the intensive mental effort made his 'brain reel'. It had a sequel of nervous debility with insomnia that laid him aside for several weeks. Similar episodes were to recur in his working life. He was shielded from their worst effects by a temperament enviably free from morbid introspection.

Lord Bryce (1838–1922), sometime British ambassador at Washington, said that in the Oxford of his day undergraduates 'had an inordinate fondness for measuring the intellectual growth of their contemporaries and conjecturing the kinds of eminence they might achieve'.[6] If any of APH's New College contemporaries pondered his future, they most likely set it in one of the Inns of Court. He spoke of taking the Bar examinations but did little about it, probably to the disappointment of his father, who had a fancy that APH's Selwyn blood was assurance of high legal ability and corresponding eminence. Having savoured the peculiar pleasures of print and publication, he may have found them more alluring than the law.

At that point, it suited him to join his friend Jack Parr as a volunteer helper at The Oxford House Mission in Bethnal Green. A resounding appeal to university graduates had been made by Winnington Ingram, who was head of the Mission until his appointment to the bishopric of Stepney. 'You are coming up to London to make your careers and follow your professions. Stick to them like men. I am not asking you to be parsons. But put in a bit of spare time with us in the slums. Better still, come and live with us. It's jollier to dine on a leg of mutton with a dozen Oxford men at Oxford House than to munch a solitary chop in lodgings at Hampstead. Come and try'.

That breezy and bustling Church leader, who eventually became Bishop of London, was an effective spokesman for a social service development set in motion thirty years before by two young and dedicated Christ Church men, Edward Denison and Theodore Talbot, who foreswore their prospects of inherited wealth and leisure in the cause of succouring London's poor. Their exemplary lives stirred the consciences of Oxford men of a later generation, and led to the founding in 1884 of The Oxford House Mission, in an abandoned elementary school at Bethnal Green. It was to become 'the ark and sanctuary' of the university settlement movement in the East End.

Volunteering to work in that unfamiliar milieu, APH undertook to attach himself to The Oxford House Mission for a full year, 'doing what I could'. He washed dishes, swept floors, ran errands and, on behalf of The Children's Country Holiday Fund, collected its beneficiaries from door to door in back streets and shepherded them – washed, dressed, and neatly labelled – to the railway termini. As some of us cannot forget, the sky over England that summer was wonderfully blue; perfect holiday weather.

'He did not delude himself that he was helping to solve the problem of poverty by this work; but he thought humbly that he could add a little happiness and order to the lives of a few; and he knew that he was learning much that every citizen ought to know.' In defining the no more than mildly nagging social conscience of the hero of a novel of his written years later, APH was referring back to his own feelings as a voluntary worker in Bethnal Green.[7] He certainly could not have been charged with responding to the current patronizing urge known as 'slumming'. More likely, he was aware of an element of adventure implicit in those surroundings. It was like entering a foreign enclave. Life in the East End was still raucous and rough. Policemen patrolled some of the streets in twos. The naptha flares of the market-traders' stalls had not finally dispelled the shadow of The Ripper.

At Argyll Road, Kensington, Deakie ruled a depleted household. Owen William Eugene, the second Herbert son, had qualified through Sandhurst and Woolwich to wear what Hazlitt scorned as 'the loathsome finery of the profession of blood'. Sidney Jasper, the youngest, was set on his naval course via Osborne and Dartmouth. APH was always closest to Sidney, writing later that he did not 'remember Owen so well'. How their father was passing his retirement, whether he was in any way active as a 'literary journalist', is not now known. Jack Parr was often a visitor at Argyll Road. Herbert senior made 'very little' impression on him. It seemed to him that home did not 'mean much' to APH, who was unlikely to have been confiding about it if it did.

'The position in Europe', *The Times* reported on Tuesday 4 August 1914, 'is one of breathless anticipation of the beginning of hostilities on a large scale.' APH had spent the Bank Holiday with his friend 'Cherry' Newbolt at Netherhampton, near Salisbury, 'the modest but delightful house' of Sir Henry Newbolt.[8] During a game of bowls, Sir Henry was called to the telephone. 'Germany has declared war on France', he remarked rather than announced as he returned to the lawn. The poet of *Drake's Drum* was not readily distracted by historical crises. He called across the green to APH: 'Your turn, I think'.

War was not the only excitement of those summer days for APH. He had lately met Gwendolen Harriet Quilter with some of his New College friends, and he had been greatly taken by her slender beauty and low-voiced charm. Voice attraction was the determinant of their mutual sympathies. Gwen Herbert says that the timbre of *his* voice as he called love-forty over a tennis-net at Campden Hill sealed her fate.

She was one of the daughters of Harry Quilter, MA, whose father was head of a leading City firm of accountants, Quilter, Ball and Co. Harry Quilter, who in his best years looked like a shortened version of Augustus John, was a man of extraordinary energy and versatility. After Cambridge and the Slade School, he made an impulsively sharp turn to walk the wards of Middlesex Hospital. His medical studies were soon abandoned for the law. After six months in chambers, 'during which', he wrote, 'my incipient dislike of the legal profession became a passion', he joined an Italian circus company to travel with them in the Far East. He lived adventurously in Australia, New Zealand and the South Seas. In 1892 he married by licence at St James's Church, Westminster, Mary Constance Hall, of Hove. She was twenty, he thirty-nine. 'Rank or profession of father' was stated, in each instance, to be 'Gentleman'. Mary Hall had been an art student, and her life-size bust of her husband, modelled in wax, was deemed worthy of preservation as an heirloom. She was a talented linguist, remembered in later years by one of her sons-in-law, Lance Sieveking, as 'a jolly little woman with an immense energy that found an outlet in dancing every night'.

Harry Quilter wrote a life of Giotto and other books, founded *The Universal Review*, which failed at heavy cost to himself after two years, collected old masters, strove to paint like Sickert and lectured on the visual arts wherever there was a platform at his disposal. He compiled an encyclopedic work called *What's What*, himself writing 'upwards of a thousand' of its two-thousand five-hundred articles on as many subjects. As art critic of *The Times* and *The Spectator*, he fell foul of Whistler, who pilloried him in *The Gentle Art of Making Enemies*. Whistler's derision became malignant when Quilter bought The White House, Tite Street, Chelsea, designed for the artist by the Victorian architect E. W. Godwin, who was extravagantly accused of providing every bedroom with its own staircase. Hearing that Quilter was adding a private theatre to the house, Whistler wrote to *The World* denouncing 'our 'Arry', as he scornfully called Quilter in and out of print, as a philistine. 'Shall the birthplace of art become the tomb of its parasite in Tite Street?' Whistler accused him of being 'unable to *smell* the difference between oil and water-colour'.

Quilter, whose right eyebrow was permanently cocked as if life was for him a never-ending surprise, appears in several contemporary biographies, variously described as 'a stocky, brash little man', 'aggressively short tempered', 'swaggering and bluffing his way into

Fleet Street offices'. He was one of the arresting characters of a period that abounded in them, and who now seem almost to have been freaks of nature.

His 'Important Pictures, Drawings, and Engravings' were auctioned at Christie's in 1906. They realized £14,381. By then his mercurial tastes and enthusiasms had exhausted the family inheritance that had made him, at one time, a wealthy man. His brother, Sir Cuthbert, the first baronet of the line, set up a trust of £60,000 for Harry's family. Sir Cuthbert was a pioneer investor in the national telephone service, a Suffolk member of Parliament, and the father of Roger Quilter, the composer (1877–1953).

Harry Quilter died in 1907, a cancer victim. *The Daily Telegraph* obituary notice stated that he was 'a man of many ambitions, mainly literary and artistic, who perhaps never quite attained the success which his innate abilities seemed to deserve'. It was an unkind fate that deprived APH of the opportunity of knowing the exceptional, many-sided man, touched with the Ulysses spirit, who was his father-in-law.

NOTES ON CHAPTER 2

1 Founded in 1884 in memory of Lord Beaconsfield (d. 1881). League members had to sign a document: 'I declare on my honour and faith that I will devote my best ability to the maintenance of religion, of the estates of the realm, and of the imperial ascendancy of the British Empire . . . ' Its 'Habitations' were copied from the 'Lodges' of the Orange Movement in Ireland. Membership in 1910 was 2,053,019.

2 Louis Paulhan, French pioneer aviator, won *The Daily Mail* Prize of £10,000 for the first flight from London to Manchester.

3 Oxford scholar; sometime assistant master at Haileybury; author, and editor of Roman historical studies.

4 Philip Guedalla (1889–1944) made his name in the thirties as a biographer and historian. He cultivated the pose of a successful man of letters, and was one of the best conversationalists of his day.

5 'F. Anstey' was the pen-name of T. Anstey Guthrie (1856–1934). The son of a West End military tailor, he disclosed in his autobiography, *A Long Retrospect*, that he was surprisingly failure-prone as a writer.

6 Lord Bryce: *Studies in Contemporary Biography* (1903).

7 *Holy Deadlock* (1934).

8 Sir Henry Newbolt, CH (1862–1938) gave currency to one of the most characteristic of English popular slogans: 'Play the game!'

3

War in a Classic Setting

On 5 September 1914 APH enlisted at Lambeth Pier as an Ordinary Seaman in the Royal Naval Volunteer Reserve. It was his short answer to the young East Enders at The Oxford House who caustically assumed that – to quote Jack Parr – 'we Oxford blokes would go off and take commissions and, so they erroneously concluded, be all right'.[1] He acted on another impulse; that, by joining a branch of the senior service, he would stand a better chance of 'running across' his brother Sidney. As Sidney was training as a submarine officer, the contingency was perhaps remote.

He was 'mainly persuaded', he afterwards wrote, 'that we had gone to war for a just cause'. Many others thought the same, and it was on their behalf, too, that he resented in print the raucous tone of the stage play of a later time, *O What a Lovely War!* with its mean-spirited implication that he and his like were 'duped into the Forces by damsels singing patriotic songs', or that they were hypnotized by Kitchener's 'pointing finger'. He reverted to that matter twenty years later, addressing the Oxford University Conservative Association.

'I am one of the too-fortunate survivors of that lost generation of 1914, who suffered our Schools in June of that year, and heard our fate in July. For a week or two of that brilliant summer we strutted the world, boasting about our degrees or explaining them away, and in either case considering ourselves lords of life – and then in August, or maybe September, discovered ourselves, with some astonishment, recruits or combatants in a war that was to save civilisation and be the last war of all. Yes, though we were thrilled by the bugles and the drums, and though we delighted in our flags and uniforms, we did believe that.'[2]

The Royal Naval Volunteer Reserve consisted largely of landsmen with some sea-training or experience; its numbers were made up by willing recruits who had neither. The Reserve became one of the constituent bodies of the Royal Naval Division, formed out of the twenty to thirty thousand volunteer reservists who hoped to see service afloat, but for whom the newly mobilized Royal Navy had no accommodation.

Wearing his naval rating's uniform, with bell-bottom trousers, APH escorted Gwen Quilter to Bethnal Green to meet the then head of The Oxford Mission, the Revd F. A. Iremonger, MA, DD (1878–1952). 'The most compelling of clergymen. No heathen could have withstood him for more than ten minutes' (APH). Dr Iremonger charmed Gwen Quilter into taking over the running of a women's club at the Mission.

Early in October a telegram was delivered at 4 Argyll Road. Owen Herbert, who had been commissioned as a Gunner, was 'missing, believed killed', a casualty of the retreat from Mons. He was never heard of again. APH marched with the Royal Naval Volunteer Reserve contingent in the Lord Mayor's Show procession in November 1914. A few days later he traversed part of the same route behind the gun-carriage bearing the coffin of Field Marshal Lord Roberts, VC, who, only a fortnight before had received the abjectly tearful homage of Indian troops in French hospitals. During the slow march up Ludgate Hill, he caught the glances of two New College men transformed into proud-lipped Guards' officers with incipient moustaches and drawn swords. 'We exchanged a discreet and delicate Oxford grin.'

At Oxford, 'emptiness, silence, reigns everywhere', wrote Sir Herbert Warren, the President of Magdalen. An unprecedented break had occurred in one of the oldest scholastic traditions. For the first time in five hundred years, no Wykehamist had gone up to New College for the new academic year. Of the 531 Winchester 'old boys' who were serving in 1915, or had served until they fell, nearly all had gone from school into the armed forces.

APH went back to Oxford in the last days of that autumn to sit for the written examination for the All Souls' Prize Fellowships of 1914. His motive for doing so seems to have been oddly perverse, in the light of Professor Rushbrook Wiliams' recollection. 'I sat next to him. He was in the uniform of an AB of the RNVR, a spectacle that filled me with envy because I had been rejected by the Oxford recruiting office on the score of poor eyesight only that week and told that I would be more useful in India (where I had just been appointed to a chair of Modern Indian History). I confided my feelings to APH in the intervals of our ordeal. He told me that he was only sitting for the All Souls Fellowship for a lark, as it would give him the chance to pull the legs of the examiners. As luck would have it, I got the History Fellowship and subsequently learned from the examiners that many of APH's answers to the questions on the papers had been written in the form of light (not to say frivolous) verse, for which he was renowned throughout Oxford.' Professor Rushbrook Williams thinks that some bawdy lines by APH may have offended the clerical element, 'at that time rather strong in the All Souls' Common Room', and Professor Williams adds: 'I have always thought that the College missed a real chance when they did not take him' (Letter, 15 May 1973). Like Sydney Smith's, APH's humour, similarly seasoned with logic, was an obstacle to preferment.

When he was made Acting Leading Seaman, entitled to flaunt a red anchor on his left sleeve, he said that it gave him as much pleasure as his First in Law. It was fully in character that he took his little advancement seriously, studying map-reading, semaphore and Morse signalling, with the earnestness of one trying for an Alpha-plus in all subjects. For him Morse was a coveted skill, perhaps because of its association with dramas of the sea. Keeping assignations with him in Kensington tea-shops, Gwen Quilter had to put up with him practising with a spoon on plates and cups and saucers. In furtherance of their romance, he tried – with not much success – to teach her to reply in kind.

Deakie, at Argyll Road, did not take kindly to the advent of Miss Quilter. 'Alan has picked up a girl in the East End!' she was heard to say, with alarm in her voice. Warned that he was bringing her to the house to meet his father, Deakie took the precaution of hiding a string of pearls that had belonged to his mother. After the visit, she grudgingly agreed that 'she seems quite well brought up'.

They became engaged early in December 1914, and were married in the first week of the New Year by the Revd Dr Iremonger at his church of St James the Great, Bethnal Green. The bride wore white, the bridegroom his bluejacket's uniform. Lines that he wrote later celebrated his feelings that day:

> When you consider, on this spacious star,
> How many million single men there are,

But only one incomparable bride,
Who can explain why I am at her side?
At all events, I am as proud today
As one who finds the needle in the hay.

As they left the church, the Mission organist played them out with
an improvised voluntary that contained unmistakable echoes of
Every Nice Girl Loves a Sailor. Their honeymoon was spent in rooms
in Fulham Road, where the china rang incessantly with APH's
ardour for proficiency in the Morse Code.

Receiving his commission as a sub-lieutenant RNVR early in 1915,
he was posted to Hawke Battalion of the Royal Naval Division in
camp at Blandford, Dorset. Kindred spirits were already in training
there in the late winter mud, among them Rupert Brooke, of Hood
Battalion, commanded by Colonel Arnold Quilter, APH's cousin
by marriage.[3] APH had good company in Douglas Jerrold, whose
family name was prominent in the annals of *Punch;* Arthur ('Oc')
Asquith, son of the Prime Minister; Vere Harmsworth, son of
Lord Rothermere; F.S. ('Cleg') Kelly, Oxford rowing blue from
Australia and fine musician; Denis Brown, another musician who
was to be denied the fulfilment of his gifts, and whose last letter
home was addressed to Winston Churchill's secretary, Edward
Marsh: 'I've gone now too. Goodbye'; and Bernard Freyberg, who
survived to win extraordinary military renown. It may be doubted
that APH agreed with the fellow-officer who said that 'an ideally
cheerful evening' in the Mess at Blandford Camp was one in which
there was 'oblivion after the soup'.

Jerrold maintained that 'on any statistical computation the Naval
Division was richer in personalities than any comparable formation
in the British Army', which, as a wearer of naval uniform, he affected
to disdain. Writing of the men of his battalion, he said that they
were 'distrustful of authority, indifferent to the appearances of
efficiency'. In his opinion, 'not an easy battalion to command. They
would not tolerate cant'.[4] They never sang *Tipperary* or *Keep the
Home Fires Burning*. One can believe that to APH it was an agreeable
state of life in spite of the mud.

'C' and 'D' companies of Hawke Battalion embarked for Gallipoli
early in 1915. Briefly ashore in Malta, APH and Jerrold were
accosted by a street tout offering the services of 'dancing girls'.

Jerrold long cherished his memory of the *gravitas* of APH's reply: 'No, thanks – we don't dance.'

Arriving in the Bay of Mudros on 17 May: 'We landed straight from the dining-saloon of a Cunard liner on to the very edge of a battlefield where history was still in the making.'[5] APH had been given charge of No. 11 Platoon, 'C' Company, consisting of Tynesiders who spoke what to him was an alien version of the common tongue, and who too obviously thought themselves similarly victimized, only more so, when he addressed them. Adding to the confusion were two men from a remote Durham mining valley whose dialect baffled their Northumbrian neighbours.

> Stout miners all, their ardour knew no check
> While forth we fared upon our warward way;
> They wrote long letters from the ship's safe deck,
> Behind the boom of some Aegean bay
> (Breathing the hot inflammatory soul
> Which comes, it seems, from always carving coal),
> Of how they heard the hideous cannon's roll,
> And many a vivid but invented fray.
>
> And when we sought the catacombs of strife
> The lust for slaughter yet illumed their eyes;
> On the way up they nearly took the life
> Of two black braves from Afric (our Allies);
> They longed to leap from the sandbags' screen,
> And in close combat satisfy their spleen;
> While I, who truth to tell, was not so keen,
> Hardly persuaded them it was not wise.[6]

Intent on rousing his men's interest in that classic setting, he introduced the tale of Helen of Troy into one of his platoon lectures, and was pleased to notice that 'they listened politely'. Leading a party down to the beach to bathe, and thinking of Leander and Byron, he 'shared bliss unbelievable' as they lay drying 'democratically naked' in the sun. Presently he rose and pointed eastward. 'Officer says it's the Plain of Troy over there', the platoon sergeant explained to the men, and APH was moved when some of them instantly leapt to their feet and plunged in again, 'as if inspired'.

His closest companion then was Lieutenant William Ker, Harrow and Balliol,[7] a classics man who was apparently impervious to the romantic appeal of Tynesiders disporting themselves in the Hellespont. He referred to the spectacle as 'a cross between Blackpool and the Ganges', writing in the same letter home: 'You should have seen me and A. P. Herbert the other evening bathing in the Dardanelles with the Turkish lines in sight on a ridge to our left, the Plain of Troy before us on the other side' (30 May 1915). Probably APH was drawing on that companionship when he pictured himself in verse retiring to 'a rock that stands sheer above the blue', where they could 'look across and see the Trojan Plain':

> There will we sit and talk of happy things,
>   Home and 'the High', and some far fighting friend,
> And gather strength for what tomorrow brings,
>   For that may be the end.
> It may be that we shall never swim again.
>   Never be clean and comely to the sight,
> May rot untombed and stink with all the slain.
>   Come, then, and swim. Come and be clean tonight.[8]

Ker's letters to his parents supplemented Jerrold's published account of Hawke Battalion in training and in action. APH's letters from the two war fronts on which he served have not survived. Perceptive reading of his war novel, *The Secret Battle*, leaves one in no doubt of the authenticity of its scenes and episodes, that they faithfully report his personal and sometimes shattering experiences.

'The sniping was terrible. In that first week we lost twelve men each day. They fell without a sound in the early morning as they stood up from their cooking at the brazier, fell shot through the head, and lay snoring horribly in the dust; they were sniped as they came up the communication trench with water, or carelessly raised their heads to look at the ships in the Bay; and in the night there were sudden screams where a sentry had moved his head against the moon.' That passage from *The Secret Battle* may fairly be used here to illustrate the reality of APH's war baptism.

'An extra misery', he wrote, was the recurrence of his old affliction of hay fever. The pollen of poppy and cornflower caused him 'to sneeze all the way to the front line and back'. He was ordered out one night on reconnaissance duty with two of his Tynesiders as scouts. They groped cautiously forward through the dusty scrub of no-man's land. Sub-Lieutenant Herbert was seized by a sneezing fit. The Turks immediately responded with a burst of machine-gun fire. One of the scouts was hit in the femoral artery. 'I remember terribly how the other scout and I dragged the poor fellow back through the hole in the wire into the front trench. He died later. Hay fever is no joke to me.' The episode was a searing one, painfully recalled fifty years after.

News of his father's sudden death at Bognor reached him in June 1915. Patrick Herbert, who was sixty-six, had made his will a fortnight before the outbreak of war. It was witnessed by two 'Undergraduates of Oxford University', Walter Turner Monckton and John Willoughby Parr. One of its provisions related to the sale 'of my house at Beaconsfield, Rosebank, Baring Crescent'. It confirmed family suspicions that as a widower of sixteen years he had found clandestine consolation beyond the polite purlieus of Kensington. He does not emerge from remembrance or from his eldest son's diary pages as a positive personality. A saying of his, Irish in origin, survived to serve APH's dialectical purposes when scepticism was aroused: 'Like the thirteenth stroke of a crazy clock, a shadow of doubt is cast over all previous assertions.'

APH soon acquired a distinctive reputation in the Naval Division through his *Punch* contributions. In Hawke battalion he established a secondary claim to esteem by his off-hand attitude to Army regulations. One instance of it quickly passed into legend. After a minor advance against an enemy sector shown as Point P on the staff maps, he was made responsible for consolidating the new position by erecting barricades and posting guards. Ignoring the Army formula for the instruction of sentries, he was overheard telling them: 'Now, stay where you are, men – and regard all Turks with the gravest suspicion.'

His notion that by joining the RNVR he would have a chance of meeting his naval brother Sidney proved after all to be less than fantastic. 'Blow me, he did come ashore one day from some great ship off the Gallipoli Peninsula. I took him up to the front line (in his whites, provoking the Turkish snipers).'

On 30 July 1915 his friend Ker reported in a letter that 'Herbert unfortunately developed a temperature of 103·5 (he has been unwell all along), and was taken to hospital and out of my ken'. His name appeared in 'Mr Punch's Roll of Honour' with the inaccurate announcement that he had been 'wounded at the Dardanelles'. (He was invalided home with virulent enteritis.) 'We are delighted to conclude that he is well on the road to recovery, since he has contributed from his bed some more of those excellent verses which have so often adorned these pages' (*Punch*, 1 September 1915).

Verse writing relieved the tedium of a fairly long convalescence. Hearing that James Gammell,[9] a friend from Winchester days, was wearing the red tabs of the General Staff, was an excuse for scoring off an unpopular caste.

> It does not make me laugh or whoop,
> (Though certainly the choice is droll),
> To hear that you are asked to stoop
> To join that great malignant group;
> I hasten to condole.
> Not for your frame, I fear – ah, no,
> For far as creature comforts go,
> They lack but little here below:
> I shudder for your soul.[10]

When he was passed 'fit for light duty', he was seconded to Admiralty Intelligence in Whitehall. His first assignment may have tempted him to levity of the kind he showed in the All Soul's examination room. It required his attendance, he wrote, 'at the Wallace Collection to prepare a report on, of all things, the Method of Agriculture in Egypt'.

He had been left a fifth share of his father's estate of £7,000. The lease of 'the great Kensington barn', 4 Argyll Road, was given up. Considering where to set up house as a newly married man, he recalled 'the nice little walk' that Anstey had proposed by the river in the last year of peace. He retraced it with his wife. They 'looked longingly at Kelmscott House', with its William Morris associations, then on the market at £2,000, 'which we did not have'. They strolled admiringly on towards Hammersmith Terrace, shortly afterwards fictionally described by APH with faint embellishments as 'a short half-mile of old and dignified houses, clustered irregularly in all shapes and sizes along the sunny side of the Thames, with large trees and little gardens fringing the bank across the road, and, lying opposite, the Island, a long triangle of young willows, the haunt of wild duck and heron and swan – it had a unique, incomparable character of its own. It was like neither street, nor road, nor avenue, nor garden, nor any other urban unit of place in London or indeed, it was locally supposed, in the world. It had something, perhaps, of an old village and something of a Cathedral Close, something of Venice and something of the sea. But it was *sui generis*'.[11]

A house-agent's board hung on the railings of Number 12.[12] With a neighbour's connivance, entry was accomplished without the usual order-to-view formality. A lease at £55 a year was arranged. They took possession in February 1916. No grace-and-favour tenants could have considered themselves more fortunately treated by the gods, who decreed that 12 Hammersmith Terrace, W.6, should be a fixed point of domestic and social felicity through the next fifty years. For many of us, Number 12 seemed from the first to be dedicated to the service of friendship, and life there one long house-warming party.

War had its victories: would peace bring its revenges? To a new poem, *A World Set Free*, he added a bracketed sub-title: ('An Awful Prospect').[13]

> Long, long ago, when I had not attested,
> I prized the liberties of this proud race,
> The right of speech, from haughty rulers wrested,
> The right to put one's neighbours in their place;
>   I liked to argue and I loved to pass
>   Slighting remarks on Robert, who's an ass,
>   To hint that Henry's manners were no class,
> Or simply say I did not like his face.
>
> But things are changed. Today I had a tussle
> With some low scion of an upstart line;
> Meagre his intellect, absurd his muscle,
> I should have strafed him in the days long syne;
>   I took a First, and he could hardly parse;
>   I have more eloquence but he more stars;
>   Yet (so insane the ordinance of Mars)
> I must say 'Yes sir', and salute the swine.
>
> And it was hard when that abrupt Staff-Major
> Up to the firing line one evening came
> (Unknown his motive, probably a wager),
> And said quite rudely, 'You are much to blame;
>   Those beggars yonder you should enfilade'.
>   I fingered longingly a nice grenade;
>   I said those beggars were our First Brigade,
> But might not call him by any kind of name.

Yet not for ever shall the bard be muted
  By stars and stripes, but freely, as of yore,
When swords are sheathed and I'm civilian-suited,
  I shall have speech with certain of my corps,
    Speak then the insults which I now but brood:
    'Pompous', 'incompetent', 'too fond of food',
    And fiercely taste the bliss of being rude
And unrestrained by Articles of War.

That will be great; but what if such intentions
  Are likewise present in the Tenth Platoon?
What if some labourer of huge dimensions
  Meet me defenceless in a Tube saloon,
    And hiss his catalogue of unpaid scores,
    How oft I criticised his forming fours,
    Or prisoned him behind the Depot doors,
Or kept him digging on the Fourth of June?

Painful. And then, when all these armed millions
  Unknot with zest the military noose,
Will the whole world be full of wroth civilians,
  Each one exulting in a tongue let loose?
    And who shall picture or what bard shall pen
    The crowning horror which awaits us then –
    That civil warfare of uncivil men
In one great Armageddon of abuse?

NOTES ON CHAPTER 3

1 Letter, 30 October 1973.
2 6 November, 1935.
3 Killed in action, Gallipoli, 1915.
4 Jerrold: *The Hawke Battalion* (1925).
5 Jerrold: *The Hawke Battalion* (1925).
6 From *The Paralysis of the Tenth Platoon*: A. P. Herbert, *Punch*, 24 March 1915
7 Son of Charles Ker, Glasgow chartered accountant, and nephew of W. P. Ker,
   Professor of Poetry, and Fellow and Sub-Warden of All Souls.
8 A. P. Herbert: *Half Hours at Helles* (1916). In *The Soldier* (1915) Rupert Brooke
   has the line . . . 'as swimmers into cleanness leaping'.
9 Later, Lieut-Gen. Sir James Gammell, KCB, DSO, MC.
10 A. P. Herbert: *To James. Punch*, 8 September 1915.
11 A. P. Herbert: *The House by the River* (1920).
12 'I do not think such a thing has been seen in the Terrace from that day to this'.
   – APH, 1969.
13 A. P. Herbert: *Punch*, 8 March 1916.

4

Why he wrote The Secret Battle

Like the siege of Troy, the Gallipoli campaign was 'all for naught'. The evacuation of the Peninsular was carried out early in 1916. The Royal Naval Division was transferred to the Western Front, leaving its dead to lie with those subsequently commemorated by the great monument at Helles Point, to which passing ships long afterwards dipped their flags in salute. APH rejoined Hawke Battalion at a base camp near Abbeville later that summer. He had been passed fit for active service again.

He arrived to find his fellow-officers unduly concerned with appearances, something they had not bothered much about at Gallipoli. The unsoldierly bearing of the Tynesiders in particular offended some of the Army commanders, whose critical gaze fell on them from the day of disembarkation at Marseilles. The 'Geordies' did not jump to attention smartly enough when the staff rode by. There was tedious new emphasis on drill, physical training, discipline, and proficiency in all things.

Relegation from naval to army status was anathema to APH and to Jerrold, who was a stalwart of the political Right. Both resolved to assert the precedence of the senior service. Brigadier B. B. Rackham, CBE, MC, DL, president of the Royal Naval Division Association, has no doubt that they wilfully conducted a campaign of 'needling the Army'. He was present with them when a new divisional commander, Major-General Cameron Shute, arrived at Hawke Battalion headquarters. After polite preliminaries, there was a discussion on administrative matters in the course of which Jerrold, whose voice was resonant with authority, implied that commanding a division was an inferior job to 'running Harrods'. At that, General Shute walked out. A rumour that he was planning to replace a number of Naval Division officers by others with Regular Army training did not advance his popularity.

He took exception to the Naval Division beards, singling out that of Hawke Battalion's transport officer, Lieutenant C. S. Codner – 'an incident of great moment', Jerrold wrote in his history of the Battalion. 'We could not have selected a better issue on which to challenge the military hierarchy. Our beards might be slovenly, our transport muddy, but our beards were an unassailable prerogative. If we had lost Codner's beard, for it soon became far more ours than his, we lost everything.' Its epic significance was emphasized by APH in a ballad that had the whole Division laughing when it appeared in *Punch*.

> Now Brigadier-General Blank's Brigade was
>   tidy and neat and trim,
> And the sight of a beard on *his* parade was a
>   bit too much for him:
> 'What is that' said he, with a frightful oath,
>   'of all that is wild and weird?'
> And the Staff replied, 'A curious growth, but
>   it looks very like a beard'.
>
> And the General said, 'I have seen six wars,
>   and many a ghastly sight,
> Fellows with locks that gave one shocks, and
>   buttons none too bright,
> But never a man in *my* Brigade with a face
>   all fringed with fur;
> And you'll toddle away and shave today';
>   But Codner said, 'You err'.
>
> Now Generals crowded to the spot and
>   urged him to behave,
> But Codner said, 'You talk a lot, but can
>   you *make* me shave?
> For the Navy allows a beard at the bows, and
>   a beard is the sign for me,
> That the world may know wherever I go,
>   I belong to the King's Navee.'

APH was made assistant-adjutant of the Battalion, 'in which capacity', says Jerrold, 'he became the Correspondent-in-chief with Brigade on all controversial matters'. When they were not controversial he often contrived to make them so. 'This brilliant writer can seldom have been seen to better advantage than in some of the never-ending correspondence which he conducted from this vantage point of mingled authority and irresponsibility' (Jerrold).

His promotion entitled him, nominally a naval man, to a horse, while the battalion was still behind the lines. Possibly recalling his experience at the Kensington riding school, he accepted the mount with reluctance. 'It was a self-willed black mare. When the battalion paraded in a green field this creature would eat throughout the proceedings. If her rider hauled her head up she retaliated by walking backwards very fast, not looking where she was going. My predecessor let her eat. I thought this was undignified, and acted. As the battalion moved off to the Somme the horse moved rapidly backwards into the band and put a foot through a drum.'

Another of his mounts was called White Face. 'This animal was always proudly tossing its head and hitting me on the nose. He must have been a failed show jumper. On the march, he would suddenly bound away from the head of the column, clamber up a steep bank at the side of the road, look round, charge at the nearest fence or hedge, and, to my dismay, leap over it.'[1]

The Royal Naval Division moved into the front line at Souchez, near Vimy Ridge, in July 1916. Part of the support line had been abandoned, 'on the curious ground', Jerrold wrote, 'that it was dangerous'. As there was a risk that the derelict trenches would provide cover for enemy patrols, it was decided that a semblance of reoccupation should be devised. APH put up the idea that a life-size figure of an infantryman, moulded out of *papier mâché*, and moved from point to point, might provide the necessary deception. On its first appearance the figure, named Archie, drew a shower of German rifle grenades. When APH and an NCO went to move it to a new position, they were forced to retreat under concentrated enemy fire, leaving Archie a bullet-riddled wreck.

In mid-November, Hawke Battalion took part in an attack on Beaucourt. The battalion went into action with twenty officers and 415 other ranks. Within minutes 'it ceased to exist' (Jerrold). Fewer than twenty NCOs and men mustered for roll-call after the attack. APH was one of two officers who came out unscathed. Among the killed was his friend William Ker, 'a personality', Jerrold wrote, 'of rare promise and rarer charm'. APH remembered him in lines written after returning with Sub-Lieutenant Rackham to the battle-ground.

I crossed the blood-red ribbon that once was No-man's land;
I saw a winter daybreak and a creeping minute hand:
And here the lads went over, and there was Harmsworth shot,
And there was William lying – but the new men knew them not.

And I said 'There is still the river and still the stiff stark trees
To treasure here our story, but there are only these'.
But under the white wood crosses the dead men answered low:
'The new men knew not Beaucourt, but we are here – we know'.[2]

During the attack there occurred a failure of morale that resulted
in the court-martial and execution of a sub-lieutenant in Nelson
Battalion of the Naval Division. APH may not have known personally
that victim of shatteringly cruel circumstances. He certainly knew
of him, and heard the subdued talk about the case in the Division.
What he heard seems to have shaken him to the heart's core. His
distress of mind is remembered by Basil Rackham. 'He was so
upset', a crisis of feeling that he afterwards sought to resolve in
fiction form.

After reorganization in 1916–17, the Division ceased to be 'a
semi-naval, semi-civilian force'; it was integrated in the Army as the
63rd (RN) Division. When it went into the line at Pozières in
February 1917, APH was on leave. 'His return', Jerrold wrote,
'revitalized Battalion headquarters.' He had been made adjutant,
promotion that did not inhibit him from persisting in his disrespect
for his new masters, the Army Command. Meeting Brigadier-
General Phillips, 189th Brigade, he was emboldened by Jerrold's
recent taunt to let fall the opinion that the late William Whiteley,
'the Universal Provider', of Westbourne Grove, would have been 'the
ideal brigade commander'. The jibe had 'memorable results',
according to Jerrold who, regrettably, did not state them in writing.

Hawke Battalion saw much further fighting in 1917. On
Shakespeare's Day the Division was ordered to attack Gaverelle,
west of Arras. Enemy shell-fire, blasting shrapnel in all directions,
struck APH down. Sub-Lieutenant Rackham saw him fling up his
arms and fall. 'He seemed to me to be in a bad way – dangerously
wounded, I thought at first.' At a field-dressing station, jagged bits
of shrapnel and hip-flask were found to be embedded deep in his
left buttock; ignominious wound, honourably sustained. It was
serious enough for him to be sent home again. He believed that the
brandy from his flask was an effective sterilizing agent. The theory

would have had Deakie's warm approval, her faith in the prophylac-
tic worth of brandy being a family legend.

Back in England, there was 'bitter news to hear, and bitter tears
to shed'. Those shining lights he had known at Oxford had all been
extinguished: Poulton, Palmer, Cheesman, Gillespie and the rest.
At a memorial service in New College Chapel, the Warden, Dr
Spooner ('the Spoo' to APH's generation of undergraduates)
'white-haired and full of blameless years', knelt on the bare stones
by the altar to pray that 'it may be granted to us to live such lives
as those young men who have gone before us'.

With time to spare, and leaning heavily to starboard as he sat
at his desk, APH began writing his war novel. An agreeable parenthetical event was his election to his father's old club of all the
arts and most of the talents, the Savage, then in Adelphi Terrace.
At the same time he was elevated by *Punch* to the exclusive group of
its contributors who were allowed to attach their initials to their
work; hitherto, his identity had been relegated to the index of the
bound volumes.

In March 1918 the British Third and Fifth armies recoiled from
the force of the last great German bid for supremacy on the Western
Front. Sir Douglas Haig issued his 'backs to the wall' appeal to the
troops and the nation. APH wrote a poem called *The Windmill*,
subtitled 'A Song of Victory'.[3]

> Yes, it was all like a garden glowing
>   When first we came to the hill-top there,
> And we laughed to know that the Boche was going,
>   And laughed to know that the land was fair;
> Acre by acre of green fields sleeping,
>   Hamlets hid in the tufts of wood,
> And out of the trees were church-towers peeping,
> And away on a hillock the Windmill stood.
>
> *Then, ah then, 'twas a land worth winning,*
>   *And now there is naught but the naked clay,*
> *But I can remember the Windmill spinning,*
>   *And the four sails shone in the sun that day.*
>
> But the guns came after and tore the hedges
>   And stripped the spinneys and churned the plain,
> And a man walks now on the windy ledges
>   And looks for a feather of green in vain;

Acre by acre the sad eye traces
  The rust-red bones of the earth laid bare,
And the sign-posts stand in the market places
  To say that a village was builded there.

But better the French fields stark and dying
  Than ripe for a conqueror's fat content,
And I can remember the mill-sails flying,
  Yet I cheered with the rest when the Windmill went.

Away to the East the grass-land surges
  Acre by acre across the line,
And we must go on to the end like scourges,
  Though the wilderness stretch from sea to Rhine;
But I dream some days of a great reveille,
  When the buds shall burst in the Blasted Wood,
And children chatter in Death-Trap Alley,
  And a windmill stands where the Windmill stood.

And we that remember the Windmill spinning,
  We may go under, but not in vain,
For our sons shall come in the new beginning
  And see that the Windmill spins again.

In another poem he dreamed of better days, 'when foolish men for ever sheath their foolish swords'. His front-line experiences were recurring in 'most horrible and extraordinary' nightmares. There is no doubt that his war novel was being compulsively written under the duress of frightful memories. It was to tell of the failure of a young officer like himself to come to terms with fear at the height of battle, and it owed its veracity to circumstances bitterly recollected in the Royal Naval Division; so bitterly that the chief witness for the prosecution at the court martial was ostracized throughout the Division when the dreaded verdict was made known. As an epitaph on a victim of the unprecedented stresses of war in the twentieth century, APH concluded his novel with the words: 'My friend Harry was shot for cowardice and he was the bravest man I ever knew.'

He wrote the novel 'in a few weeks,' much of it from personal experience. Reading it, one can believe that it was an attempt to exorcise the haunting effect on his mind and heart of the fate of his central character, whose identity as a comrade-in-arms was all too real to him.[4]

Writing the book was an affair of greater urgency than finding a publisher for it. For the time being he made no move in that direction. The end of the war was imminent. A further period of service in his amphibious role lay ahead of him.

NOTES ON CHAPTER 4

1 A. P. Herbert: unpublished article.
2 A. P. Herbert: *Beaucourt Revisited*, from *The Mudhook*, journal of the 63rd (RN) Division, September 1917. Lieut. the Hon. Vere Harmsworth had recently written to his father, Lord Rothermere: 'I may have been born just to live my 21 years and then fade away.'
3 A. P. Herbert: *Punch*, 10 April 1918.
4 The name of the young officer who was court-martialled was first published in Horatio Bottomley's *John Bull*; more recently, in *The Thin Yellow Line* by William Moore (1974).

5

Convoy Alarms — and Excursions

On 2 October 1918 he sailed out of Liverpool in a convoy bound for Alexandria. He was rated 'Assistant to Commodore'. His experiences were pencilled in a diary that testifies to his discretion in that post. It gives no hint of the nature and purpose of the convoy, not even whether it was laden or unladen.

From the first day out he realized some of the difficulties of a convoy commodore, '(a) in finding his position, peering through the rain and spray, and wondering whether or when to alter course; (b) in trying to collect the bits of escort and convoy scattered by our sailing in darkness, and by the wind'. Two days later, the commodore was laid low by influenza, a victim of the epidemic that swept over Europe that autumn. As his amateur right-hand man, APH was apprehensive. 'Hope to goodness he doesn't succumb' (*Diary*). Then came the convoy's first loss by enemy submarine attack. Women and children went down in the stricken ship – 'an awful blow'. Vessels that lagged behind, fell out of line, or wandered off course, became an increasing and constant worry.

'Great excitement on the bridge' one night: a collision seemed imminent. 'The captain, the commodore, officers, signalmen and all sorts were peering into the pitchy darkness and expecting at any moment to cannon into the other ship. It was extremely lucky that no bump took place' (*Diary*). Other moments of crisis were ascribed to 'periscopes, porpoises and false alarms'. The diary vividly annotates the routine of a wartime convoy officer's days and nights.

Relaxing, APH read novels by Wells, Conrad and Compton Mackenzie, and talked with the ship's doctor, 'a probationary surgeon with an intellectual face and a small beard who knows all about Nietzsche and who, tho' a doctor, refuses to be inoculated'. The ship had a newly acquired mascot, 'a little old Yorkshire terrier with a feeble bark'. It had been rescued from the sea, 'floating legs upward', after a torpedo attack.

Aided by Mothersill's, APH survived 'enormous seas' and what
he feared would be calamity, 'a terrifying angle of rolling, 30 or
40 degrees. We thought she was going.' After being shown round the
engine-room by the chief engineer, he wrote: 'I hate engines', and
pondered the likely fate of men immured there during a torpedo
attack. 'It is very disturbing, I was longing to get on deck again.'
He was depressed by the working conditions and pay of the lascars,
who had 'one of the worst jobs going, hidden away down there.
They only get 22–30 rupees a month.'

Port Said was 'a dirty, uninteresting place, the natives always
amusing but, my goodness, how rapacious!' He was given a free
pass to Cairo. 'The first thing I saw was COLMAN's MUSTARD on a
signal box.' He was cheered by the news that the Allies had taken
Lille and Ostend.

In the spice market he was shown 'the famous letter from Mrs
Asquith to the proprietor of "a small cigarette stall".' The letter
was 'much tattered but obviously genuine'. It was written to remind
the stallholder that Sir Ernest Cassel[1] had ordered him to send
Mrs Asquith a supply of Egyptian cigarettes every week but that
'for 2 weeks they have not arrived. I hope that you will not make him
pay for them.'

The convoy left Port Said in the last week of October, sailing
along the North African coast: 'no submarine alarm for four days'.
APH took the chance of going ashore at Tunis, Bizerta, Algiers and
Oran, making unaccompanied excursions inland. Tunis was 'a
funny, sleepy place, where everything is topsy-turvy and the very
cocks crow at midnight'. It was there he heard that 'Turkey has
thrown her hand in', great news for one who had fought at Gallipoli.
He had always hoped to visit Carthage. Now he was there, finding
the ruins 'sparse but interesting', with the exception of the theatre,
'which really is rather impressive'. Dismissing the 'rather irritating'
guide, he came to the place where, he presumed, 'Dido was burned, a
marvellous site' for a funeral pyre. Judging by the diary, nowhere
did his classical knowledge inspire him to more than prosaic comment. Later, discussing sightseeing in a *Punch* article, he supposed
that he was 'singularly lacking in the Sense of the Sublime', and
asked himself: 'What is the matter with me? Freud would know, I
suppose', but APH on the couch might have been a misleading case.

Constantine, 'a surprisingly good place to see', was 'rather like
Shaftesbury'. From the train going there he had looked out over

fields of red earth that 'remind you of Devonshire'. Continuing by train to Algiers, the flattest part of the landscape was 'very moist and fertile and cultivated, most like England'. Algiers was 'a little disappointing – rather like a clean edition of Hastings'. Dining with three officers of the Royal Navy, 'it was a relief to meet some English folk again'. An Algerian music-hall was 'a rotten show', compared unfavourably with the Chiswick Empire.

On 11 November he went by train from Oran to Tlemcen, 'which everyone assured me it was my duty to do. Curiously enough, exactly at 11.00 we heard that the Armistice had been signed'. Soon the flags were out: 'nearly all French, numbers of American, but very few Union Jacks'.

Caught up in an excited multi-coloured crowd, he was conducted into the presence of the mayor on a balcony, where he was cheered and toasted in champagne. 'I must have been the only Englishman for at least 80 miles.' A self-appointed master of ceremonies induced him to sing *Tipperary*. 'He then flung himself upon me and kissed me violently on both cheeks (he was extremely prickly).'

After the compliments, which included no more than half-hearted acknowledgment 'of the part played by Angleterre', APH 'rose in duty bound and spoke a few appropriate remarks in halting French, a feeble attempt'. People packed the streets, bands played, drums were banged, processions marched back and forth, the scene becoming highly theatrical with the lighting of torches after dark. At one stage in the festivities, 'a Boche suddenly approached me and asked if I spoke Allemand. I was amazed. He had a French wife, so I could not have slain him if I had felt like it'. He finished the evening 'promenading with 2 amusing French officers, and was quite glad to get to bed'. His encounter with the German was more disturbing than he knew.

On 17 November he noted in the diary 'a most unpleasant' war nightmare in which he faced a crowd of Germans in field grey, all armed with carving knives. 'One being menacing to me, I realised that I had only a fish knife. This I stuck into his throat. It was sufficiently horrible but I did not make a good job of it. Jerrold appeared with a carving knife and finished the disgusting deed', a dream of inadequacy that may have been as revealing of Jerrold as of the dreamer. A less recondite aspect of his nature was disclosed in the diary entry he made after shopping for souvenirs: 'Don't think I am very good at bargaining.'

Shore leave at Gibraltar enabled him to cross to Algeciras, where the hotel 'was not a great ugly barrack but really a dream, set in beautiful grounds with orange and palm and rose trees. Altogether very attractive but of course a *leetle* expensive – 25 pesetas a day now.'[2] He was happy among his own kind again. 'A lot of good fellows over from the Rock to lunch – Scott, Watts, C'r Pape & others.' A crowd of young American officers 'made fools of themselves and a frightful noise from about 10 to 2 a.m.'

In the same week of November 1918, 'showering pesetas right and left', he took train for Seville, 'passing through the great cork forests before Ronda; after that everything is olives and ploughland and neat vineyards on the hills'. An abortive appointment with the vice-consul, named Hartley, provoked the diary comment: 'Either one has no company or the company you have messes up your arrangements. However, the Cathedral a very fine building, a wonderful picture gallery of Murillos'. He went to vespers: 'the rest of the public consisted of 2 Spaniards, chatting and laughing at the service, and 2 motionless old ladies in black. Service impressed me unfavourably.' The behaviour of the choirboys was 'incredibly bad, charging about, talking, laughing, and now and then spitting, (I even saw one priest spit in the choir), and genuflecting with wild hilarity like clowns in an arena'. Walking the streets, 'extraordinary number of cross-eyed people you see here'.

He was 'not at all pleased with Cordoba', though agreeing that 'it might have looked well if the sun had shone'. There were 'stacks of oranges all over the town', and the streets were 'full of donkeys with enormous panniers carrying earth from over the river'. Vespers at the cathedral there too, 'the service a little better than Seville but I disliked very much the regiment of fat and self-satisfied priests. One old chap was colossal. He swam in and out with obvious difficulty, only just threading his way between the columns. It shows what an immense place it is that as he disappeared down the interminable vistas of arches even he began to seem small.'

He was 'quite glad to leave the place', for frequently he was mistaken 'for a Boche', and sneering remarks were made, accompanied by derisive laughter, at his expense. 'I have turned on one or two & explained hotly, as far as that is possible in my Spanish, that I am Inglese. They are a low crowd here & I have no doubt that they were all for the Boche a few weeks back.'

He arrived in Madrid on 22 November, lunching that day with

the embassy naval attaché, Captain Harvey, 'a nice bluff fellow'; Filson Young,[3] 'with whom I argued, to his surprise & disgust'; one Merry del Val;[4] and others'. Madrid was 'not attractive in the rain', and it was lacking in beautiful buildings, 'rather like an inland Brighton'. Evidently a sweet-toothed city: 'thousands of high-class confectioners with an immense wealth of chocolates and cakes'. He concluded his notes on Madrid with the critical observation: 'Considering that we gave them a good deal of coal, I don't think the Spaniards should be allowed to waste so much on illuminated advertisements.'

He did not record the homeward voyage. The war had ended but for him, as for so many others, its tensions remained. He had suffered psychic wounds that were long in healing. His nightmares persisted into the new decade. His agitation at their climax was often terrible. He would throw off the bedclothes and stumble about in the dark screaming words of command. One night, returning to London *via* Paris, he flung himself from the hotel bed and would have opened the window at his peril had he not been restrained. Those episodes became so alarming that Gwen, his wife, tied her wrist to his in bed as a warning device. His anguish vibrates in a poem he called *The War Dream:*

> I wish I did not dream of France,
>   And spend my nights in mortal dread . . .

A willing actor in the drama of 1914–18, which Yeats from his critics' box dismissed as 'a bloody frivolity', APH played his part, like the rest of the enormous cast, in obedience to primitive promptings translated by rhetoric into ideals. If the experience of war helped him to attain a measure of self-knowledge, there was no sign that it brought him a sense of fulfilment, though anyone looking him in the eye might have discerned there a flicker of pride at duty done. He mostly enjoyed the inescapable propinquity of his fellow men, especially of those who reaffirmed the heroic element in human nature. He emerged from the comradeship of fire apparently as self-sufficient as before: untouched by the radical disillusionment that produced better poetry than his for the post-war anthologies; cherishing an undeclared resolve to hold to the standards and loyalties of his companions who had died; committed to no personal affinities that imperatively mattered outside the home; dedicated, as the consequence of unforgettable tragedy, to the defence of the individual against every kind of organized tyranny or threat to his freedom.

NOTES ON CHAPTER 5

1   Sir Ernest Cassel (1852–1921), a German-Jewish merchant banker who had been a close friend of Edward VII.
2   The peseta was then the equivalent of 9d.
3   Filson Young (1876–1938) was editor of *The Saturday Review*, a *Manchester Guardian* special correspondent, and author of books on music and travel.
4   Brother of the Spanish ambassador in London.

6

Pen v *Wig*

Punch Office,
10 Bouverie Street,
London, E.C.4.
25 January 1919

Dear Mr Herbert,   At the last minute I have had to sub-
stitute your Jazz verses for those about Rabbits. You will
see that I ventured to correct a grammatical slip. 'Fair as
her' ought I fancy to be 'Fair as she'.

Good luck to your
novel. I hope you will let Methuens see it first.

Yours sincerely,
E. V. L.

I never saw a letter from E. V. Lucas (1868–1938) in which the left-
hand margin did not widen down the page until his famous initials
formed the apex of an inverted pyramid of mostly illegible words.
One wonders what an inspired graphologist would have made of it.
Perhaps it was one of the pointers to aspects of his personality that
puzzled his friends, who were numerous, admiring, and affectionate.

He was the devoted biographer of Charles Lamb. He was also
just about the most prolific light essayist of his time, his gifts as
attractively displayed in the pages of *Punch* as in his weekly column
in the *Sunday Times*. His travel books were widely read and long
enduring in print. At that time of writing to APH he was filling the
dual role of literary editor of *Punch* and chief reader for Methuens,
the publishers, in Essex Street, Strand.

E.V., as he was familiarly known, was of old Quaker stock, the V
indicating kinship with the far-flung Verrall family of that persuasion. A reluctant pupil at a succession of Brighton schools, he would
doubtless have agreed that his education began when, at sixteen,
he was taken on to the staff of a local newspaper. He first sat at the
Punch table in 1904, filling the chair of Phil May, by way of augment-

ing the literary side against a preponderance of artists. He had a quiet magisterial presence from which in the right company he lapsed easily into conviviality, his curious twisted smile often suggesting judgment deferred on utterances too readily pronounced or too eagerly accepted by others.

His interest in the novel APH was writing led to the finished work presently arriving on his desk at Methuens. Having recommended it for publication, he arranged for APH to meet Sir Algernon Methuen, the head of the firm. Sir Algernon was addicted to the use of the speaking-tube, already an antique method of internal communication in the business world. 'It doesn't cost you money to write a book,' he brusquely reminded his caller. 'It does cost *us* money to publish it. Books, you know, don't grow on trees, Mr Herbert. Books have to be printed – they have to be bound'. Shuffling the papers on his desk, Sir Algernon asked: 'I wonder if you have the slightest idea what our bill for paper was last year, Mr Herbert?' A whistle into the speaking-tube brought the required answer. 'Then there is our binding bill, which amounted to – let me see', and another whistle produced the information, passed on to APH. Sir Algernon then began to speak more explicitly of overheads. APH had never heard the word before. He said that he was made to feel like a penitent. 'I shambled out of that office almost ready to apologise for having written a book.' A contract followed, giving him an advance of £25, afterwards amended to £50.

The Secret Battle was announced in Methuen's spring list for 1919. It was critically appraised as a young man's novel, winning favour by its crystal-clear style and hard truth. The crushing power of the Army system over the individual was depicted with a quiet force that left readers chilled with dismay, the more so because, as *The Times Literary Supplement* reviewer observed, it enhanced the impression that 'something very like it must have happened over and over again'. (Those of us who served on the Western Front can have no doubt of it.)

The book was 'read all night' by Lloyd George, who, APH was told, commended it to the attention of Winston Churchill, then Secretary of State for War. APH believed that court martial arrangements were subsequently 'altered in some way'. H. A. L. Fisher, the historian of Europe, admired the book as 'a masterpiece of construction'. A war leader of the future, General Montgomery, considered it 'the best story of front line war'. As recently as 1970 it was recalled in *The Times Literary Supplement* as 'a masterpiece of realistic fiction'.

Unanimous approval did not mean soaring sales. Readers, it seemed, were tired of war as a dramatic theme; it had been too much with them in the past five years.[1] The sumptuous Christmas Number of *The Bookman* (1919) contained a full-page advertisement listing sixty current Methuen titles. *The Secret Battle* was not among them. Its failure at the crucial stage may be seen as having an important effect on its author's professional development. Had the book been a success in the counting house he might well have settled down to the career of a novelist, in emulation, say, of Galsworthy, with whose public spirit he had much in common, and with whom there was also an affinity of style; both were more concerned with what they had to say than with how they said it. As literature, *The Secret Battle* was and remains APH's best book. Because it gave him no guarantees for the future he was driven to take an economic decision that deflected his talent from the drama to *divertissement*. A subtler self-protective factor may have been at work. The dark side of life had been too much with him in recent times, instilling in him a mistrust of the imagination, with a consequent loss of creative force. Laughter was a solvent of fear, humorous journalism an antidote to the terrors of the night.

He was called to the Bar by the Inner Temple, and entered the chambers of Leslie Scott, K.C. (1869–1950), Conservative MP for the Exchange Division of Liverpool, sometime Solicitor General, and a Lord of Appeal. Two of APH's Oxford friends, Walter Monckton and Harry Strauss (later Lord Conesford), joined him there. Lord Conesford was sure that APH never seriously considered a career at the Bar. 'We three were called the same night. Alan was an excellent lawyer, but he was too many-sided to find the workaday life in chambers tolerable'.[2]

No doubt he would have been a good advocate, though hardly for the devil. One can imagine him forcefully arguing a case (with much blinking and head-jerking). He would have been less likely to shine as examining counsel. He was capable of clinical detachment but his inhibitions would have had the last word, his impregnable inner privacy a shield for others as well as for himself. There was also the matter of rewards. Bar practice could be as precarious as freelance journalism.

Doubt about the relative satisfactions of the wig and the pen might have been more immediately resolved for him could he have foreseen the result of his review in *Punch* (19 November 1919) of a little book called *Tales of Talbot House*, a history of the Army spiritual welfare movement known as Toc H, founded by the Revd P. B. Clayton in memory of Gilbert Talbot, one of APH's fellow-lodgers at Oxford. In the review APH endorsed a plan to 'keep alive this Christian fellowship of the War'. Sixteen years later, 'Tubby' Clayton wrote to him: 'Your review in *Punch* was the first step which brought Toc H in Flanders to rebirth.' The letter was signed 'Your debtor'.

For the hardly congruous reason that a legal career might have yielded material for 'a knock-out novel' (his phrase), APH afterwards affected to regret that he had not 'answered the call' to the Bar. Having made the decision, he indulged in sentimental recollections of his brief period in the Inner Temple. Lawyers were 'a much maligned but beneficent body of men'. If he laughed at them, it was 'with affection and respect'. He especially treasured his memories of dining in Hall on Grand Night. The panelling, the pictures, 'every stately decanter of port', glowed in his memory. They were 'eloquent of the antiquity and indestructability of the traditions of English law'. He declared himself 'for ever sorry' that he was 'not of the proud and faithful brotherhood who serve the laws of England'.

Domestically, he was preoccupied by the 'overheads' to which Methuen, the publisher, had cryptically alluded. The household at Hammersmith Terrace could not be supported on *Punch*'s eccentric rates of payment, e.g. £2 14s. for 'a set of verses'. His first prose contribution appeared there in March 1920, and again the cheque implied patronage rather than just reward.

Other sources of income had to be found. With the masterful will-power that he was capable of imposing on every purpose, great and small, he wrote *The House by the River* (1920) in two months. It was a crime novel with a difference in that its chief character, a poet who inadvertently becomes a murderer, is presented in comedy terms without diminishing the underlying drama. Some of its river scenes, depicted with delicacy and charm, show that already APH had surrendered absolutely to the lure of the Upper Thames. His rendering of the more frenetic aspects of the post-war dancing-fever is a contribution to social history. If the novel added little to his reputation, it deserved more critical notice than it received for its evidence of a good mind at work on a murder story that, in other hands, might have been merely sensational.

He had handed his literary business to the leading agent, A. P. Watt, who sold the American rights in *The House by the River* to Knopf in New York. Watt also secured volume publication of some of his prose pieces from *Punch* under the title *Light Articles Only* (Methuen, 1921), dedicated 'with respect' to Leslie Scott, KC, MP. His sense of fun interlaced every subject, whether it was the House of Lords in session as the nation's supreme court of appeal; an early morning visit to Billingsgate fish market; Bradshaw's *Railway Guide*; or the art of poetry.

Punch readers expected him to have fun with *vers libre*, and he did not fail them. They did not know then that while it was a form that he tended to parody a little too self-consciously, he could and did express himself with fine assurance in it. In the same place he gave it as gospel that 'the limerick is the most difficult form of the metric art'.

NOTES ON CHAPTER 6

1 *Tell England*, by Ernest Raymond, published two years after *The Secret Battle*, contained Gallipoli scenes but it was not a war novel.
2 Letter: 16 June, 1973.

7

'Across the Pond'

In 1921 he crossed the Atlantic with Logan Pearsall Smith and J. C. Squire, a conjunction of personalities promising if not guaranteeing an invigorating voyage. Pearsall Smith (1865–1949),[1] an American citizen turned Englishman by adoption, had been at Balliol under Jowett. He was respected by the literary *cognoscenti* as the author of the *Trivia* books, collections of aphoristic writings representing his life's ambition 'to live on after my funeral in a perfect phrase'. He was going to the Johns Hopkins Hospital, Baltimore, 'for an operation on the ignoble parts of my anatomy' – more explicitly, for prostate surgery. Squire (1884–1958), poet, essayist, parodist, 'Solomon Eagle' of the *New Statesman* and founder-editor of the *London Mercury*, had lecture engagements in Philadelphia, Baltimore and Washington, as part of a campaign to promote his magazine among American readers. APH was commissioned by *Punch* to write half a dozen articles on the trip under the general title of *Across the Pond*. He hoped for profitable meetings with New York publishers and editors. Pearsall Smith reported in a letter that his companions were 'as kind and charming as two human beings can be'. Afterwards it appeared that he was not greatly attracted by Squire.

APH's often illegibly pencilled diary of the trip barely acknowledges Pearsall Smith's existence. 'We have a man called Smith with us', he wrote in the first of his *Punch* articles, in which Squire is disguised as 'Hodge'.[2] While there may not have been the gulf between them that Pearsall Smith maintained there was between himself and those who disliked oysters or did not enjoy Jane Austen, they seem to have had little in common. Affinity between the disciple of Pater and the acolyte of *Punch* may have been too much to expect.

Strolling the deck of 'this not wholly satisfactory good ship *Albania*', of the Southern Ocean Steamship Line, APH would have heard good talk, though he may often have felt himself excluded from it, for Pearsall Smith's prime topic was books and literary style, and Squire was well equipped to engage in any such discussion. At the Savage Club in the thirties a group of members – Earle Welby, D. B. Wyndham Lewis, Edward Shanks, T. Michael Pope, Clennell Wilkinson, Victor Bridges, James Agate and others – kept book-talk flourishing there as never since. A memory survives of APH standing by, glass in hand, sagely blinking, saying little; in that company, a periphery man. I never knew him to draw a conversation into literary channels.

On the voyage to New York, 'my first view of Ireland', he wrote on 16 October, when the ship put in at Queenstown. 'It looked misty and wet and unnaturally green in patches and generally as distressful as it ought to look'. The harbour was 'very fine', the town like a 'small Hastings'. Forty-five 'peasant-like' new passengers were taken on board, 'many weeping'. Early in the voyage, a rumour went round the ship that Pearsall Smith was the Bishop of Bermuda and APH his private chaplain.

'The Queens' were not yet ruling the Atlantic waves but their predecessors of the twenties had already acquired prestige as floating hotels, prompting APH to comment that 'our ship is more like a floating boarding-house', and that it should be renamed 'Seaview' or 'No. 1 Marine Parade'. By the fifth day out, 'the charm of this ocean has been greatly exaggerated', he wrote. His literary *ambiance* having been discovered, he had to prepare himself for such confrontations as that of the woman passenger from Belfast, who exhorted him: 'Do tell me what books I *ought* to read.'

He ruminated on the fate of a swallow 'that suddenly appeared in the smoking room and flew round and round, very frightened and tired'. The Venerable Bede's great simile evidently did not occur to him, though he wondered: 'Where can it have come from?' An appealing thought struck him: ' – perhaps from Chiswick Eyot!'

Staten Island looked 'jolly and English'. Having to file past 'a cross-eyed American doctor' before landing led to 'an awful bungle' because he had 'seen some of the same people twice'. As for 'the Customs business, it was absurd'. Pearsall Smith's account of their treatment by American officialdom was far more scathing. 'We arrived yesterday', he reported in a letter to James Whitall, 26 October, 'broken in spirit & degraded & consternated by all the awful formalities of landing. They herded us about like swine & we were submitted to every kind of insult & degradation.'

Pearsall Smith went off to the hospital in Baltimore. APH and Squire booked in at the Albert Hotel, 42 East 11th Street, denounced by APH a week later as 'cheap, God-forsaken, and miserable' because he could not be served with early-morning tea. For a further week it was the base from which he and Squire sallied forth to meet and be met as part of an impromptu programme of welcome that more than once sent APH to bed 'dazed, bewildered, over-whelmed, stunned – no words to describe our condition of mind. American hospitality is positively homicidal. The American heart is built on the same scale as the skyscrapers.'

Early one evening he strolled alone 'nearly the whole way down fifth Avenue, a glorious street' His pleasure in it was marred by the 'appalling injunction: No LOITERING – KEEP MOVING – CITY ORDINANCE', in what he supposed was 'just about the best loitering place in the world.' Prohibition, which he suggested should be called Discouragement, was the subject of recurring exclamatory notes in the diary. He was nervous of wood-alcohol, and after a disturbed night he feared that he had been poisoned by it. He noted shifts of moral behaviour among highly respectable persons, and was a guest in several houses where the hosts, normally law-abiding, had hidden stocks of whisky, gin and wine. In one or two they were so well hidden that they could not be found when wanted. He witnessed frantic upstairs and below-stairs searches.

The New York social pace was too much for him. He was often 'tired to death'. His depleted nerves led to a neurotic reaction as he looked down from the top of the Woolworth Building, the height of which, he noted, was 792 ft. 1 in. 'Never had before so strong an inclination to throw myself over. Normally, I don't have that feeling. Up there it was awful.'

Invited to meet Pearsall Smith's maternal relatives, the Whitalls, at their home 'in a sort of Wimbledon, only better', between New York and Philadelphia, he endured an afternoon of intellectual disadvantage. 'Jack and Mr Whitall[3] talked "book shop" until 6 p.m. I would have preferred to sit quietly outside but was too polite.'

Princeton was 'a curious mixture of awful old buildings and new good ones, especially those in the Oxford pseudo-Gothic style'. He saw startling evidence of the anarchic impulses that have been trans-formed by present-day cant into student protest. It appeared to him that 'nearly all the buildings seemed to have been burned down at some time or other'. Passing 'a large heap of stones', he was told that 'they were the chapel'. He had the impression that 'they eventually burn any building they don't like', and he wondered 'which is the next on the list'. The visit had its rejuvenating moments. 'Made us feel quite young again to see every one walking about without hats.' His appreciation of 'the very pronounced Oxford atmosphere' was heightened when he met a certain Professor Macdonald, 'who was indistinguishable from an Englishman'. Young Schuyler Jackson, writer and poetry editor to be, was 'very pleasant and intelligent, not to say dynamic'. He produced 'some whisky that had been hidden away'.

Philadelphia had no charms for him: 'a huge, sprawling, ugly industrial town. The best thing, the old State Hall', surrounded by 'wide old buildings, rather like Kensington Square'. A local club reminded him of the Savage; 'a surprising number' of the members claimed to have read *The House by the River*.

In Baltimore he stayed with a Quaker family, Dr and Mrs Carey; 'a pleasant old couple but the old boy inclined to prose on a bit. If you ask him a simple question he begins by explaining the creation of the world.' The doctor produced some whisky, 'obtained by medical prescription. Oh, for a decent glass of wine!' Baltimore was 'quite a nice little town (considering it has about three-quarters of a million inhabitants), much nicer than Philadelphia'. Pearsall Smith wrote to James Whitall from his hospital bed: 'Squire & Herbert have just been in. They are having a roaring time & their talk is all of the evasions of the Prohibition laws. The sweetness of forbidden drink seems irresistible' (7 November 1921). APH's diary tells us nothing of that hospital visit or of the patient.

He thought it worth noting that 'you never see a bicycle in this country'. He had seen two or three at Princeton; that was all; none in the streets. 'Everybody here has a Ford. Very soon they will have forgotten how to walk.'

On 8 November 1921 APH and Squire left for Washington to meet 'Judge' Bingham.[4] At the Shoreham Hotel they were handed a message postponing the appointment. 'Unfortunately, we had provided ourselves with no introductions, so felt unusually lost. Wandered about the town for some time. It is like a small Paris, without the shops, and entirely inhabited by motors. Never saw anything like the cars alongside the pavements, which are absolutely deserted. Why they have pavements I don't know. Walking is practically illegal. There seem to be more cars than people.' After no more than two days he was 'rather bored' with Washington and 'its architecture of the dead'.

With nothing else to do one afternoon, he and Squire dropped into 'a kind of music-hall place (standing room). A very good show', which included 'a comedian who was an actor gone wrong'. As they were leaving, 'we discovered that Woodrow Wilson[5] was in the house'. He had gone there to see 'the Unknown Soldier film', his appearance in which was 'loudly cheered'. He was 'loudly cheered' again as he left. 'Caught a good glimpse of him in the theatre and in the car outside. Apparently he is becoming popular again. He looked very old and white-haired but smiled and waved his hat quite actively.'

In the train to Charlottesville, Virginia: 'The country open and pretty, and in the distance the Blue Ridge Mountains (made famous by the *Lonesome Pine* song). Very like England in many ways except (a) nothing seems to be done with any of the land, very little corn and only a few cattle, the decay of the South plainly visible; (b) we missed the little villages and church towers; (c) all the houses of wood.'

Observing that among 'the rows and rows of eating-shops' in Charlottesville 'some bore the sign: *For Whites Only*', he scribbled down his recollection of what a British diplomat had earlier told him, that 'the first article of the Transvaal Constitution begins: "There is no equality of White and Black in Church and State." That at any rate is frank, which is more than can be said of the American, which begins: "All men are free and equal".'

At Lexington, centre of the tobacco-growing industry, where Bingham was campaigning for a co-operative movement, APH came to the conclusion that 'this is where the old stock still carries on. The great majority not only look but speak like Englishmen.' Many might have been mistaken 'for wise and elderly London solicitors. Not one of them was bronzed, not one of them carried a gun.'

Seen from the train, St Louis was 'an extraordinarily dirty town, looking very like the outskirts of Bristol, nothing but tall chimneys and smoke'. He and Squire were *en route* to Springfield, Illinois, to meet Vachel Lindsay, 'the jazz poet'. Lindsay was adapting verse to the new ragtime rhythms and, as an apostle of what was called 'the higher vaudeville', poetry for public declamation, was evoking an excitement akin to that of negro revivalist meetings. He was a pop figure of his time and – well ahead of ours – was making a reputation based largely on childish ideas and mindless noise, only faintly redeemed by the music-hall gusto of *The Santa Fé Trail* and *The Fireman's Ball*.

A meal at the poet's home consisted of 'some really horrible dishes', one of them 'a loathsome sticky sweet concoction of ginger and yellow tomatoes'. Lindsay's mother was 'a nice but maddening old thing' who had 'an awful habit of butting in', prompting the wry comment in the diary: 'I don't wonder that Lindsay is going to travel for a year'.

They were taken on a sight-seeing tour of the Chicago stockyards of 'Messrs Swift & Son, the meat packers', an experience that cast a sombre shadow over their last days in the US. Received at the entrance by 'a genial old man, the Treasurer, Mr Cotton', they were asked: 'Won't you stay to lunch after you've seen the sticking – proof of the pudding, you know?' The invitation was declined. Possibly primed by Upton Sinclair's sensational novel, *The Jungle*[6] (1906), 'we had already imagined enough of what we were going to see'.

They braced themselves to watch 'the really terrible' cattle slaughtering. 'Saw calves hanging heads downward and being slit. They were *not* knocked on the head first because, the guide said, it would spoil the brains. The cattle, though, are stunned with a sledge hammer first, and we saw them being driven along a narrow pen, two by two, and sledge hammered by an invisible man, at which they crumpled up and were hauled away for "sticking".'

> They were strangely silent,
> But once from them came most quiet and pitiful
> A brief little lowing, a little plaintive moo,
> Like a question that got no answer.[7]

'An incredibly horrible scene', APH wrote of the final act of killing the cattle. Men were walking about 'in a sea of blood, slitting the animals' throats, and over all the horrible smell', which Squire in his poem described as 'the smell of death, the odour of death, that hangs over Chicago'.

Sheep were led to their fate by a white goat, 'trained to lead them into the pen (they won't go otherwise)'. Having enticed one batch to the slaughtering place, the white goat went back for the next, and the next; and so on, 'for eight hours a day'.

Rhine wine diluted with water was served at lunch with 'some of the *litterateurs* of Chicago', who gave him the impression of being 'rather on the defensive about American books'. One of them, Carl Sandburg, 'a maddish free verse poet and rebel',[8] argued with Squire about *The Times'* art critic.[9] Another writer, 'Mr Hecht,[10] was sore because a book of his had been slated by *The Times*. There was also Mr Sherwood Anderson, who seemed a clever fellow'.[11]

The diary closes with an account of a football game, Michigan *v* Minnesota, mostly transcribed from a local newspaper, and affirming his unfailing response to the quotidian, the inexhaustible appeal to him of the living present, his existential indifference to time past and to come. The bland surface of life was his domain, not the troubled depths. At no point in his daily notation of his American experiences is there evidence of a probing mind, of his asking a searchingly relevant question, or exploring even the most prosaic avenues of inquiry. He was a singularly incurious man who behaved as if he was in thrall to a nursery ordinance that equated inquisitiveness with bad manners. He returned from the United States with an assortment of memories and impressions as his mental luggage but, unlike Squire, with nothing of intellectual value to declare.

Logan Pearsall Smith to James Whitall:

> The Deanery, Bryn Mawr,
> Penna.
> 28th January, 1922.
>
> . . . I hear many echoes of Squire's & Herbert's progress through America. They seemed to cause as much astonishment as they received. There was a formal dinner party in New York to which the Flexners went, and Squire was invited. He brought Herbert along, uninvited, in his genial way & Herbert entered with a pair of un-washed socks in his hand which he had borrowed from Simon Flexner[12] & which he thought appropriate to return on this occasion. This, as you can imagine, created a sensation.

At home the year was one of political uncertainties, especially in the Conservative and Unionist ranks. Anglo-French relations were under strain. The possibility of war with Turkey was a source of rising anxiety. The long dominance of Lloyd George was coming to an end in a cloud of recrimination about his handling of foreign affairs and, even more bitter, about the sale of honours and the profit they brought to his Party funds and allegedly to himself. His resignation in the autumn was followed by a general election. APH went up to Liverpool to help his former chief in chambers, Sir Leslie Scott, who was holding his Conservative seat against Joe Devlin, the Irish Nationalist candidate. APH's arrival on that scene was the subject of an entry in the diary of Sir Archibald Salvidge, PC, a commanding figure in the civic life of Liverpool. He could not understand 'what exactly was APH's part' in the campaign.

'As one of the foremost leaders of the Bar, Scott is not in need of a prominent author to marshal his arguments or supply him with a flow of words. And as he killed Devlin with clear logic and cold facts and not by adopting ridicule or banter, APH did not come in on the latter score. However, everyone likes Herbert, so he is always an asset. He works like a Trojan at whatever Scott gives him to do and goes about everywhere, blinking rapidly behind his glasses with a sort of nervous intensity.'

At dinner one night Sir Archibald showed him a rhyme that he intended using in a speech supporting Scott, a play on the words "Great Scott! Don't let the Devl'in!" 'APH kept touching up the lines between courses, and at the end of the meal he handed me a marvellously improved version of the doggerel which went splendidly when later I fired it off from the platform.'

NOTES ON CHAPTER 7

1 He was the brother-in-law of Bertrand Russell and Bernard Berenson.
2 He reappeared in the same guise in A. G. Macdonell's *England, Their England* (1929).
3 A glass-bottle manufacturer of distinguished Quaker lineage.
4 Robert W. Bingham (1871–1937), newspaper proprietor, US ambassador in London, 1932–37.
5 President of the USA, 1913–21.
6 *The Jungle* shocked the American reading public and led to a Government investigation of conditions in the Chicago stockyards.
7 J. C. Squire: *The Stockyard*, a long blank verse poem dedicated to Robert Frost. It was published in the *London Mercury*, June 1922.
8 Carl Sandburg, poet of the Middle West, often spoken of as Walt Whitman's chief disciple.
9 At that time, A. Clutton Brock.
10 Presumably Ben Hecht, Jewish-American newspaperman and film scriptwriter; notorious after World War Two for his anti-British attitude.
11 Sherwood Anderson, the first American novelist to present his characters in Freudian terms.
12 Director of the Rockefeller Institude for Medical Research.

8

An Invitation from 'Mr Punch'

From the early twenties APH's name became a hardy annual in the publishers' lists, chiefly Methuen's. Verse and prose of his from *Punch* came out in a succession of volumes that had a particular appeal to readers who rarely opened any other kind of book. Like most professional humorists (Leacock and Wodehouse, for example) he wrote for a largely uncritical public. Some of his verse was compared with Belloc's *Cautionary Tales for Children* (1907). The affinity was superficial; even so, one has the impression that he was well aware of Belloc's overshadowing presence in the light verse *genre*; and that aggressive satirist might well have given an approving nod to APH's *Song for a Socialist Sunday School :*[1]

> All are born equal, counter this who can.
> Place in his cot some scion of the rich,
> Lay at his side an infant artisan,
> And who shall say for certain which is which?

> *By reason, not ruction,*
> *We soar to the skies;*
> *The means of production*
> *We nationalise;*
> *With rapture surprising*
> *We bring within range*
> *By nationalising*
> *The means of exchange.*

> How comes it then that as the seasons pass
> These equal babes enjoy a different lot?
> One steers the ship, one polishes the brass,
> While one is beautiful, the other is not.

> *By reason, . . . etc.*

APH acknowledged Belloc as one of his 'prime heroes, who alarmed me a little'. They first met at close quarters in 1923. Squire and APH sailed with him in his *Nona*, a craft that was to achieve a place in the literature of the sea. Their previous encounters had been over casual pints in the Fleet Street tavern near the *London Mercury* office in Poppins Court. The up-Channel cruise started at Torquay – Belloc at the tiller, which he would entrust to no other hand. To APH he was not the scourge of venerated historians, the hero of legendary walks, the writer of novels, biographies and essays, but a W. W. Jacobs character in 'a peaked cap, an old blue jersey, and jacket', affecting the superstitions of an old salt. 'Stop that whistling!' he commanded APH. 'You'll bring on a gale.'

It soon appeared that Belloc's prejudices were freshened by the Channel breezes. 'When the sun shone and the wind was fair there might be a little lecture on the glories of the Tudors; when it was foul we heard about the machinations of the Jews.' Because he could not get 'a jorum of water' at Lyme Regis, he strode the streets of the little town proclaiming the superiority of an earlier age. Black clouds ahead, he steered discreetly into West Bay, Bridport, rather than face the hazards of rounding Portland Bill, which he respectfully referred to as William.

When they stepped on to the Wessex shore, Squire proposed that they call on Thomas Hardy at Max Gate, Dorchester, sixteen miles away. According to Squire, he went ahead of the others to ascertain whether they would be welcome, and that when he mentioned Belloc's name Hardy enquired: 'Do you mean that Catholic journalist?' Belloc – again according to Squire – spoke of Hardy as 'that atheist novelist'.

APH's version of the visit was that 'the three of us crammed into a taxi and drove up to Dorchester to see Thomas Hardy, whom I had never met'. Max Gate was 'a modest villa with a small suburban crescent approach round a shrubbery'. It was wonderful, he wrote, to see Belloc 'who had been lording it along the coast', bullying harbour officials and others, 'enter the little drawing-room, cap in hand, and bow reverently before the Master'.

The Master, it seemed, was not in his 'best form'. A day or two earlier he had been told of another octogenarian who had bicycled to visit relatives several miles away. Rashly attempting to emulate if not eclipse that feat, Hardy had overdone it. His visitors found him recovering 'from this excess'. None the less, the author of

The Dynasts engaged in lively talk with the author of *The Path to Rome*, 'both passionate about history' (Squire), their chief topic 'a great legendary storm off Portland Bill'. Not a compulsive listener, Squire 'faded into the background', his own admission, while APH was reduced to mute anonymity: 'I never said a word'. Nor was he able afterwards to recall even the gist of what had passed between those two disparate intellects temporarily in equilibrium.

Sailing on eastward to the Isle of Wight, *Nona* breasted what APH described as 'the most confused sea I ever saw'. He had a vivid phrase for the turmoil around them: 'The angry waves stood up like corn stooks and fell flat upon the deck'. He mistrusted *Nona's* fitness to stand the strain. 'At last we lumbered into civilised water.'

In the Solent they were surrounded by the yachting aristocracy assembled for Cowes' week. Squire, who had been spinning for mackerel, was glistening with fish-scales. All three men were unshaven. 'Wind-swept, weary and hungry' (APH) they landed at Ryde and made for the nearest hotel, conspicuously out of place among 'the pressed white flannels and yachting caps' (Squire). Managerial *hauteur* was broken down only when Belloc 'made his presence felt, and began talking about the laws (he had recently been a legislator)'.[2] A screen was put round the table at which they had breakfast.

As a breadwinner, APH was still not sure of an income sufficient to buttress his self-esteem as the head of a growing family. The Quilter Trust, from which his wife benefited with her sisters, was a prop, not the mainstay, of the household at Hammersmith Terrace. The lights of Shaftesbury Avenue glittered attractively. Had not A. A. Milne, sometime assistant-editor of *Punch*, found fortune with his plays, *Mr Pim Passes By* and *Dover Road*? Whether or not APH was seized by an if-he-can-do-it-so-can-I impulse, he wrote a series of one-act plays in quick succession, and tried his hand at sketches for the revues that were a fount of much West End gaiety in the twenties. A verse monologue of his, *I Can't Come Out Tonight*, was one of the encored items in the *Punch Bowl Revue*, produced at the Duke of York's Theatre by a new young impresario, Archie de Bear.[3] The monologue, originally written for Angela Baddeley, was recited by a delightful young actress, Polly Ward (now Mrs Ward Freeman), impersonating a lovelorn 'slavey'. Thirty years later, when through illness APH was unable to be at a party given by the Ward Freemans, he telegraphed with adroit remembrance: *I can't come out tonight.*

He also experimented with comic opera in one-act form; a chance to display his gifts as a librettist. *Blue Peter*, with music by Armstrong Gibbs, one of the young composers of a post-war group that included William Walton and Benjamin Britten; *The Policeman's Serenade*, for which Alfred Reynolds, his collaborator in later more ambitious works, wrote the music; *The King of the Castle*, with music by Dennis Arundell: all those were trial flights of a talent that in time would be recognized by the curtain-calls of wider appreciation.

The King of the Castle, a Christmas play put on at the Liverpool Playhouse by William Armstrong, brought kindly commendation from Sir James Barrie, OM (1860–1937). As a sequel, E. V. Lucas took APH to meet Barrie in his 'large and lovely flat' in Adelphi Terrace, overlooking the Thames between Waterloo and Westminster. Ensconced in a dark corner by a blazing log fire, Barrie, a heavy pipe-smoker, was 'coughing his heart out', and APH wondered 'how the small frame could stand it'.

In money terms APH's early efforts to gain a footing in the theatre were of small account. Much more to be desired was the weekly royalty cheque from the run of a full length drama or comedy. He had begun writing a play about politics, based on his experiences in two general elections in Liverpool as Sir Leslie Scott's aide. He drafted a first act and then put aside his work on it in deference to a request for his services from Winston Churchill, the Free Liberal candidate in a by-election at West Leicester in 1923. They had been brought together at the annual November reunion dinners of the Royal Naval Division. Churchill's part in the Dardanelles failure had not been forgotten. It was a subject of hostile heckling during the by-election campaign. APH was able to give him moral support, as one who had seen active service in that theatre of war and who believed that Churchill had been 'right in his strategy'.

One evening, after a noisy meeting in the constituency, APH dined at the Grand Hotel, Leicester, with Churchill, Brendan Bracken and Cecil Roberts, the debonair young editor of the *Nottingham Journal*. Churchill's prospects had slumped. Gloom was in the air.[4] Attempting to dispel it, APH began intoning some verse he had written on the recent birth of Princess Mary's first child.

Cecil Roberts, soon to forsake newspaper work in the first flush of his success as a novelist, remembers Churchill and APH joining together in a psalmodic rendering of the lines: *O let us be jubilant and gay/ Let every Englishman take off his hat and pray/ Drink and be merry, for 'tis not every day/ That Princess Mary has a baby . . . Then let our Colonies, with loyal cries/ Some simple, manly telegrams devise/ To share their Motherland's unique surprise/ That Princess Mary has a baby . . . The hour is dark, the dogs of war are stealing/ Civilisation rocks from floor to ceiling/ But there is joy in Wimbledon and Ealing/ Now that Princess Mary has a baby . . .*

APH's private doxology was an unfailing source of merriment to those of us who gathered round him at the piano in the drawing-room at Hammersmith Terrace. His metrical settings of passages from Hansard; Asquith's 'We shall not sheathe the sword' speech of World War One; King's Regulations – '*Disembarkations are carried out in a similar manner to em-bark-ations*' – and extracts from leading articles in *The Times*, could be extremely funny. That effect owed much to the *sostenuto* gravity of his vocal performances.

The Editor of *Punch* to A. P. Herbert:

> *Punch* Office,
> 10 Bouverie Street,
> London E.C.4.
> 19 Jan. 1924
>
> My dear Herbert,　I am sending you this formal invitation from the Proprietors and myself to join the Staff of *Punch* and attend the dinner here on Wednesday February 6th at 7.0 p.m. You will find a hearty welcome awaiting you. I shall look to you then, and always, to come armed with two or more ideas for the cartoons . . .

The editor, Owen Seaman, went on to explain that *Punch* was engaged on a programme of post-war expansion. He hoped that APH would write a weekly article; and he opened the door of opportunity still wider by intimating that he would 'always be glad to receive from you any matter on any subject additional to the regular contribution, such additional matter to be paid for at the ordinary *Punch* rates.' The letter contained instructions about proof corrections and stressed the necessity of keeping to the printer's time schedules. There was a postscript: 'This letter seems to be very pedagogic for an invitation.'

In the same week E. V. Lucas heard from John Galsworthy, who was wintering in Portugal. He had been reading some of APH's freelance writings in *Punch*. 'I do think he's a valuable youth',[5] he wrote. 'He amuses, and he hits things that ought to be hit quite nice and hard.' Lucas had already made up his mind that 'one skin down, APH is a pure reformer'.[6]

The summons to the *Punch* Table was more momentous for APH than his call to the Bar. For once the sense of the past was strong upon him as he took his place on that inaugural occasion. Aware of Thackeray's solemnization of the Table as 'The Mahogany Tree', he had not expected it to be of a more pliant wood; fortunately so, for as a newcomer he was required to cut his initials on 'the sacred board' (his phrase). Churchwarden pipes were still laid out on it, but rarely used, relics of the time of Jerrold and Leech. Those, and other *Punch* worthies, looked down from the walls of 'the pleasant old room' where Burnand, Tenniel and Keene had settled down after dinner to earnest discussion of the next issue of 'the paper' over coffee and brandy.

Present at APH's initiation were Seaman, headmasterish at his end of the Table; Philip Agnew, of the proprietorial family, at the other; C. L. Graves, general editorial assistant – by then at the 'dear old boy' stage of seniority; E. V. Lucas, who looked after 'Our Booking Office' and the reviewers who serviced it; Bernard Partridge, the chief cartoonist, who had acted professionally in the plays of Pinero and Shaw; L. Raven-Hill, his more politically minded second string; Frank Reynolds, the art editor; and two staff artists, the almost morbidly shy George Morrow, of whom Lucas said that 'it is a wonder of the world that a man can have so many comic thoughts'; and Ernest H. Shepard, whose humorous drawings had raised morale in many a wardroom and dugout during the war.

Punch was still commonly regarded as the safe deposit of the national humour, especially by those who saw copies of it only at the dentist's. Tenniel's great 'Dropping the Pilot' cartoon had not been eclipsed by any of his successors, whose work was rarely more than politely caustic. The gaffes of the 'temporary gentlemen' of the war being no longer source material for the comic artists, they were replenishing their stock-in-trade from surviving class differences, *outré* fashions, and débutante inanities, with Cynthia apparently registered as the most popular feminine name of the period. Return ing to those *Punch* volumes of the twenties it is not easy to believe in the paper's radical origins.

Extra-murally, APH was received like a favourite son into the coterie of *Punch* writers and artists who were not of the elect but who, by long tradition, maintained their own sacrosanct table at the Savage Club, which has a famous *Punch* name on its founders' roll of 1856. Among the *Punch* men he foregathered with there were the artists George Belcher, G. L. Stampa, Bert Thomas, G. D. Armour, Heath Robinson: the writers, Basil Macdonald Hastings, Ashley Sterne, Harris Deans, Anthony Armstrong. Here was the nucleus of the exceptionally varied acquaintanceship drawn from the arts, journalism, publishing and the stage that swarmed about him down the years.

His accession to the staff of *Punch* assured him the then good salary of £50 a week (income tax, 4s. 6d). In return, the proprietors acquired the full copyright in all that he wrote for the paper, with a share in the book rights. With the contract there went the privilege of sending his 'copy' direct to the printer. The editorial eye did not fall on what he wrote until the proof stage. Another agreeable perquisite was the weekly dinner in Bouverie Street, though the price in mental effort to produce cartoon ideas may have been considerable. There is no way of estimating his usefulness in that line.

Punch published the first of his *Misleading Cases* that year; editorially, a good omen for the new contract. Those 'frolics in jurisprudence', as he called them, were to develop a popularity that made them a lasting asset to him and the paper.

He finished his full-length play about provincial politics and showed the script to Nigel Playfair, who lived within neighbourly range at Said House, Chiswick Mall. Playfair turned it down for his theatre, the Lyric at Hammersmith, but undertook to produce it for a charity matinée at the Aldwych Theatre, Strand, suggesting that it might be launched from there into a West End run.

With Athene Seyler, Angela Baddeley and Claud Rains in the cast, the play was presented under the nondescript title of *At The Same Time* on a sultry Sunday afternoon in July 1925. It was an hilarious flop. APH believed that the stalls were filled not by the wealthy women who took tickets but by their domestic staffs, with a preponderance of ladies' maids. No West End managers or their scouts bothered to see the play. A frock-coated fund-raiser embarrassingly prolonged an interval by his speech from the stage extolling the charity. The audience also had to endure the memory lapses of a comedian who had lunched unwisely.

Feeling aggrieved, APH complained that Playfair had 'ruined' (his word) the play's chances in the West End by producing it in a charity context. Finally, he wrote it off as 'a laughable but sad experience'. It was soon relegated to insignificance by his unexpected nomination as *Punch* representative at the forthcoming Imperial Press Conference in Australia.

NOTES ON CHAPTER 8

1   A. P. Herbert: *A Book of Ballads.*
2   Not so recently; he was a Liberal MP, 1906–10.
3   Sometime private secretary to Arnold Bennett, and to Sir Basil Zaharoff, the armaments 'king'.
4   Churchill was defeated in the West Leicester by-election. It seems that he never forgave Leicester. 'Beastly place', he snapped when, twenty-five years later, Harold Nicolson told him that his son was contesting a seat there.
5   The 'valuable youth' was then thirty-four.
6   E. V. Lucas: *Reading, Writing and Remembering* (1932).

9

A Man with a 'Happy Mind'

Led by Lord Burnham of the London *Daily Telegraph*, the United Kingdom delegation to the Third Imperial Press Conference at Melbourne in 1925 consisted of newspaper proprietors, managers and editors, an hierarchical company in which APH may have felt professionally misplaced. 'I was only a humble young contributor to *Punch*.' One of his fellow-delegates was Anthony Eden, MP, representing a family interest in the *Yorkshire Post*, for which he was writing articles on the tour. In one of them, straining for effect as a descriptive reporter, he wrote of clouds over Quebec as 'a sky to make a painter's palette itch'.[1] APH referred to him as 'looking very young and Etonian, making a good impression with two or three speeches'.

APH had cause later to bless the day on which the delegation was joined at Victoria, Vancouver Island, by John J. Astor[2] of *The Times* and his wife, Lady Violet. It was the beginning of a typical APH friendship, harmony without intimacy, an accord that was to hold fast through the years to come.

At Honolulu he revelled in what he afterwards recalled as 'one of the magical mornings of my life'. The official itinerary involved a visit to a pineapple cannery, which did not appeal to him at all: 'hideous' was his word for it. Stopping his ears against repeated cries of 'Alan, where are you?' he hid in a lavatory until the cavalcade of cars with the rest of the delegation moved off. He then returned to his hotel room, put on his antiquated university bathing-costume and, hoping not to be noticed, made his way eagerly down to the beach to take the plunge as a novice at surf-riding. 'With the gorgeous luck of a beginner, I stood – *stood!* – on my first wave', to be borne 'at about the speed of a Derby winner', three hundred yards to the shore. The sensation was 'blissful; one of the most luminous, unforgettable mornings of my life'.

In New Zealand, 'many told me that they recognised my Selwyn nose'. In Australia the conference trip became a super beanfeast of receptions, banquets, gala events, spectacular excursions, to a running accompaniment of uninspired speeches on emigration, the freedom of the press, and Empire trade. 'One day I listened to twenty-seven speeches. We became stupefied by speeches, half-mad with speeches.'

Except for his undergraduate efforts at the Union, he had no experience of public speaking beyond responding to toasts at the annual dinner of the Royal Naval Division. His speech to a large assembly at Melbourne at the close of the conference was described as 'delectably witty' – the verdict of the founding father of the Imperial Press Conference, Sir Harry Brittain.

His hope of good fortune in the theatre was revived when Nigel Playfair invited him to write 'an entertainment' for the Lyric at Hammersmith. It was to be 'a new departure, a highbrow revue'. He was 'thrilled and delighted' to be asked to write it. The result was *Riverside Nights*, with music by Alfred Reynolds; presented at the Lyric in April 1926. He had a personal triumph with his Chekov sketch, *Loves Lies Bleeding*: 'Parody of the very highest order', James Agate told his *Sunday Times'* readers: 'it entitles Mr Herbert to sit down even in the presence of Mr Max Beerbohm.' Galsworthy thought it 'delicious entertainment'. One of APH's lyrics, *It May be Life*, was also a hit, singled out by Agate as 'a little masterpiece of writing by Mr Herbert'. It brought down-stage a disappearing social type that long haunted APH's imagination, the romantically yearning servant-girl comparing her dismal lot with the glamorous life of the film stars.

> I wish I wore a wicked hat;
> I've got the face for it, I know.
> I'm tired of scrubbing floors and that,
> It may be life – but ain't it slow?

A class awareness of the virtues of humble folk stamped much of his verse in the twenties and thirties. Increasingly, he combined polished lyrical expression with a social sensitivity that was consciously benevolent, unconsciously patronizing.

Threatened in the beginning by the General Strike, as a consequence of which it was uprooted and taken to the West End, *Riverside Nights* returned to the Lyric at Hammersmith for a run that petered out after eight months. APH's reputation in the theatre was enhanced. For Nigel Playfair there was no happy ending: he had to face a loss of £4,000.

APH followed *Riverside Nights* with a straight play called *The White Witch*, dramatizing the situation of a couple in a divorce suit who protested their innocence of adultery, a plea that he said was 'hardly ever believed in the courts'. The play was accepted for the Haymarket Theatre and produced there, with Fay Compton and Leo Quartermaine in the leading parts, on 29 September 1926.

That week Arnold Bennett wrote in his diary: 'We had supper at the Herberts. Only one servant; they had no coal[3] and cooked meals on a gas ring. We chiefly helped ourselves. A general air of picknicking.' He described it as 'an uproarious evening'; also present: the Wadsworths,[4] the Kenningtons,[5] and J. R. Ackerley.[6] 'Mrs Wadsworth argued too much but seemed quite all right.' Bennett reserved his highest compliment for the hostess of the evening. 'Gwen Herbert grows more and more admirable and lovable.'

In a letter Bennett told APH that he liked *The White Witch*; in his diary he wrote: 'I was very disappointed indeed.' After the Haymarket first night APH had telephoned Bennett, who assumed that 'he wanted my views on the play. Fortunately I was out' (30 September 1926). Galsworthy thought that the cross-examination scene in the play was 'very clever – like your *Punch* satire on the same subject, badly needed'. Slumbering Quaker prejudice was roused in the offices of Methuen the publishers.

> 36 Essex Street,
> Strand.
> 30th September 1926

> My dear Herbert, I'm sorry not to be able to be enthusi-
> astic, but then I loathe adultery discussions in public. The
> theatre, in my opinion, should be jollier than that and a
> place to which family parties can go.
>
> I am in a minority, I know, but there it is. I am really in
> distress not to be able to congratulate you.

> Yours ever, true-ly,
> E. V. L.

That austere view prevailed more widely than was realized. *The White Witch* came off after six weeks. APH put its failure down to a lapse of imagination on his part. 'Nobody made love. That was fatal.' The play, which had tangential relevance to the private lives of Bennett, Galsworthy, and Lucas was his first experiment in translating his zeal for reform from the pages of *Punch* to the theatre. He was not plagued by the artistic temperament, so called, and he bore his disappointment well. For reassurance he could turn to the book reviewers. They were uniformly amiable in their notices of the successive volumes of his collected verse and prose, mainly compiled from *Punch: Ballads for Broadbrows; Wisdom for the Wise; A Book of Ballads; Tinker, Tailor . . .*, etc., etc. The general critical sentiment was summarized in a *Times Literary Supplement* observation that he had 'a happy mind'. As a humorist, he might have retorted that as much could be said of the village idiot. Not that his sanity was ever in doubt, even among those staunch upholders of rational behaviour, the bank managers.

In its issue for August/September 1927, the *Westminster Magazine*, house organ of the then Westminster Bank, reproduced a photograph of 'one of the most remarkable cheques ever negotiated. It was drawn in pencil at the Savage Club on a table napkin and duly paid in by the payee to his account at Golders Green branch, where it was dealt with in the usual way.' The cheque was for £1, payable to G. L. Stampa, and signed 'Alan P. Herbert'. The payee himself had sketched on the napkin two others present at the table, Albert Toft, a well-known sculptor, and Sir Stanley Woodwark, the foppish general practioner with a Harley Street address.

APH had a habit of calling at Heppells, the Strand chemists, for a tonic specially concocted for him – or so he was persuaded. If you were with him, you would be expected to partake of it. Once I went with him near midnight to the ever-open Boots' branch in Piccadilly Circus, where they dispensed the same formula. 'Coupled with the name of Heppell', he said, raising his glass.

He believed in the restorative power of Turkish baths and indulged in them regularly through most of his active life. Sir Percy Harris, Liberal MP for Bethnal Green, commended to him the Hornibrook system of physical exercises, which Arnold Bennett also extolled. F. J. Hornibrook, an atheist from County Cork, was a self-taught physiotherapist who had served with the Royal Army Medical Corps in south-east Africa in the First World War. From local tribal practices he took ideas that provided the basis for his book, *The Culture of the Abdomen*. There were queues at the bookshops the day after Bennett reviewed it in the *Evening Standard*. APH became a lifelong addict of the Hornibrook belly rotation formula, with its comically earnest associated ritual called 'liver massage': it involved 'pressing your buttocks together a hundred times, standing or lying down'. As a supplementary routine, he 'took a hundred deep breaths out of doors the last thing at night'. Hornibrook, he said, had corrected his sitting posture. 'You press the base of your spine against the back of your chair and draw your stomach in,' and showed me how it should be done.

His interest in health matters was never so obsessive as to qualify him for the brotherhood of the hypochondriacs. His health reserves were limited; and his recourse to exercises, tonics and pills suggested that he was aware of it. He was an early captive of the vitamins cult and before long was claiming that he had 'studied them for years', though in the beginning they served him as a topic for rhyming persiflage:

> Vitamin 'A'
> Keeps the rickets away,
> And succours the meagre and nervy;
>   'B's what you lack
>   If the stomach is slack,
> And 'C' is the foe of the scurvy;
>   So when a man dines
>   Let him murmur these lines,
> Or sure he will live to deplore it –
>   Just ask yourself 'What
>   Disease have I got,
> And which is the vitamin for it?'[7]

The jaunty approach was soon abandoned. Vitamins, he became convinced, were 'one of the secrets of life', and, especially, an insurance against lowered vitality. Given the opportunity, he would have preached a sermon on the importance of replacing those vitamins allegedly destroyed by cooking or alcoholic indulgence. Scandinavian rose-hip juice, magnesium from the Dolomites, dessicated liver tablets, with others in the vitamin alphabet, were prominent in his health armoury, regularly replenished.

Having adopted Arnold Bennett's suggestion that he should follow the Hornibrook way to well-being, APH reciprocated with some advice of his own when, one evening at the Lyric Theatre at Hammersmith, Bennett confided to him certain current worries. Domestic strife was bearing heavily on Bennett who, APH said, was 'the most human and natural' of the 'literary swells' he knew at that time. Having heard Bennett's recital of various recent crises in his household, APH advised him: 'Don't let 'em get too dependent, don't let 'em get too dependent!' Concluding that APH spoke with 'the passion of experience', Bennett exclaimed in his diary: 'How wise!'

That note of Bennett's fixed APH in an amusingly unfamiliar posture. Donning an invisible wig, he could hold forth with authority on legal aspects of the conjugal state. His pose as an instant oracle on sex relations was a joke. His declamatory advice to Bennett has the ring of remembered stage dialogue, perhaps from a play by Wilde, Pinero or Shaw, or possibly it echoed a distracted fellow clubman's 'passion of experience'.

Arnold Bennett was finding more than advice to appreciate in APH a new-found friend of the late twenties. After dining at what Bennett liked to call his 'rather noble thing in houses', 75 Cadogan Square, APH 'sang his song about Princess Mary, and it is really masterly'. APH's one-act play, *Two Gentlemen of Soho*, was billed with *The Critic* by Sheridan at the Lyric, Hammersmith. Bennett judged it to have 'little or no dramatic quality but very many marvellously funny lines – in fact, as good as Sheridan's'. It could fairly be insisted that *Two Gentlemen of Soho* is a cut above the *jeu d'esprit* that Bennett's comment suggested. It was singled out by John Press in *The Fire and the Fountain* (1955) as 'delicious parody'. Peter Fleming daringly proposed in the *Sunday Telegraph*, 27 September 1970, that it contains 'the best Shakespearean couplet not actually written by Shakespeare':

> Man, like a pebble on a glacier,
> Moves imperceptibly, but always down.

He might also have quoted:

> But down the windy parallels of Time
> Echoes again that interrogative
> Which mocked our entrances . . .

APH was proud of his *Two Gentlemen of Soho*: he said so. In its five-hundred lines of Elizabethan swagger there are intimations of a gift consigned to abeyance by the demands of 'the laborious week'. That it could have expressed itself at a transcendent level may be questioned. He was too much at home in a world in which there were axes to be ground, pomposities to be pricked, rights to be defended, busybodies to be routed. His voice was heard more authentically in his *Ballads for Broadbrows* (1930), for example:

> Let's stop everybody from doing something!
>   Everybody does too much.
> People seem to think they've a right to eat and drink,
> Talk and walk and respirate and rink,
>   Bicycle and bathe and such.
> So let's have lots of little regulations,
> Let's make laws and jobs for our relations,
> There's too much kissing at the railway stations,
> Let's find out what everyone is doing,
>   And then stop everyone from doing it.

NOTES ON CHAPTER 9

1 Anthony Eden: *Places in the Sun* (1926).
2 Later Lord Astor of Hever, chief proprietor of *The Times*.
3 There was a miners' strike.
4 Edward Wadsworth (1889–1949) had been a prominent member of the New English Art Club and of the Chantry Bequest Committee. He was an accomplished painter.
5 Eric Kennington, RA, sculptor and later official war artist.
6 J. R. Ackerley, author of *Hindoo Holiday*, etc. His autobiography *My Father and Myself*, described with candour and pathos his life as a homosexual. He was literary editor of the *Listener*.
7 A. P. Herbert: *A Book of Ballads* (1931).

10

His 'Not Inconsiderable' Influence

He supposed that he had written more verse than 'any Briton alive'; and he might have made a parallel claim as a writer of letters to *The Times*. In 1933 Sir Leslie Scott wrote congratulating him on '100 A1 letters to *The Times*'. A trial count made twenty years later indicated that his final total then exceeded five hundred; he himself thought 'perhaps a thousand', between the wars and after.

He wrote to *The Times*, he said, because he was 'bursting with something to say'; once he had written 'Sir', the compulsion was not to be checked. The result was usually a fusion of good sense and good nature capable of sweetening the temper of the most irascible commuter in a crowded 9.15. Enjoying, relishing even, the prominence of the best platform of the kind in daily journalism, he made it a pretended grievance that if he had been paid for every letter of his printed in *The Times* he would have been able to buy the proprietor's ocean-going yacht (in which he had the compensatory pleasure of enjoyable cruises). This is not to say that he was given to equating public spirit with cash rewards; far from it.

'The correspondence column is a pillar of democracy, a forum, a pulpit, thought incubator, safety valve. Two thousand words of free writing on every subject under the sun – better writing, very often, than the leading article next door.' He suggested that the editor should be more grateful than he appeared to be for those gratuitous contributions. 'The haughty fellow behaves as if he were doing us a favour by letting us write the best part of the paper for nothing. Why do we do it? It is exacting toil and prolific of trouble.' He recalled with amusement that an editor of *The Times* 'solemnly rebuked' him in writing for sending a letter to the *Daily Telegraph*. 'My answer should have been: "Sir, You talk as if you *paid* me to correspond with you. By the way, why don't you?"[1] When it was put to APH that his time and energy might be more productively employed, he was content to reflect that his 'itch to write to *The Times*' occasionally served 'a worthy purpose'. It earned him long remembrance in Printing House Square as 'a good friend of the Paper'.

As far back as 1927 the then associate editor of *The Times*, G. Murray Brumwell, 'spoke very highly' to J. H. Morgan, KC, Reader in Constitutional History to the Inns of Court, about a letter of APH's on Socialist jargon. 'He said that you were the only man who could laugh the Communist Party out of existence.'[2] The letter in question made sardonic play with the Socialist concept of brotherhood, and quoted a series of 'fraternal epithets' applied to the 'victims of capitalism' in a newly published proletarian song-book: slaves, serfs, cringers, boneheads, boobs, dolts, dupes, duffers, fools, tools, catspaws, cowards, cravens, dogs, beasts of burden; making laughable nonsense, he contended, of the great Socialist ideal.

The risk of 'running a correspondence in *The Times*', he discovered, was that 'one brief, witty reply may blow you to pieces'. There is no sign that he suffered that fate. On the contrary, he emerged unscathed from a duel in that newspaper's correspondence columns with Bernard Shaw over simplified spelling, proud to be able to say: 'I silenced Mr Shaw', as decisively, it seems, as the young Burke had silenced Dr Johnson at the dinner table. He admitted that he often gave more time and thought to composing a letter to the editor than to his money-getting labours. 'Every sentence, every word, is a worry. How I fuss!' He fussed over whether a letter would merely evoke the customary courteous acknowledgment that implied rejection, whether it would draw a daunting riposte from an equally adroit fencer with the pen, whether the chosen topic would die the death before retired admirals at Southsea or dons at Oxford found time to reply.

He initiated and enlivened numerous public controversies in those august columns, as often as not in protest against impediments to just causes. Many of his letters were embryo leading articles. The sum of them alone over half a century warranted the verdict of a reviewer in *The Times Literary Supplement* that 'his impact on the affairs of the nation has not been inconsiderable'.[3]

In the twenties and early thirties he attended Old Wykehamist dinners, most often with Francis Toye, music critic of the *Morning Post*. Each needed the other's support, feeling 'a little out of the picture' and that their professional activities were regarded as less credible to the college than those of other alumni distinguished in the Church, the learned professions, the civil service and politics. 'Everyone was friendly; everyone was genuinely delighted to see us', Toye wrote, 'but we did not fit in with the Wykehamist pattern. We were just writers.'[4]

Whether or not APH was as sensitive to reputation as that contemporary of his, whether or not he shared Byron's greater regard for the life of the man of action than for that of the writer, he may well have aspired to be named among those whom his old school held in such high esteem. Or he may have been unconsciously complying with the Johnsonian dictum that 'every man has a lurking wish to appear considerable in his native place'.

The chief impact of his no doubt quantitatively unequalled out-pouring of verse may after all have been personal. Where others in the twenties were 'schooling the noddle' (Arnold Bennett) by means of the widely advertised Pelman System of Mental Training, APH was achieving similar results, without forking out the guineas, by exercising his verse-writing flair which, he afterwards said, faintly echoing Dr Johnson in another context, 'clears and sharpens the mind'. Probably aided by the peculiar discipline of 'Toys' at Winchester, he developed an abnormally high critical point of noise-tolerance. It enabled him to work with the dynamism of a Wagner overture flooding his study. His young women secretaries, each in her turn, had to endure taking dictation and typing to whatever musical accompaniment he chose to inflict on them. If spring-cleaning compelled his retreat to the nursery upstairs, he worked there with the same serene imperviousness to the distractions around him. Richard Hughes noted his extraordinary indifference to the social din. 'He was able to write at the very hub of the hubbub of a cocktail party as undisturbed as when alone in his deck chair by the river'.[5]

Similarly, in the theatre, where near-chaos often reigned as an opening date drew near: from a seat in the stalls, with a scribbling-pad on his knees, he would rewrite a light opera scene or a revue sketch with an effortless concentration that defied the prevailing confusions. Wendy Toye, who directed a number of notable Cochran productions, has memories of APH 'calmly writing away' amid the clamour of rehearsals. She often had to demand 'Quiet, please!' from the cast; never in deference to him.

As a writer of verse he was awarded few poetic laurels and not often favoured by the anthologists. Yet he has a place in the Praed, Calverley, Dobson tradition, with the forgotten Arthur Clement Hilton and W. S. Gilbert, R. C. Lehmann, Belloc, Chesterton, Squire, E. V. Knox, Harry Graham; that talented company. He resented the notion that light verse is necessarily inferior poetry; a sore point with him, never healed. Holding that the writing of light verse – he disliked the term – was 'not sufficiently esteemed as a difficult and important form of literary art', he maintained that its practitioners were as worthy of respect as the currently canonized poets, Eliot, Auden and others whose 'slovenly habits' he called on them to repent. His general contention was reinforced by Cyril Connolly, reviewing *Nineteenth Century Minor Poets*: 'One must conclude that the Light Versifiers have greater technical skill than all the rest; the massed felicity of Hood, Praed, Barham, Clough and Calverley is consummate.'[6] APH never forgot his delight in discovering Calverley at Winchester, though it was Clough, not Calverley, who was known as 'the pet poet' of the universities.

APH could have argued that the lush blooming of poetry in England had its roots in light verse. *Of a rose, a lovely rose, Of a rose is al myn song*, was a seedling of *c.* 1550. 'Till the Elizabethans, all poetry was light', Auden reminded readers of his introduction to *The Oxford Book of Light Verse* (1938); and the voice of APH is heard again insisting: 'This is an important Muse', whether styled light verse, humorous verse, *vers d'occasion*, *vers de société*, parody, satire or libretto. 'This', he repeated, 'is a very hard school of writing. No other form of writing requires and accepts so stern a discipline.'

He could have invoked the poet Cowper, writing about the verse of Matthew Prior (1644–71): 'To make verse speak the language of prose, without being prosaic, to marshal the words of it in such an order as they might naturally take in falling from the lips of an extemporary speaker, yet without meanness, harmoniously, elegantly, and without seeming to displace a syllable for the sake of a rhyme, is one of the most arduous tasks that a poet could undertake.' In his preface to *Lyra Elegantiarum*, Frederick Locker agreed that 'the writing of *vers de société* is a difficult accomplishment'; even so, he reckoned it 'an inferior branch of the art of versification'.[7] A. A. Milne, whose reputation in Bouverie Street and beyond immediately preceded APH's, was dogmatic in his view that 'the practice of no

form of writing demands such a height of technical perfection as the
writing of light verse in the Calverley and *Punch* tradition'.[8]

To be hailed as 'a direct and forceful poet' in the authorized
version of the history of *Punch*[9] was undoubtedly gratifying to APH,
whose early promise was frustrated by his lack of a wholly poetical
temperament. His assertion of equality with 'the serious lads of
poetry' (his phrase) was thought eccentric, as when he dismantled
the opening lines of *The Waste Land* and reassembled them as 'a
blameless piece of prose'. He was genuinely perplexed. 'Try as I
may, I cannot see what it is that entitles this passage to the name of
poetry.' In his judgment, 'rhyme is a positive part of the poetic
process, adding force to the poet's message'. As for the light verse
genre, he would have blinked hard at the suggestion that it has more
often been the poetry of proficiency than of inspiration.

T. S. Eliot said that 'some forms of ill-health, anaemia or debility,
may produce an efflux of poetry'. The theory, which was nothing
new, may be cited with nonchalant relevance to APH's resort to
the ship's doctor during a homeward voyage from Ceylon in the
Orient liner *Otranto* at the end of the twenties. He was worrying
about a sore on his tongue and its possible connection with pipe-
smoking. Waiting in the doctor's cabin, he picked up the nearest
book, a surgical treatise. His furtive perusal of it caused him to
reflect how little he, as a married man, knew about 'the female form
divine'. His muse, which had been disconcertingly unresponsive as
he worked on a new light opera for the Lyric at Hammersmith to
be called *Tantivy Towers*, was suddenly quickened. Returning to the
promenade deck, he wrote his *Lines on a Book Borrowed from the
Ship's Doctor*, four mildly erotic stanzas that he afterwards feared
by the perversity of fate would survive as the sole proof of his
poetic powers.

> The portions of a woman which appeal to man's depravity
>   Are constructed with considerable care,
> And what appears to you to be a simple cavity
>   Is really quite an elaborate affair . . .

Intending the lines only for the private entertainment of a small
shipboard circle, he destroyed his original pencilled copy. But the
purser, who collected 'parodies of Kipling and other literary
curiosities', had noted them down, and it was he who sped them

forth to a wider audience. It seemed that there was no West End club in which they were not familiarly recited. As a word-of-mouth transmission they crossed every boundary of the masculine world. He met men who had 'come across them in Australia'; others who first heard them in the USA. He was 'neither ashamed nor proud of them', he said, though there was a hint of self-justification in his opinion that they would not have survived if they had been expressed in prose – 'or in verse without metre or rhyme'. He regretted them only when, increasingly, he was credited with the authorship of bawdy verses invented by others. 'Many such works have been put down to me with which I had nothing to do – indeed, with some distress I have seen typewritten copies with my initials at the bottom: this was the only one to which I confess.'[10] There were no crudities in his attitude to women. If he was somewhat less than worshipful of the sex, he was more than somewhat respectful of it.

His spontaneous lyrical wit was displayed with similar results during another voyage in the same vessel – his name in the passenger list appearing there by courtesy of the public relations department. Lord Marchwood writes that his father, a friend and fellow-passenger of APH's, 'well remembered the incident' that evoked the *Ode to a Seagull* as the ship approached Gibraltar.

> O seagull, we're grieving
>   To see you relieving
> Yourself on the merchant marine.
>   You have very good sight
>   And should see, in this light,
> The *Otranto* is not a latrine.
>   God gave you the oceans
>   For your little motions,
> And Spain's a convenient po;
>   But if it feels finer
>   To aim at a liner –
> Well, why not a nice P & O?[11]

Mr Gerry Stewart, of Melbourne, Cambridgeshire, whose father was 'a regular *Orient* Line traveller', says that it was put about that APH's reference in that context to the P & O 'caused a certain amount of offence' (Letter, 13 May 1973).

APH identified himself for the first time with a prominent public issue in 1928; the occasion, the prosecution on obscenity grounds of

The Well of Loneliness by Radclyffe Hall. Having read the book, he 'could not understand what all the fuss was about'. He considered it 'a sincere, courageous, unexciting plea for a tolerant understanding of the unfortunate Lesbians'. He attended a protest meeting of authors that was addressed by Shaw in one of his more perverse moods. He added his name to those of the several score volunteer witnesses, none of whom was called. The book was banned and in one quarter burned.

APH's own novel *The Secret Battle* reappeared in the bookshops in 1930; like *All Quiet on the Western Front*, and the play *Journey's End*, a sign of revived interest in the great war of 1914–18. Winston Churchill wrote a foreword recalling that after its first publication in 1919 the book had been 'a little swept aside by the revulsion of the public mind from anything to do with the awful period just ended'. Re-reading it, he did not doubt its entitlement to 'a permanent place in war literature, a soldier's tale cut in stone to melt all hearts'. Five new editions followed, and the book was accorded a place among the First World War classics, the works of Blunden, Sassoon, Zweig, Barbusse and Graves.[12]

The Times Literary Supplement of 18 September 1970 stated that *The Secret Battle* 'led to reform in court-martial procedure'. While research has revealed no official documentary evidence for that claim, the Deputy Judge Advocate has written: 'I understand that certain changes were indeed made in courts-martial procedure during the period to which you refer. The most important of these appears to be the right of an accused to have competent counsel to represent him in addition to the "prisoner's friend" ' (Letter, 18 January 1974).

The powerful emotional effect of the book may have influenced the campaign against the Army death penalty promoted in the House of Commons by Ernest Thurtle and Oliver Baldwin, son of the Prime Minister and a friend of APH's. No member of the committee on courts-martial procedures set up in 1938 who read *The Secret Battle* can have been indifferent to its message.

NOTES ON CHAPTER 10

1   A. P. Herbert: unpublished notes.
2   J. H. Morgan, KC to A. P. Herbert; 4 November 1927.
3   18 September 1970.

4　Francis Toye: *For What We Have Received* (1950).
5　*The Author*, Spring 1974.
6　*Sunday Times*, 2 July 1967.
7　He was capable of writing trite verse; e.g. *At Her Window* (Oxford Book of English Verse, 1900).
8　A. A. Milne: *It's Too Late Now* (1939).
9　R. G. G. Price: *History of Punch* (1957).
10　A. P. Herbert: *Independent Member*.
11　Referred to as an 'incomparable ode' in Sir Alec Douglas Home's introduction to *Within the Fringe* by Lord Stuart of Findhorn (1967).
12　*The Secret Battle* is still in print (1975).

The Thames, a Ruling Passion

His novel of canal life in England, *The Water Gipsies*, was published in June 1930; two new editions quickly followed, foreshadowing a popular success that carried it on to a final sales total of a quarter of a million copies. The first welcoming letter he received was from Vita Sackville-West: 'It is a long time since I have enjoyed a novel more.' H. G. Wells read it in Paris, and thought it 'humane and true'. Galsworthy joined in the appreciative chorus: 'A most excellent and pathetic book. It has the breath of life.' Those personal compliments were endorsed by the reviewers. There were rather venturesome comparisons with Dickens. APH, it was said, had the master's instinct for character. 'He has the Dickensian fecundity. He is drawn to the odd,' said *The Times Literary Supplement*. The reviewer added that APH's 'young women would fail to get a character from the creator of Little Nell'. *The Water Gipsies* lifted the veil from what for most readers and reviewers were a secret people, the nomads of the inland waterways who remained uninfluenced in thought and habit by the social and political changes in the world beyond 'the Cut'. It roved delightfully through a milieu that was relatively unfamiliar to APH himself – 'a new, beautiful, and friendly world'.

His experience of the canals was at that time limited to his home stretch of the Thames. Recently he had bought a seven-foot clinker-built dinghy from Gamage's, price three guineas a foot, and had taught himself the rudiments of handling it from a textbook. Soon it was not enough for him to tack back and forth over the length of Hammersmith Terrace.

Boldly he set out to make a landfall at Westminster, seven river miles, steering by oar and plotting a course that was to become familiar to him in strikingly different circumstances later. At Westminster Bridge he turned homeward with misgivings about the strongly running tide. His problem was solved by a passing Brentford-bound lighterman, who beckoned him aboard and then leaned over and plucked the dinghy out of the water with the ease of a boy recovering a toy yacht from the Round Pond. APH said he felt humiliated, a feeling heightened by his glimpse of a group of MPs 'watching with broad grins' from their Terrace. He said it was then that he made a vow: 'One day I'll be there.'

He acquired 'a fifteen footer with a good beam', and became a member of the London Corinthian Sailing Club and an entrant in its competitions. 'How magical it is to be about in my own boat.' He commemorated his pleasure in one of his few anthologized poems, *My Ship*.[1]

> My ship is my delight,
>   And she's the one I woo
> When in the shiny night
>   We dance across the blue,
> With whispering sail and spar
>   As live as ladies are,
> And twenty times as true.
>
> My ship is my delight,
>   I made her, she is mine,
> I built her trim and tight,
>   I dreamed her gracious line;
> No wooden thing is she
>   But some proud part of me,
> I made her, she is mine.
>
> Then at the helm I stand
>   And not alone are we.
> Two lovers hand in hand,
>   We ask no company.
> So, by some lover's art
>   I think she knows my heart
> And sings or sighs with me.

Raglan Squire, a boy in the thirties, remembers APH's voice upraised in song as he sailed up and down betwixt Chiswick Eyot and Hammersmith Bridge on the right kind of day. '*O Shenandoah* . . .!' He could make himself heard on either shore. 'It became a neighbourhood joke.'

Gwen Herbert's friend Betty Carver, a widow of the First World War who lived on Chiswick Mall, was at 12 Hammersmith Terrace one afternoon when the doorbell announced a caller who asked peremptorily: 'Is Betty here?' The visitor was a soldier of the Warwickshire Regiment named Montgomery, the field-marshal to be. He knew another soldier, Percy Hobart, a future commander of armoured forces in battle, who had an old flat-bottomed canal-boat for disposal. That was how APH became the owner of *The Ark*, in which he made his first voyage into canal territory, plodding along the Grand Union from Brentford Lock to Uxbridge and Rickmansworth, picking up bits of canal lore on successive trips that occasionally extended to Berkhamsted. He never went beyond the urban bounds, and for that reason his later elevation to the status of patron saint of the narrow-boats was a mystery to some observers of that scene.

He had discovered the special pleasure of handling a sailing-boat on the river. Canal navigation offered nothing to compare with it. He wrote as if the ship's sail was first among man's inventions, more worth while than the ploughshare or the wheel. 'What a sense of mastery is in that light hand on the tiller as you fill your sails and dance away over the water! What a wonder it is that with two stretches of cotton, some rope, and some wood, you can make wind and water your slaves. A great yacht gives excitements to many but one man in a small boat is as independent, as lordly, as a conjuror.'

The river became a ruling passion from the day when, 'greatly daring', he took *The Ark* down the tideway into dockland and beyond to Gravesend Reach, where ships of the nations were being piloted in and out of that seaward gateway to the Thames. Here was the grand climax of the barely perceptible rippling movement of the water that he so often waited for and watched from his Hammersmith window, the turning of the tide in obedience to a law not of this world. 'A moment as difficult to catch as the opening of a flower', he wrote in later years. 'You turn your head, and there, it has happened; all that water is on the move again'. It was a kind of revelation, his first realization of the Thames as 'a powerful shaper of our history'. There in the lower reaches Nelson had learned his seamanship. In the sailing-ship days, master-mariners spoke of London's river as 'the highroad to China'. APH's first tentative exploration of it had whetted his appetite for further voyages of discovery in those waters. *The Ark* was replaced by a vessel built to his requirements in a Hammersmith boatyard and named *Water Gipsy*. 'A queer, uncommon craft', he agreed; length thirty-nine feet, beam nine feet, drawing only two feet six inches; fitted with two nine horse-power petrol engines by Thornycroft.

He was of the variously distinguished company that met at the Adelphi Hotel, Strand, in July 1930 to make the most of Belloc's sixtieth birthday; a dinner party that Chesterton, who presided, ebulliently proclaimed 'an immortal feast'. Much merriment ensued from a practical joke in which each speaker credited his right-hand neighbour with being the prime mover of the celebration, and so on, round the table. Chesterton gave the palm to APH. 'We all know that he is an admirable author. I never knew before that he is an admirable actor. I shall never forget the exactitude of the accent in which he said: "I'm sure, friends, we're all very pleased to see ex-Druid Chesterton among us this evening".'[2]

In the recollection of many survivors from the thirties APH reappears vividly as host at the annual Boat Race party at Hammersmith Terrace. It was 'open house' on a scale that has passed into legend as a central social event of the year for many friends of the family as well as for the uninvited for whom the open door at Number 12 and the sounds of revelry within were an irresistible provocation to trespass. 'Our mad gatherings', was APH's phrase for those parties; 'sometimes the house almost exploded', recalling the besieging throng that took possession of it, clambered on the roof, crowded the staircases, filled every room with a view. It was my experience that the pleasures of exciting propinquity often exceeded those of watching the flashing oars on the river. Concerning the rival crews, APH would tell newcomers: 'They used to say that rowing in the Boat Race took ten years off a young fellow's life.'

He wrote to me on 25 September 1930: 'I was *forty* yesterday and I am feeling my age.' His letter was an appeal for my editorial consideration of the work of his friend E. V.'s daughter, Audrey, 'who has an overdraft'. He was capable of much decent concern of that kind: more than one young writer came to me, and no doubt to other editors, with generous commendations from him – not always apposite. He abounded in good nature while reserving the right to excommunicate fools, hypocrites and purveyors of cant.

In those years one never heard him ill-spoken of; that came later, with the broadening of his public activities. Those who did not find him delightfully easy to know, as most did, may have been sensitive to his perfunctory handshake, an outward and could-be disconcerting sign of the locked-in part of his personality, a private emotional reserve probably subconsciously dedicated to the mother who died untimely. No one ever found the key. Assumptions of intimacy were likely to be repelled. 'I don't understand him', an actor well known to us both complained to me. 'He knows my voice better than he knows his own. When I telephoned him for the second time this morning he pretended that he didn't. "Who did you say you are?" he asked in a very off-hand way. I might have been a stranger.' A quondam brother-in-law of APH's, Lance Sieveking of the BBC, was baffled 'by the veil that surrounds the core of his personality'. Sievking 'used to wonder' whether the fault was in himself. 'Then I discovered that it was everyone's experience. Even a daughter badly needing her father's sympathy and advice could not discover the open sesame.'[3]

That it was 'everyone's experience' may be questioned. The ingrained reticence did not detract from his charm or success as a social being. Nor was self-centredness the problem. He related remarkably little to himself or to his work. It was not easy, and many found it impossible, to manoeuvre him into the position of discussing either.

One remembers him from the thirties as the most companionable if the least confiding of men; equable in temper, except for the rare outbursts of his 'little volcano'; seldom cast down, never bored. Recalling his lithe figure, that was of small profit to Savile Row, his irregular striding walk, his habit of greeting one with both hands limply outstretched, one also remembers that he was without affectations, being under no middle-class duress to equip himself with a pseudo-*persona* like, for example, his fellow professional Noël Coward. He was content, even happy, to be himself. He had no grievances against fate; none of discontent at being born in the wrong century or with the wrong shape. He had every reason to be satisfied with his natural endowment of a good height and good looks embellished by a readily-induced smile that was never insincere. His faunish cast of countenance was moulded imperceptibly after middle-age into a refined facsimile of Mr Punch's.

In short, except perhaps to see his name exalted in the theatre, he wanted little more than he already had: a happy marriage and family; free play for his talents; a good understanding with his bank manager; a multiplying acquaintance with kindred spirits, and ample opportunities for disengaging himself from them when the mood was on him. In much of his life-style he warranted Tennyson's 'good old name' of gentleman. He kept his word and scorned the lie. It was self-disclosure when he made the narrator of his novel *The Singing Swan* say: 'I was not cut out for mendacity or double dealing.' He was contemptuous of the oppressors. He was an unequivocal patriot. 'Love your country and defend her institutions (for they are pretty good, when all is said),' he wrote as counsel to the young. If philosophy and religion ever engaged him in earnest thought he was unlikely to have put it into words. Nor was there reason to expect from him a coherent view of life. Most probably he would have agreed that a Persian poet had spoken for him:

> What is heaven that we should seek it?
>   Wherefore question, How and Why?
> See, the roses are in bloom: see, the sun is in the sky,
> See, the land is lit with summer; let us live before we die.[4]

I stayed a night with him at Hammersmith during that autumn of 1930. Gwen, his wife, was away on one of her painting holidays. He and I had cold supper in the river-level dining-room, made gay with her aquarium murals. He then proposed to reveal to me the charms of his favourite riverside resorts, the Dove and the Black Lion public houses. He made much of their attraction for him, and one's passing impression that it derived from the salutes of admiring recognition accorded him as we entered was dispelled by his obvious approval of 'something Belloc said – that pubs are the heart of England'. As we came to the Dove he remembered that James Thomson – 'you know, *The Seasons* poet' – had lived there or close by. He grew peaches on his garden wall and had a trick of eating them straight from the branch with his hands in his pockets. Eccentricity of that order delighted APH, whose own defiance of the humdrum could take equally amusing forms, e.g. walking the pavements with one foot in the gutter, and drawing those unorthodox cheques.

That part of our outing completed, we walked across Hammersmith Broadway for a drink with Nigel Playfair at his Lyric Theatre. He welcomed us with a warmth that did not conceal his underlying anxieties as a producer who was often ahead of his time. APH afterwards explained to me that to 'get out' each week the Lyric had to take £1,000. Reaching, let alone sustaining, that level of income was a continuing struggle. APH disclosed that 'so far' he had 'made nothing' out of the Lyric. Not that he complained. It was the scene of his apprenticeship as a writer for the stage. He appreciated the chance that had been given him there, and wished very much that 'dear Nigel' could repeat his great success with *The Beggar's Opera*.

I have a clear recollection of asking APH on our homeward way that night why he did not stand for Parliament. He answered that he could not afford it, and that the only seat of interest to him would be Oxford University, where he had no reason to think he would be welcomed. He had mentioned to me earlier that, sailing past the House on a summer afternoon, he had seen 'quite a few members out on the Terrace, doing themselves well, it seemed to me, with lady friends, strawberries and cream, drinks, and so on'.

We discussed family expenses and an accountant's scheme to ease taxes for us by a trust arrangement. Typically, because I could not grasp the financial complexities, I dropped out, while he, typically, persevered until he did grasp them, though with what result I never heard. I wrote in my diary that 'he has three girls, all with pre-Raphaelite faces, and one boy, down for Winchester'.[5] He thought four children 'about right', while agreeing that family life gives a man 'something to live and work for apart from himself; very important', he said. He was not by nature philoprogenitive, nor was he emotionally demonstrative; no ride-a-cock-horse abandon for him.

> The artless prattle of a child
> Drives nearly everybody wild.
> And who that for an hour beguiled
> A babe, however clever,
> For all the riches of the rich
> Could contemplate a life in which
> They lived at that exhausting pitch
> Day after day, for ever?[6]

His attitude to the young was chiefly expressed in kindly tolerance, rarely in affectionate display. He was not wanting in warmth of feeling: his nearest were his dearest, but he would not have thought it necessary to say so. He and Gwen seemed to me ideally unpossessive parents.

Waking early at Hammersmith Terrace the next morning, I was driven back under the sheets by an abominable river smell. 'You get used to it,' he said; 'it's supposed to be healthy.' Breakfast, which he had airily celebrated in verse as 'the meal of my heart',[7] was partaken of in a silence imposed by his resolute preoccupation with *The Times*. When communication was restored, he corrected my use of the term 'bargees' which, he said, should be 'bargemen'. He seemed to me to have an awesome knowledge of the tidal mysteries of the river. He described the 'destructive potential' of the Thames in flood. Did I know that in 1928 people were drowned in riverside basements half a mile away? 'It couldn't happen in Paris. Why in London?' There had been various plans for a protective barrage at Greenwich; they should be looked at again. He intended 'to do something about it'.

My indulgence in toast and marmalade provoked a change of subject. 'You should cut down the carbohydrates.' I was lectured on the principles and merits of the Hay diet, the latest health fad. The gospel was issued in pocket-book form. I had seen him consult it during meals at the Café Royal. I mentioned that my newspaper work tended 'to get into my sleep'. That was a signal for him to disclose the formula with which he banished worries at the end of the day. It consisted of repeating a set of words in conjunction with deep breathing. 'Fear nothing. Why worry? Thank God. All's well'. According to him, the incantatory process, combined with the breathing, was an infallible recipe for 'a good night'.

His was a mainly practical mind, versatile and lucid but not profound. He had a lawyer's aversion from the abstract, the speculative, from elaborate fancies and strained interpretations. In conversation he would fall into the Socratic habit and demand, sometimes embarrassingly, definitions and precise meanings. He liked argument and it pleased him to say, as he did to young Raglan Squire after discussing a radical topic: 'Of course, you know that I could just as easly argue it from your side, if I wanted to.' He had an ear for pleonasms, and would not hesitate to draw attention to them in the most light-hearted exchanges if the mood was on him.

He was not so fastidious about his personal appearance. Style and fashion had no interest for him. I see him in those years invariably walking abroad in uncreased grey flannel trousers with turn-ups and what was probably the first jacket to hand in his rarely replenished wardrobe. I was assured from within the family that he never went willingly to a tailor. We both laughed, I remember, when he arrived in a new suit to join me at lunch with a friend of mine from New York, George Jean Nathan, then the leading American drama critic. Neither sartorially nor socially was he a devotee of the old school tie, and I never saw him wearing one, which is not to say that he was a dissenter from the values it represented. Like many First World War survivors, he had not reverted to civilian headwear. The hatless habit was repugnant to his friend E.V., who one day enticed him into a Dunn's shop in the Strand. APH came out wearing a soft brown felt hat with the brim turned down in front. As soon as he had parted from Lucas in Essex Street, he rolled up the hat, stuffed it into his pocket, and never wore it again.

He asked me to go with him to the private showing in Wardour Street of a documentary film called *Windjammer*, for which he wrote the commentary. While we were there he introduced me to a sweet-faced young actress named Celia Johnson. He suggested that I should squire her to the Carlton for a cocktail and await him there. When he appeared, his macintosh over a shoulder, as usual, he stood miming to us from the foyer. With him was a young man, also ungroomed-looking, his bronzed wiry hair pushed untidily back from his forehead – Anthony Asquith. 'Not in 'ere, signor! Not in 'ere!' a waiter was beseeching APH, who called out to us: 'Can't you two see what's happening? They won't let us in!' Nor would they. As my diary reminds me, 'we all had to go cowering into a little side bar'.

His light opera in three acts on a hunting theme, *Tantivy Towers*, opened at the Lyric, Hammersmith, in January 1931. It was in the true opera tradition: no spoken dialogue and a minimum of recitative. Thomas Dunhill wrote the music; his brother, head of the well-known St James's pipe and tobacco firm, supplied some of the finance. It had a run of 170 performances.

APH believed that he had devised an original theme for an opera, 'the Counties *v* Chelsea, Bloodsports *v* Bohemia'. At one of the early performances Anthony Eden and his wife were present with four friends from the shires. It was arranged that in an interval they would adjourn to the bar to meet APH. Meanwhile, the hero had to sing the lines:

> . . . do not ask me to enjoy
>   This pretty sport, for, as a boy,
> I've seen your butcher's work, and had my fill.
>   You fouled the charming country's breath
> With scent of blood and boast of death . . .

APH went to keep his appointment in the bar. Anthony Eden appeared alone to tell him: 'They're not coming up. You should have heard what they were saying: "Not drinking with *that* fellow!" '

NOTES ON CHAPTER 11

1　*Poems of Today:* Second Series (1950).
2　G. K. Chesterton: *Autobiography* (1936).
3　Lance Sieveking: *The Eyes of the Beholder* (1957).
4　*Poems of Shensheddin Mohammed Hafiz of Shiraz:* trs. Payne.
5　The young Herberts were thought to be the originals of the children in Richard Hughes' *High Wind in Jamaica*. He tells me his fictional family did not 'derive specifically from any family I knew at the time', who included, 'as well as the Herberts, the young Williams-Ellises, and Robert Graves's first brood' (Letter, 23 April, 1974).
6　A. P. Herbert: *A Book of Ballads*.
7　A. P. Herbert: *A Book of Ballads*.

12

'Life is Sweet, however Disgusting'

Helen, the operetta that APH adapted from *La Belle Hélène*, with Offenbach's music, was presented by C. B. Cochran at the Adelphi Theatre, London, in January 1932. Artistically, it was a triumph in which its producer said that he had 'never more nearly realized theatrical perfection'. For APH it was 'the richest, grandest, most beautiful show I was ever in'.

It was an event for him in another sense, bringing him into a close working association with the last of the great stage impresarios. Cochran had lately put on *Cavalcade*, and had been caught up in disputes about it with Noel Coward. Impatient by nature and given to sharp retorts, Cochran was also capable of exerting insidious charm. One had to curb one's vanity against his initial greeting: 'I've always wanted to meet you.' With APH he started off on terms that soon warmed into mutual admiration, a bonding that may have been the firmer for the disparity in their sense of humour. Cochran's was mainly limited to bad puns.

As the librettist of *Helen* APH, happily exercising his talents on an Euripidean theme, was obliged to compete with enchanting music and a generally eye-ravishing production. In the judgment of the *Sunday Times*' drama critic, 'no other adapter could have been wittier'. In Cochran's opinion, the libretto was 'a genuinely creative work', and he urged those who had not seen the play to 'buy the book and revel in its wit'.

Having sold some of his Toulouse-Lautrecs to provide necessary cash, Cochran took APH with him to Berlin to see a Reinhardt revival of *La Belle Hélène*. They went on to Salzburg to confer with Reinhardt at his Schloss Leopoldskron, with its vast rooms and splendid Alpine views. APH thought him 'daunting in his dark castle'. He was glad to meet again 'the charming Rudolf Kommer', Reinhardt's personal assistant. One remembers Kommer weaving his way familiarly among the tables of the Savoy Grill in those early thirties.

APH was 'never so warmly surprised' as when Reinhardt agreed to his 'audacious plan' to write a third act for the operetta, with Helen appearing at the walls of Troy before returning to her neglected husband Menelaus. She was to move towards his waiting ship singing the naughtily defiant lines written for her by APH as the climax of the piece:

There's no life without love, and no love without pain;
I have lived, I have loved – and I will not complain.
I have opened my heart like a rose in the rain,
I have played a great part – I would play it again.

Working with Cochran, consulting with Reinhardt, rehearsing with a cast of seventy-one headed by Evelyn Laye and George Robey, was technically exhilarating and professionally unsettling, at moments to a point at which he felt himself to be 'an upstart from Hammersmith'. He had his consolations. Winston Churchill borrowed one of his lines, given to Menelaus, for frequent private quotation: 'Life is sweet, however disgusting.' His programme notes, offered as 'Some Interval Reading For Those Who Have Neglected Their Classical Studies', were a treasured souvenir for many play-goers. Above all, there was Cochran's faith in APH's ability to work with him on still more ambitious ventures. As to that, APH said that he would like to be 'given a go at Grand Opera'.

Helen had 'a magnificent start' (Cochran); unanimous critical approval, full houses week after week; all seeming set fair for a long and successful run. Then, inexplicably, public interest melted away. The curtain came down for the last time after only 163 performances. In a *post mortem* account of the production, Cochran blamed some of the players, saying that but for the libel laws he would name them for their lack of spirit. He was a disappointed man. He had always objected to revivals on principle. *Helen* was the one exception he was prepared to make. The opportunity never came, though he continued to hope that it might.

Undaunted, APH looked for better things from *Derby Day*, 'a comic opera in three acts', written for Playfair at the Lyric. It took him back into a milieu in which he was more at home, in and out of the precincts. 'Nigel Playfair was our neighbour. There were bathing parties from our garden wall; we talked shop while drying, or even in the water. I was very fond of him.' He always had 'a

soft spot', he wrote, for *Derby Day*, appreciating especially Alfred
Reynolds's music for it. 'His tunes were delightful. He was a true
musician', whose varied life included a period as organist at the
British Embassy church in Berlin. A most likable man, his personal
style was that of an eminently trustworthy family solicitor. He had a
fixed association in APH's memory with 'those happy if humble
times at the little Lyric. I still pine for them', looking back over
twenty years.

Derby Day,[1] which ran for several months on a capital of £1,000,
of which APH contributed one-tenth, was the end of Nigel Playfair's
brave and honourable reign at that modest suburban theatre –
before his time locally known as the Blood and Fleapit, a home of
melodrama at its goriest. He had tried hard to regain for it the
prestige associated with his fine productions of *The Beggar's Opera*
and *The Way of the World*. The struggle had worn him down.
Buoyancy had gone from him. By 1932 APH 'had the feeling that
he had lost the will to live'. Within two years he was dead. He had
made theatre-history with his eighteenth-century revivals and his
imaginative employment of the gifts of the brilliant and sadly
short-lived young stage-designer, Lovat Fraser.

APH did not see his hundred pounds again. So far, his work for
the theatre had shown only a meagre pecuniary profit, rewarding
though it otherwise was; for instance, in technical experience and
social enrichment. As part of the experience, he had to contrive
that his second-act curtain always came down before 10 p.m., the
hour at which the local licensing justices required the bar to close;
and revenue from that source was important. It was at the Lyric
too that he discovered the reality of first-night nerves. Gwen
Herbert has not forgotten his intimidating silences as they drove
together to the theatre for those occasions.

Playfair had never been able to pay him more than a hundred or
two in advance of royalties at five per cent. Cochran could make
better terms; advances of five hundred pounds on royalties that
were subject to revision if things went badly. Subsidiary rights
came more prominently into the contracts, fees from amateur
performances, and so on.

About those theatre transactions, about his finances in general,
APH was as uncommunicative as he was about his inner life. His
wife never had a clear view of his financial situation at any time.
When she asked him what he paid a secretary, he replied: 'Oh, I

sign her weekly cheque and she fills it in.' At intervals he would make imperious demands to see the household bills, which he would scrutinize item by item as if crisis impended. If crisis came, he managed to keep it a matter between himself and the bank; the household went on as before. *Punch* apart, his income was unpredictable. More than once when he had money to spare he yielded to a Quixotic impulse to propose to his publishers that he should contribute to their production costs. I understood from him that he sold War Loan as insurance against loss on one of his propaganda books, *No Boats on the River* (1932), in which he accused authority, central and local, of grossly neglecting 'the mighty Thames'. Unexpected royalty receipts were likely to be spent on maintaining even more hospitable 'open house' at Hammersmith Terrace, or on late night supper parties at the Savoy or on still later ones at the Gargoyle, the then exclusive night-club in Dean Street, Soho. Yet at the Savage Club, where he was always one of the most warmly welcomed members, he is still spoken of as having been more ready to join in a round of drinks than to pay for one. He had no great regard for the ritual that requires a man to drink, as Kipling said, 'because the other chap is thirsty'.

Sir Owen Seaman's retirement from the editorship of *Punch* in 1932, an affair of backstage manoeuvring, he being coldly unheeding of hints that 'the time has come', was an event in APH's career. To him Seaman remained a man of consequence, inspiringly helpful from the beginning with his reiterated: 'I think you can do better.' It was from Seaman that he acquired the habit of sending his 'copy' to the printer in handwriting, dubiously justifying that archaic practice by claiming that 'all the great stylists wrote in longhand'. When he bought his first typewriter, 'the comps', he was told were 'very annoyed'. Wits had been sharpened in the composing room by the weekly game of deciphering his often faintly pencilled manuscripts.

Seaman's place was taken by E. V. Knox, a man of rueful countenance and subtle humour who had been working for the paper for years as 'Evoe'. He was steeped in its atmosphere and traditions, and patiently endured classification as a *Punch* versifier, though he was in truth an accomplished poet – almost a banned term in the office. He was to last seventeen years as editor, gathering to himself much goodwill and regard from those around him. Oddly, APH barely mentions him in his autobiography. There may have been a want of sympathy; hardly of respect. Knox had been one of the *Punch* seniors who objected to the contract of £50 a week that Seaman had made with APH.

As a *Punch* humorist, APH was asked in 1932 to address a literary society at Bridlington on humour. He composed a lecture for the occasion entitled 'On Being Funny'.[2] Having delivered it to an audience whose appreciation was rarely expressed in laughter, he received a request from the Customs and Excise for a *précis* of it to enable them to judge whether its content was educational or entertaining. Deciding that its educational value was nil, the authorities charged the society entertainment tax. It was the impetus of one of APH's most pertinacious campaigns in the public interest.

He reported a humorous sequel to the Bridlington episode. As a preamble to lecturing to an audience consisting mainly of school-girls, he suggested ironically that to avert the imposition of tax they had better not laugh at any amusing story he might tell. They sat 'in solemn silence' throughout.

E. V. Lucas to A. P. Herbert:

36 Essex Street,
Strand.
October 27th, 1932.

Dear Alan,   Please be an honest English gentleman and don't traffic any more with the stage until your novel is written. Such success as you had in *The Water Gipsies* should be followed up, and you are abandoning it. I speak for us both, you and this firm.[3]

Always yours,
E. V.

The new novel was to be a not too solemn *exposé* of English divorce law, which demanded adultery from those who had no desire to commit it. The theme was worked out during a trip down the Brittany coast in General Spears's yacht *Bittern*.[4] APH filled a sketchbook with notes on the characters and scenes that he intended bringing into the story.

His host had a more recondite preoccupation, the many relics of the ancient world scattered along that shore. 'The moment Owner sees a menhir', APH wrote, 'he casts anchor and staggers inland. I can *not* see the charm of Druids. I cannot follow the workings of Owner's mind. He is a devout Christian but gazes on heathen cromlechs with the reverence he gives to Quimper cathedral. Owner's wife detests Druids. She is a woman of great intelligence.'[5] He pondered the problem of his inability to enjoy sightseeing, particularly the ruins of past ages. 'Can it be', he asked himself again, 'that I have no sense of the sublime?' He had forgotten his rapture at first seeing the plain of Troy seventeen years before.

During the summer of 1933 he went down to Chartwell, Westerham, to spend a day with Winston Churchill. A National Government was in power, Churchill out of office. 'To think', he remarked to APH over lunch, 'that the reins of this great Empire are in the nerveless hands of Ramsay MacDonald and Stanley Baldwin!' APH was 'deeply sorry' for him. 'I would have betted ten thousand to one against his becoming Prime Minister.' He watched him feed his black swans, some named after politicians who were out of favour with him. APH sat with him in the garden studio, surrounded by what Churchill later spoke of to me as his 'poor daubs', the paintings that had solaced those years of his public abeyance. 'I have my birds, my paintbox, my dear family,' he told APH, counting his blessings. 'He talked like Cincinnatus', APH wrote after the visit, 'and tried to persuade himself that, with so much to keep him happily busy, he should not worry because he wasn't wanted.' One of his remarks that day APH never forgot: 'It is easy to exaggerate one's importance.' Before APH took his leave, Churchill said ruminatively again: 'To think that the reins of this great Empire . . .'

APH had lately joined a group of writers who met for monthly dinners in Soho under the auspices of the *Week-End Review*, founded and edited by Gerald Barry, rebounding from the summary termination of his editorship of the *Saturday Review*. Still tied by his *Punch* contract, APH was free to write elsewhere only 'by kind permission of the Proprietors', to quote their condescending formula for all acknowledgements of their copyright. Judging by the frequency of his name in the correspondence pages of the *Review* in 1933, his function was to impart the note of controversy to them. He may have been content to be paid in dinners, though intellectual profit was to be had from the lively minds assembled at that table. Anyone knowing T. Earle Welby, for instance, a fine literary critic,[6] would value the chance to hear his conversational flow. Others usually present were L. P. Hartley, Ivor Brown, Edward Shanks, Anthony Bertram and Dyneley Hussey.

His *Misleading Cases* had been a success with *Punch* readers for the
past nine years, and had sold well in the bookshops. When *More
Misleading Cases* came out in the autumn of 1933, Lord Trenchard,
the Commissioner of Metropolitan Police, wrote from New Scotland
Yard: 'I should like your brains here to help me with all my
misleading cases.' In October of that year Sir Leslie Scott wrote
to him: 'What about Germany?' He was expressing the general
unease created by the rise of Nazi power. APH wrote some verses
for *Punch*:

> It's sad to think that Science, nobly slaving,
>   Has made it much more easy than before
> To ascertain how everyone's behaving
>   And disseminate the news from shore to shore.
> And the one result (except for cricket scoring)
>   Is that any ass can propagate a roar,
> That Gobble can be cosmically boring
>   And we can't escape from Goring any more.
> I think it's time the Press began ignoring
>   The kind of information I deplore.
> Well, does it matter what was said by Goring
>   Or what uniform it was that Gobble wore?
> But all the same, each morning finds me poring
>   O'er the news concerning one or other bore,
> And the avenue which I am now exploring
>   Is familiar, I dare say, to many more.

A letter from Berta Ruck, the novelist, on holiday in Austria,
told him that she had 'cried with laughing until two handkerchiefs
were finished for the day. You see, I am here in the middle of it.'
As an indication of the surrounding tensions, she thought it wise,
she wrote, *not* to pass on her copy of *Punch* to Austrian friends.

Frau Dircksen, wife of the German ambassador in London,
addressed APH a little too pointedly at a party: 'They tell me,
Mr Herbert,' she said when he was introduced, 'that you are a
humorist. Please, what are humorists?' His reply went the round of
the clubs. 'Madam, I find that difficult to explain. You see, you
don't have them in your country.'

Holy Deadlock, his divorce novel, was published in April 1934;
essentially, a tract for the times presented as fiction, the author a
propagandist masquerading as a story-teller. The message was clear:

existing divorce law was unworthy of England's statute book. Rudyard Kipling, to APH, 16 May 1934: 'I've read your *Holy Deadlock*. It made me sick. I knew things were pretty heathen in that department of our "civilisation", but I didn't realise that they were worse than heathen.'

APH had recently been made a member of Grillion's, the exclusive political dining-club (founded in 1812). There he met Kipling for the first time, as a neighbour at the dining-table. Towards the end of dinner, Kipling rose abruptly, tapped him on the shoulder, bidding him good-night, and left. APH was fearful of having 'bored the great man'. Sir Owen Seaman was at hand as joint honorary secretary to reassure him. 'Not at all,' he told APH; 'He has to be home by ten', adding, after a significant pause, 'always'. I myself had been a witness of the domestic duress to which Kipling was subject. He and his wife were present at the Garrick Theatre for the first night of *Rain*, a play based on a story by Somerset Maugham. At the end of the first act, Kipling's wife rose from her stall and, pulling at his sleeve, led him to an exit: they did not return.

Holy Deadlock sold well; more than ninety thousand copies. Predictably, the book brought an abnormal postal response; overtime work for his secretary rather than for himself, who seldom bothered to read, and even more rarely to answer, unsolicited letters. Some of them were from correspondents who wished to believe that *Holy Deadlock* was written out of its author's private discontents with the married state. They overlooked the dedication to 'Mrs A. P. Herbert on the nineteenth anniversary of her marriage'. The inscription had sentimental implications that were to remain intact through the next four decades.

Holy Deadlock was an entertaining novel with a serious purpose. It set out, with accuracy and wit, the processes of obtaining a divorce at that time. It was sympathetic to the Roman Catholic view of marriage as a sacramental contract, though its author's own approach was latitudinarian. Nowhere did it show penetrating insight into the realities of the married state. Its note of generalizing propaganda was struck in the names given to the two principal characters, John Adam and Mary Eve. In another guise, C. B. Cochran was given a supporting role in the story.

Works of fiction have been credited with influencing affairs in the practical world: Marryat's *The King's Own*, changes in naval administration; Galsworthy's *Justice*, prison legislation. The novels of

Dickens and Harriet Beecher Stowe are usually cited as having had a social impact. APH's war novel, *The Secret Battle*, has its relevance here, while for *Holy Deadlock* he was content to claim that 'it helped to create a more favourable attitude' to divorce law reform.[7]

He became a father-in-law for the first time when, in 1934, his eldest daughter Crystal married John Pudney. On the wedding day, while he waited to escort her to Chiswick parish church, he played Handel's *Largo* twice to her on the piano 'for soothing purposes'. At the altar he caused a minor mishap to the routine by taking his place on the wrong side of the bride at the moment of 'giving away'. Parting with a daughter brought the usual paternal antipathies to the surface. They took the form in his case of a disinclination to speak of or introduce John Pudney by name: he was always 'my son-in-law'.

Over supper at Rules in Maiden Lane, APH announced that he was 'proceeding' against the Kitchen Committee of the House of Commons for some violation or other of the licensing laws. He was one of those rare people who could talk obsessively about matters of greater interest to himself than to anyone else without being a bore. I heard more of that legal exploit of his, spending the night with him in *Water Gipsy*, tied up near some lighters by Waterloo Bridge. Awakened by him at five-forty-five the next morning, he splashing water over his torso from a bucket, I observed that the bridge and the cross of St Paul's were no longer in sight. We had swung round during the night, and were now being inspected by Big Ben. I felt that I was part of a mystery. The headlong behaviour of the river tug-boats added to one's sense of unreality: they appeared to be racing by at top speed as if on desperately urgent business. APH said that, of course, it was an optical illusion, a baffling one that he had talked about with his friend E.V. and could not explain.

He looked more like a figurehead than a helmsman, with a nose that identified him to many on the river. Once, when we were following the tide down to the Pool, a policeman on London Bridge leaned over the parapet and saluted him. As he remarked, it was 'a change from being spat upon by urchins on Blackfriars bridge', whose conduct drove him to work off his indignation in a piece for *Punch* about 'the glories' of fifty years of free compulsory education.

We were heading for the Prospect of Whitby, at Shadwell; from

a distance it looked like a white-painted outsized piano dumped
on the riverside. He was on the friendliest of terms with the landlord,
Jim Bean, 'a genial barrel of a man', a former waterman. APH
afterwards regretted in print that the Prospect of Whitby had been
'discovered and spoilt by the gay world', ignoring his own part in
its rise to popularity as 'a famous little pub'.[8]

His appearance at Bow Street magistrates' court in May 1934 to
'lay an information' against the House of Commons Kitchen Committee may or may not have been a sequel of his glimpse some time
before of MPs 'doing themselves well' on their Terrace. He now
wished to ascertain whether they were enjoying a privilege that
defied the law. There were heavy penalties against the sale of
liquor on unlicensed premises. Did the House of Commons enjoy
immunity and, if so, by what sanction?

Traipsing the Westminster corridors, he had found 'a complete
absence of conscience or respect towards the Licensing Laws'.
Satisfying himself by personal research and inquiry that the Kitchen
Committee had no legal right to sell beer, wines and spirits on
their premises, he decided to do what 'nobody in history, not even
Bradlaugh,[9] had attempted before', namely, to prosecute the House
of Commons. He found only one member willing to support him
in his confessedly 'mad enterprise', Lord Hugh Cecil,[10] who represented Oxford in Parliament. 'He said that I had raised a serious
constitutional point of law which ought to be settled, and that he
would assist me. I shall never forget a charming morning we spent
at the House when Lord Hugh took me round the various places of
refreshment, and showed me everything he could.'[11]

Unshaken by the possibility of his being committed to the Clock
Tower for contempt of Parliament – and Erskine May was com-
petently quoted for the warning – APH consulted two good friends
of his Oxford and Inner Temple time, Walter Monckton and Harry
Strauss and, with the help and a fighting fund for which he could
raise only £115, he applied at Bow Street for a summons against the
Kitchen Committee. The Chief Metropolitan Magistrate, Sir Rollo
Graham Campbell, declined jurisdiction. Unlike APH, he was not
prepared to risk being 'in contempt'.

The next move was to apply to the King's Bench Divisional Court
for a *mandamus* which, if granted, would require Sir Rollo to take
the case. 'It was here', writes Brian Davidson, CBE, then a junior

in Walter Monckton's chambers and devilling for him, 'that the fun, and my small part in it, began. The evidence to the Divisional Court had to be given on affidavit, and it was my agreeable task to translate into that form APH's racy account of his activities in collecting evidence in the House to show that the Kitchen Committee were contravening the law. I remember one passage that caused me particular difficulty. This was: "I went into the Smoking Room and found Nancy Astor there. 'Nancy, old horse', I said, 'have a White Lady!'" '12

The High Court gave him, he agreed, 'a courteous and fair hearing', but refused him the writ. Parliamentary privilege was upheld in spite of impressive misgivings. He felt entitled to assert that 'through my rash act the liberties of the faithful Commons were proclaimed and freed from doubt by the High Court of Justice, and established for ever'.13 A memorial plaque to him in the Smoking Room or Bar, he thought, would have been suitable recompense.

The Lord Chief Justice proposed that costs – which might have been put at £700 or so – should not be given against him. 'We have had a rare and refreshing diversion from the ordinary routine of this Court.' At the end of the day, APH was £45 out of pocket. 'A brave attempt', said the *Law Times*, 'to make the House of Commons feel the pressure of the Licensing Laws which it had itself created.' APH's appearance in the courts in 1934 was his initiation as a crusader whose championship of the peoples' rights and freedoms knighted him in the esteem of many long before he received the Sovereign's accolade.

I was with him at Romano's one evening at that time when he lectured a waiter on the nonsense of a law that required us to order sandwiches, which we didn't want, with our drinks. The man stood by respectfully for twenty minutes, not saying a word, occasionally bowing as if in agreement and glancing helplessly at me, until at last he was peremptorily called away. 'Afraid it was wasted effort,' I remarked. 'Not at all,' APH retorted. 'The light is never wasted.'

Returning with him to Hammersmith, I was made a temporary member of his skittles' team at the Black Lion. His passion for the river had reduced his relaxations as a landsman. He was no longer turning out so often or so eagerly to bowl a good length ball at cricket with The Invalids, the weekend-team founded and captained by Jack Squire, and from which A. G. Macdonell drew the experiences converted into the memorable cricket match in *England*,

Their England. Skittles had become his only active recreation ashore. Under his patronage, skittles at the Black Lion developed into a Hammersmith cult. 'The game is very old here,' he said, recalling that 'the officer who struck Queen Victoria over the head with his cane often played at the Black Lion after he was cashiered.' He enticed Sir James Barrie from his Adelphi chimney-corner to 'throw a cheese' with him there. As a test of his persuasive power, it equalled his achievement in inducing Sir Austen Chamberlain[14] to spend an evening with him at the Café Royal, an apparition 'that astonished the Bohemians'.

Free and easy though he was as a social being, APH preferred the Savoy Grill to the Café Royal, where propinquity with the less attractive elements of Bohemia was sometimes unavoidable. 'Of all the gilded eating-places in London the Savoy Grill has always had my heart.' He liked it because 'most of the company are people who have work to do in the world and have earned their right to be there by doing it well'. He resented 'the perverse modern snobbery which holds automatically that those who have come to the top are no good. I like to see them enjoying the fruits of their labours.'[15]

He was at work on the libretto of a new Cochran revue, *Streamline*, produced at the Palace Theatre, Shaftesbury Avenue, in September 1934. One of its 'hits' was his Gilbert and Sullivan pastiche, *Perseverance*, which the critics unanimously praised. When one of them referred to him as 'another Gilbert', he reacted with annoyance. 'It makes me sick.'

The new revue brought him in touch with the young composer Vivian Ellis. A 'long and happy' collaboration ensued. Ellis's setting of *Other People's Babies*, APH's affectionate commemoration of the English 'nanny', ensured its great success in the revue and its subsequent longevity elsewhere.

> Babies? It's a gift, my dear, and I should say I know,
> For I've been pushing prams about for forty years or so,
> Thirty-seven babies – or is it thirty-nine?
> No, I'm wrong; it's thirty-six – but none of them was mine.

>> Other people's babies –
>> That's my life!
>> Mother to dozens,
>> And nobody's wife . . .

Streamline was a personal success for him as the librettist. He had another reason for remembering it: 'One of the rare theatrical enterprises I had a hand in that actually made money.'

Out on the river on a hot Sunday afternoon that month, he yielded to a Byronic urge to be 'the first man of letters' to swim from Waterloo Bridge to Westminster Bridge: 'a mad impulse', he being by no means a strong swimmer. Powered by tenacity, he plunged in and completed the course. As he frequently said, reviewing more responsible activities of his: 'Nothing would make me give up.' Between the bridges he heard himself identified over a river steamer's loud-hailer: 'The gentleman swimming in the water on your right is Mr A. P. Herbert, the famous novelist.' When, much later, Harold Nicolson told him that Byron had swum from Lambeth to Southwark, APH revised his claim. 'I am the only president of the Society of Authors to have swum between the two bridges.'

E. V. Lucas had passed on to his fellow clubmen at the Garrick APH's saying about Dean Inge, that he was 'a pillar of the Church and two columns in the *Evening Standard*', with which newspaper the Dean had a writing contract. E.V. now had cause to give it a new lease of life. He had recently been at a public dinner at which the Dean, whose deafness was severe, repeated the remark, telling the chairman afterwards: 'I have quite often referred to that quip of A. P. Herbert's in my speeches, but never so successfully as this evening. I could see them roaring with laughter.' He had not realized, and probably never knew, that the speaker preceding him had quoted it.

NOTES ON CHAPTER 12

1 'Why does no one revive *Derby Day*, in its kind as irresistible a work of English popular art as *The Beggar's Opera* or *HMS Pinafore?*' – Sir Arthur Bryant, *Illustrated London News*, 12 August 1967.
2 Reprinted in the *Library Assistant*, the official journal of the Association of Assistant Librarians (1932).
3 Methuen.
4 Major-General Sir Edward Spears, Bt., KBE, CB, MC. He escorted General de Gaulle to England on his flight from France in 1940.
5 Mary Borden, the American novelist.
6 Author of *The Cellar Key*, *The Dinner Knell*, *Back Numbers*, etc.
7 A project for a film of *Holy Deadlock* was vetoed by the film censor because, according to APH, that official 'has always been a Catholic'.
8 A. P. Herbert: *The Thames* (1966).

9 Charles Bradlaugh (1833–91) MP and a leader of the English Radical movement.
10 Later Lord Quickswood (1869–1956), 5th son of the 3rd Marquess of Salisbury, the Victorian Prime Minister.
11 A. P. Herbert: Unpublished notes.
12 Letter, 11 May 1973.
13 A. P. Herbert: *Independent Member* (1950).
14 Sir Austen Chamberlain (1863–1937), sometime Secretary of State for Foreign Affairs; Chancellor of the Exchequer; Secretary of State for India.
15 A. P. Herbert: *The Singing Swan.*

The Archbishop was Amused

In September 1935 a message was delivered to me at Rodmell:
'Sailing Barge Plinlimmon, Newhaven Harbour. We are in this
expensive port for the weekend. Bring the family down to see us
and the boat. APH.'

The *Plinlimmon* had been a Medway racing barge. She was now
on charter for holidays; her interior, I observed with surprise, was
'about as big as our village hall'. Over sausages and mash, 'cooked
by Gwen and the girls in an appetising galley haze' (my diary),
APH mentioned a trip he had made as third hand in a spritsail
barge, the *Paglesham*, loading in Surrey Commercial Dock with
grain for Colchester. It was his induction into the freemasonry of the
sailing bargemen. 'They delighted me much.' He revelled in their
rich and ripe characters, their river and weather lore, their exclusive
forms of speech. His Suffolk skipper, seeing him strip off one chilly
morning for a wash in a bucket of water drawn from the Orwell
at Pinmill, had called out to him: 'Oh, Mr 'erbert, 'ow can you
stand there in this bitter east wind, unrindin' yourself like that?'

Later in the evening at Newhaven he proposed that I should sail
as a crew member round to Dover, the next stage in his itinerary.
As a Weldishman,[1] I have an inborn suspicion of the sea, and I
declined. We all went to the fair in the meadows by the Ouse (once
better named the Mydwynd). I wrote in my diary: 'Walked the four
miles home towards midnight, bearing cokernuts. Tired and happy.'

Great peril befell the *Plinlimmon* as she stood off Beachy Head,
caught in an unheralded storm of wind and wave. Her steering
chains broke. She was at risk of being driven on to the rocks at the
foot of those towering chalk cliffs. Her last flare was fired. It was
seen by a collier, from which a boat was launched to the rescue.
Behind the newspaper headlines was the sober truth that it had
indeed been 'a near thing'.

He had been a *Punch* staff man for eleven years. No new accession to the Table had occurred since his arrival in 1924. Still the junior member, he was expected by tradition to wait on his seniors when they were in session. How dutiful he was in fetching and carrying for them one can but guess. There was never a doubt about his loyalty to the *Punch* customs. H. F. Ellis,[2] who joined the Table in 1936, recalls that APH had 'a strong feeling (probably derived from Owen Seaman) for what was right and proper'.

One of the customs was that in the editor's absence from the Wednesday conference a deputy was put in charge to 'take the Table'. There was always concern not to choose anyone likely to fancy that his temporary elevation was a pointer to the editorial succession. APH was never asked to preside. He was never considered for the editorship, for all that he had the prime qualification of personifying the inspired amateur, a type that conspicuously influenced the fortunes of *Punch* down the years. Presumably, the proprietorial Bradburys and Agnews were saying in their own way what Reynolds said of Gainsborough: 'Damn the fellow, how various he is!' Of course he would have liked to be offered 'the chair'; parenthetically, more than any other occupant of it he would have looked the part, notably so as he grew older. What may be doubted was his readiness to accept the sacrifice of personal freedom that always meant so much to him. He had chosen to go through life on his own terms and at his own pace. Only in time of war was he a willing slave to discipline, and then with reservations that often breached it.

His work for *Punch* during that time helped to 'sell the paper', as the circulation men of Fleet Street would say; a fairly rare compliment from that quarter to a writer. R. G. G. Price states in his *History of Punch* that 'to many readers *Punch* was A.P.H.' His *Topsy* series of letters ostensibly written by a scatterbrained 'deb' type of the twenties became extremely popular.[3] As Anthony Hope had done in the *Dolly Dialogues*, he set out to create character through speech. He claimed that through Topsy he made 'some lasting additions to the language – one of them "It's the done thing" '. Another of her sayings, 'quite definitely unmagnetic', became a character smear at cocktail parties. Another character devised by him to support a protracted series of monologues was Mr Mafferty, an Irishman who was made to hold forth on a variety of topics with a gaiety and a gusto suggesting that his creator saw him as a specimen of a vanishing race. Perhaps APH had no intention other than to establish in readers' minds his own familiarity with 'the brogue'. He often lapsed into it in casual conversation, without convincing anyone that he was even half Irish.

It was to Sir Owen Seaman's credit that he gave APH the freedom of *Punch* as a platform for promoting his 'small causes', some of them not so small; not all of them likely to 'sell the paper'. In *Punch* he first flexed his muscles as a reformer, at times to the detriment of his reputation as a humorist. That, in turn, occasionally prejudiced him adversely. The funny man who aspires to be taken seriously is always in danger of rousing uncongenial laughter. APH contrived a fusion which, while it scarcely warranted the status claimed for him as 'the greatest English journalist of his time',[4] entitled him to be accounted a paladin of more than the pen. *Punch* readers were well prepared for his advent as a campaigner on the national scale. They were aware of his attitude to a number of issues of social importance. *Punch* was the springboard from which, to no one's surprise greater than his, he was propelled in 1935 into the political arena at Westminster. '*Punch* gave a first appearance to many notions that were later paraded in Parliament.'[5]

Divorce law reform had come to be the loudest buzzing bee in his bonnet by the late thirties. He knew all the arguments. He had listened to the chief protagonists: E. S. P. Haynes, solicitor and prolific author; May Louise Seaton-Tiedman, the comfortably married honorary secretary of the Divorce Law Reform Union; Claude Mullins, metropolitan magistrate and vice-president of the London Marriage Guidance Council; the Revd W. F. Geikie-Cobb, rector of St Ethelburga the Virgin, Within Bishopsgate. Haynes had founded the Divorce Law Reform Union in 1909 with Commander Ramsay-Fairfax, who 'lost a considerable fortune from relatives who disapproved his activities', Haynes wrote. Mrs Seaton-Tiedman put up her portable rostrum every Sunday afternoon at Hyde Park Corner, rain or shine, to preach against the law's neglect. No doubt the toneless voice of the bore was heard from time to time in the discussions; as to that, APH was discreetly silent. In October 1935 the often cloudy atmosphere of reform was illumined by the Lord Chief Justice, Lord Hewart, who discussed in the *Daily Telegraph* the question: Is it now almost time for something to be done about the law of divorce?

Concurrently, APH was conducting a different kind of campaign,

his 'Word War' in *Punch*. 'Piratical, ruffianly, masked, braggart and
ill-bred words invade our language and lay waste our thought
every day . . . Instead of "fun", we speak of "entertainment value";
instead of Tories we have "the forces of reaction"; instead of games
"recreational facilities".' It brought him a flood of letters, more
than a thousand, from the clergy, schoolmasters, professors of this
and that, dons, civil servants and fellow writers. One of his correspondents, Lord Trenchard, soon to retire from New Scotland Yard,
cited the misuse of a word in a letter sent from his office to the
victim of a recent wrongful arrest. The 'poor innocent man' was
asked to accept official regret for the 'inconvenience' caused him. 'I
gave him an unqualified apology.'

The vice-chairman of the London Passenger Transport Board,
Frank Pick, told APH that he had ordered the staff of his 'public
letters section' to study the 'Word War' articles in *Punch* 'as part of
their official duty' (18 October 1935). The articles came out in
book form under the title *What a Word!* (Methuen). Two new
editions quickly followed. Enlivened by APH's witty index, the book
retains its missionary zest these forty years after.

Business jargon in particular drew the shafts of his scorn. Why,
he asked, do 'office people' write that they are 'prepared' when they
mean 'willing'? An employer writes that he is 'prepared' to visit
New York 'when he has not even begun to pack'. As for the average
businessman's addiction to the use of Latin abbreviations that he
does not understand:

> I heard the happy lark exult,
> Too soon, for it was early ult.;
> And now the land with rain is rinsed –
> Ah, mournful is the month of inst.;
> Love, like a lizard in the rocks,
> Is hungry for the suns of prox.
>
> Boy Cupid with his catapult
> Could find but sorry sport in ult.;
> But through the woods, with bluebells chintzed,
> My lady comes to me in inst.;
> And O may Cupid speed the clocks,
> For she will marry me in prox.![6]

The unanimously approving response did more than confirm the
popularity of his choice of subject to write about. It supplied

particular reassurance when, towards the end of the year, he became a parliamentary candidate.

His *Misleading Cases* were setting up new records in literary longevity. An omnibus volume, *Uncommon Law* (1935) was reprinted twelve times. 'A warming letter' from an Ontario lawyer, informed him: 'I have not hesitated to quote you in our Courts . . . and your words have never failed to receive due appreciation and to illuminate the subject under discussion.' His First in Law at Oxford brought him a renown that he would have been much less likely to achieve at the Bar, though he continued to be sorry, not quite so fervently as before, that he had not had that experience – 'Well, for a year, say'. *Misleading Cases* acquired the panache of quotation in the Royal Courts of Justice, the House of Lords, the Supreme Court of the United States and in Congress.

Writing an introduction to the sixth edition, Lord Hewart guessed that 'Mr Herbert may have decided that it is more agreeable on the whole to suffer an "Introduction" than to be committed for contempt of Court'. Recognizing that aversion from the law and courts of law 'is naturally strong in the human mind', he did not doubt that 'many thousands of distinctly respectable persons would chuckle, and chuckle again and again, over the neatness, the deftness, and the dexterity – the sense, the satire, and the scholarship – of these criticisms wrapped in the pleasant guise of parody'. Typical specimen:

SUET *v.* HADDOCK

STATUS OF AUTHORS

With his lordship's address to the jury this case approached its conclusion today. He said:

Gentlemen, in this case the plaintiff is a manufacturer, and the defendant, Mr Haddock, is, among other things, an author, which fact should alone dispose you in the plaintiff's favour; for, while the life-blood of our country is its trade and commerce, we do not, fortunately, depend upon our literature for anything that matters.

The defendant Haddock does not appear to have been uniformly successful in any of the regular departments of writing; or at any rate he has not grown rich, which, as I ruled at an earlier stage of the case, is *prima facie* evidence of incapacity. Recently, however, he has devised and practised a style of writing which is quite new to this country, and, like other novelties, has proved most profitable.

Calling himself a 'Commercial Critic', he writes each week, in a
paper called *Veritas*, a reasoned article appraising the latest products
of British or foreign manufacturers. He uses the style and manner
of the fashionable literary or dramatic critic, and, as you have
heard, he contends that the public need for expert and impartial
guidance is at least as strong in the commercial as in the literary
field . . .

The Rolls Royce Company sent him for review a copy of their
1928 model, and you will remember the patronising manner in
which he wrote about it:

> '*The work shows promise. This young Company, whose name is new to me,
> have evidently the root of the matter in them, and, if they will try again, may
> well produce something which is really worth while.*'

The sometimes grudging character of his praise, however, did
not prevent other firms, confident in the excellence of their wares,
from pressing them upon him. Mr Haddock has now a small fleet
of motor-cars for review, he lives in a review house, his clothes and
his furniture are free samples, he has more free pianos, gramophones,
billiard-tables, and wireless sets than he is able to enjoy with
comfort . . . .

Whether or not he has been impartial it will be for you to say.
There is abundant evidence that he has not been afraid to cause
annoyance . . . His habit of comparing unfavourably the British
manufacturers of today with the products of past centuries and
foreign countries has given especial pain. His constant references to
Chippendale and Sheraton have admittedly irritated the modern
furniture trade. And his comment on a British piano, 'Not a bad
piano, but how much better they do these things in Germany!' was
not considered helpful . . .

While he may have had no overt intention at any time of submitting
himself to the electorate, one was not surprised to read in after
years his confession of 'secret longings to serve in that great place',[7]
the House of Commons. It was my experience that he never rejected
outright a suggestion that he should do so. Always there was the
proviso that he would want to represent his university only; no
other constituency would do. My own unimportant promptings
were less casual after meeting a Socialist MP named Harry Day, a
variety artists' agent who answered, when I asked him why he had
gone into Parliament: 'For the publicity.' Thereafter, when I heard

it said, as it often was, that APH was 'the kind of man we need at Westminster', my response was fervent. There was weighty encouragement for him within the House. Austen Chamberlain and Stanley Baldwin hoped to see him on the green benches. The spur was increasingly being applied by those outside who knew that in spite of his sauntering style he was capable of extraordinary exertions. Visiting us again at Rodmell, he made a mock-political speech from the balcony above our garage, his audience our respective families, and Edward Wadsworth with his wife and daughter, assembled on the lawn below. His gesticulating posture as a hero of the hustings that afternoon in Sussex seemed afterwards to have been a rehearsal for the singular event to come. It was a coincidence that a day or two afterwards, in our country town of Lewes, four miles away, I was shown an old print of Tom Paine, some time Excise man there. 'A large-nosed, faun mouthed man', I noted, 'with a passable resemblance to A. P. Herbert.'

At *Punch* he was 'lectured by one of the proprietors', he said, for 'dragging near-politics' into his articles. The Table had become 'a sort of Shadow Cabinet', the pressure of events compelling more political talk than usual at the Wednesday dinners. Succeeding Ramsay MacDonald as head of the National Government in 1935, Stanley Baldwin called a general election in November. German re-armament, the Abyssinian crisis, the fate of the League of Nations, national defence, were the great issues.

Pondering his unexpected adoption as a candidate for Parliament, APH regarded himself as the plaything of chance. Chance, he had no doubt, altered the course of his life at that time; and the effects of chance always impressed him as much as the consequences of design. It would have been hard to convince him of the polarizing power of the imagination. He was half-way through a new novel – it was to be about Thames barge life – and he was beginning to feel that it was stale and unprofitable labour. A welcome break came with an invitation to join a party attending the official opening of a new ICI coal-into-oil conversion plant at Billingham, Co. Durham. As a scientific development it had no interest for him, but he welcomed the outing, which proved to be germinally important.

One of his companions on the north-eastern train journey was Gilbert Frankau, the successful novelist and unsuccessful editor, who lectured APH on the folly of prejudicing his prospects as a novelist by dissipating his energies on 'writing articles about divorce' and miscellaneous topics. Frankau was engagingly serious, APH a willing listener. 'He convinced me, utterly.'

Feeling convicted of intellectual perversity, APH privately decided to reform his professional life; at which point a stranger passed that way. Someone at the dining-car table looked up in greeting. 'Hullo, Lindemann!'[8] The name was not as well known then as it was to be half a decade later. It had a particular interest for APH because Professor Lindemann had just been rejected as a prospective candidate in the forthcoming general election by the Conservative establishment at Oxford University. 'The Prof. felt deeply humiliated.'[9] No one introduced APH to Lindemann. APH civilly regretted that the Professor had not been adopted and enquired: 'Any chance, would you think, of an Independent being nominated?'

Lindemann was not encouraging; time was too short, he thought, with the election only three weeks away. The University electors were mainly postal voters, scattered throughout the kingdom. Probably not more than seven hundred or so were Oxford residents. Addresses would have to be obtained; all very difficult. So saying, Lindemann moved to his place along the train.

APH had no expectation of meeting him again. But on the return that evening to St Pancras, he caught up with Lindemann's burly figure on the platform and bade him good-night, adding on an impulse: 'If you know anyone in Oxford who would be interested . . .' Lindemann enquired vaguely: 'Interested in what?' APH reminded him of their brief encounter on the train. 'Oh, that', the Professor said, and went on his way.

A week later a box-file of names and addresses of the 22,000 voters on the university electoral roll was delivered conspiratorially after dark at 12 Hammersmith Terrace, the work of would-be supporters in Oxford. Candidates in the university elections were not permitted to canvass, display posters, or hold public meetings. They were free to circulate an election address. APH set out his aspirations as a candidate for Parliament in a series of clauses embodying, he afterwards wrote, 'some wild and ignorant stuff, no doubt, but also a good many promises, and prophecies, that came true'. He felt safe in asserting that most of the subjects referred to in it 'were not mentioned in any other Address in the land'.

Undoubtedly it was an original document of its kind; for students of parliamentary history, a collectors' piece. For example, under the heading 'Capitalism and the Socialist', he wrote: 'My reason, such as it is, rebels when I am asked to believe that, after thousands of years of a not wholly fruitless civilisation, not merely a new but the best and only way of managing this complicated world has been revealed to my old football-captain, Sir Stafford Cripps.' His Clause 9 is still quoted: 'I know nothing about Agriculture.'

On divorce law: 'If His Majesty's Government do not, as they should, accept the responsibility for this reform, I shall myself do what I can.' On liberty: 'I am a firm believer in the good sense and robust control of the British people; and therefore, until the contrary is shown, I should prefer to trust and educate rather than restrict. But where, as upon the roads, liberty is abused, I support the firmest measures.'

On education: 'I conceive that for the statesman education should embrace the whole wide world of mental enrichment, including literature, art and music. In this wide field I think the State is lamentably idle and unhelpful. It is absurd with one hand to distribute free education, and with the other to lay a punitive tax upon drama and concerts, and the takings of the BBC. The Entertainments Tax (a duty of 20 per cent on receipts, not profits) is a barbarous relic of the Great War.' He wished the State to 'more actively encourage the arts and graces of life, by the assistance of such enterprises as a National Theatre and Opera House . . . the preservation of ancient buildings and national beauties' and, ultimately, by the institution of a Ministry of Fine Arts.

Posting copies of the address to the voters in time called for dedication to exhaustion-point by himself and his family and friends, among them Peter Fleming, Lance Sieveking, Eric Linklater and a Hammersmith neighbour named Frank Bluff, who was a director of a printing firm. An earnest, near-sighted young Christ Church tutor named Frank Pakenham (later Lord Longford) proposed himself as APH's election agent.

As the day of decision drew near, when APH had to hand in his nomination paper with the statutory deposit of £150, he was sorely troubled. At one moment he considered his candidature 'a preposterous enterprise', at another, 'absurd, impertinent, and dangerous'. He worried that if he lost the deposit money he would be awkwardly out of pocket, and even more so if he won. He was fearful of being humbled, imagining it being said on every side: 'What an ass!'

Two days before the poll he told Sir Harry (later Lord) McGowan, head of ICI: 'I've no chance of getting in – not a hope.'

Considering himself immune from charges of impropriety in that undergraduates did not have the vote, he accepted an invitation to address them at the Union. 'I was terrified, as I always was there.' The closing words of the only speech that he made during the campaign brought the young men to their feet. 'You represent the true spirit of Oxford. You will go out into many corners of the community in which the name of Oxford does not stand so high as we should like to think it did and as we know it deserves to. In that hard, jealous world, among the Philistines, the Bohemians, the camps of Demos and the Temple of Mammon, I have carried the flag of Oxford, I hope with some effect. And now, returning, I ask that I may be trusted to carry that flag in the counsels of the nation and among His Majesty's faithful Commons.' Ivor Brown, who was in the escort party, said that 'APH was admirable'.

A message from C. B. Cochran awaited him at home. Cochran wrote from a sickbed in Naples. 'Don't tell anybody, please', a reminder of the occupational hazards of an impresario arranging finance for a new show. It was important that his backers should not hear adverse rumours about his health.

Envelope-addressing and tea-drinking were continuing into the small hours at 12 Hammersmith Terrace. Lance Sieveking took it on himself to flatter various addressees by exalting their social status. Under his hand BAs became MAs, captains and colonels were promoted, mere Reverends were made Canons. He also admitted to knighting a few whose names seemed to warrant it. The signatures of twelve Oxford sponsors were secured for APH's nomination form. Mostly they came from the staff of the Dragon School. There was no support from the dons. He sensed a general expectation that he would lose his deposit, for which the only consolation was that the £150 would be forfeit, not to the Crown, as in other constituencies, but to the university. He did not know then that bets were being taken against him at All Souls. Word was passed to him that the Archbishop of Canterbury considered his candidature 'a joke'.

There was a strong belief that the clergy, representing an important section of the electorate and opposed to his divorce views, would rally to defeat him. Privately, he assured himself that he could count on the support of a large body of professional people, an opinion based on the mass of correspondence that he had received during his most recent *Punch* campaign. It proved to be a shrewdly accurate guess.

At a late hour there was alarm lest his printed election address exceeded the allowable postal weight for such communications. A comedy element ensued. The family kitchen-scales were out of order. A hurried foray along the Terrace produced a replacement. That breathless emergency passed, someone remembered that there was an official regulation affecting the size of the envelopes. 'It looked as if we might have to begin all over again.' Tact and official good sense prevailed; the first of the GPO collection vans arrived at the door; 'and away the fateful documents went' (APH).

The transferable vote system operating in the university election meant a protracted counting process. While it was going on, APH walked the streets of Oxford alone in the rain, 'wondering why I had got myself into this mess'. The tension was 'worse than any First Night'. He came second in each of the four counts, and was duly elected Junior Burgess. Lord Hugh Cecil retained his place as Senior Burgess, held from 1910. When Gwen Herbert met APH at Paddington Station, he stumbled from the train looking dishevelled and anxious. 'God, I've got in!' he gasped, forgetting that he had telephoned the news to her two hours before.

What he had feared was folly proved to be triumph. Surprise was the keynote of much of the congratulatory deluge, typically expressed by Duff Cooper: 'I never thought you would get in.' Kipling, writing from his flooded Sussex valley, was 'more pleased' than he could 'decently say'. Responding to APH's recent assault on business jargon, he added: 'Trusting your good self has not been unduly affected *qua* your esteemed health by the political events which have transpired subsequent to your entry into the Public Arena . . .'

Amid the jubilation, a note of dissent was sounded by Lord Hugh Cecil: 'Sincerity obliges me to say that I deeply and keenly regret, on public grounds, your election to the University seat.' APH reflected, in writing, that 'all the Cecils feel strongly about divorce'.

NOTES ON CHAPTER 13

1 The old, forgotten name for a native of the Sussex Weald.
2 H. F. Ellis, a classics scholar and schoolmaster, was a highly esteemed *Punch* writer through three decades. APH admired his 'polished wit'.
3 Stanley Baldwin was one of her fans.

4 R. G. G. Price: *History of Punch*, p. 239.
5 A. P. Herbert: *Punch*, 26 August 1970.
6 A. P. Herbert: *What a Word!* (1935).
7 *Time and Tide:* 6 December 1952.
8 F. A. Lindemann, FRS, sometime Professor of Experimental Philosophy. Oxford University; personal assistant to the Prime Minister, 1940; later, Lord Cherwell.
9 Roy Harrod: '*The Prof.*' (1959).

14

A True Sense of Awe

His politics were not so much a creed as a cast of mind. He entered the House of Commons as an Independent supporter of the National Government. He fully realized the worth of the Party system. He could never have merged himself in it, not only because he was 'cursed with a judicial temper'. He had to be free to come and go at his own bidding. Not for him the vassalage of Party, the discipline of the Whips, any more than he could have accepted the ties of editorship or the daily servitude of a leader-writer. He was the freelance *par excellence*.

He took his place in the long line of men of letters who were members of Parliament from Chaucer onward: Addison, Steele, Walpole, Burke, Gibbon, Sheridan, through to Bulwer Lytton, Macaulay, Praed, Disraeli, Mill; and, in our era, Morley, Birrell, Labouchere, Belloc, Churchill, Buchan, Mason, Nicolson. A contemporary reference to a Victorian MP with a literary reputation, Richard Monckton Milnes, afterwards Lord Houghton, exactly fitted APH. 'His good humour is infinite . . . one of the most valuable companions in London . . . a little careless and slovenly in his dress.' Milnes also wrote verse, an accomplishment that his father feared would impede his progress as a politician.

It was not of that long and honourable pedigree that APH was most aware when, for the first time, 'with pride and astonishment', and an accelerated pulse-beat, he strode through the members' entrance on 26 November 1935. 'I had a true sense of awe as I walked past the huge figures of Burke, Pitt and the others, thinking that they were once mere new members too.' His strongest first physical impression was of 'the churchy smell of the place'.

Against the sagest advice, he made his maiden speech on the second day of the opening session of the new Parliament. Afterwards, he wondered at his temerity in defying the counsel of Sir Austen

Chamberlain who had urged him: 'Wait. Sit in the House. Absorb the atmosphere. And study procedure.' Girded presumably by the acclamation that marked his success at the poll, goaded certainly by what seemed to him the Government's cavalier attitude to private members' rights, he faced a packed House 'in a mist of apprehension', remembering what Macaulay had said, that 'there is no more terrible audience in the world'. APH was terrified – his word.

The point at issue was clouded by procedural subtleties. He was provoked to challenge the Prime Minister, Baldwin, on his motion that Government business should have precedence over all private members' bills, *pro tem*. It was not unreasonable in the circumstances of the hour, as APH later agreed. But his 'little volcano' was smouldering within him or, as he put it, 'the devil was in me and nothing would make me give up'. The might of the parliamentary machine was being brought to bear on the independent members, and it had to be resisted.

With the backing of the infinitesimal Independent Labour Party, led by James Maxton, APH denounced the motion. 'Mr Speaker, Sir, I rise with more than the usual trepidation on a point of principle, on a point of conscience. I am the Junior Burgess of the University of Oxford, the elected mouthpiece of innumerable clergymen, the trumpet – or second trumpet – of twenty thousand bachelors of art, and I have been sent here by my constituents to stop, or try to stop, the kind of thinking behind this motion.'[1]

He remembered long afterwards 'the dazzle of nameless faces on the terraced benches', as he came to the climax of his speech. 'I have in my hand a Bill which I am ready to introduce next Friday, or on the Friday after, or on all the Fridays, until it is passed into law; and I swear that it shall be passed before this Parliament is over', at which point laughter, the laughter of incredulity, rolled over him. Adopting Disraeli's stance as a novice in the House, he retorted: 'Honourable members may laugh. I must remind them that all the serious politicians laughed when I disclosed my obscene designs on my almost virgin university. Therefore I would ask honourable members to consider again before they laugh at my intentions.' Rashly, he started his parliamentary life by combining with a radical minority in forcing a division against the Government. He went into the 'No' lobby with the Independent Labour Party. The 'Ayes had it' by 232 to 5.

Of the leading parliamentarians present, only Churchill came
forward with compliments. What he said in the Smoking Room
about APH's 'brazen hussy of a maiden speech' has been quoted
often enough. Ignoring mutterings of disgust at APH's association
with Maxton and his men, Churchill also spoke words of generous
private encouragement. APH said that Sir Austen Chamberlain,
whose cautionary advice he had thrown to the wind, was 'pained, I
know'. That monocled veteran of the House was critical only of
APH's taste in shirts. The wise ones of Printing House Square,
acknowledging in a leading article that 'he has lost no time in
showing that he is an original Member', reproved him for his
impetuosity, conceding that it was for want of 'a little more
experience'.

MPs' pay then was £400 a year. The problem for APH was to
reconcile his writing life with the demands of Parliament. He did
not regard his arrival in the House of Commons as the beginning
of a new public career; far from it. Career politics did not command
much respect from him, and professional politicians were never
among his favourite men. He had no conceit about making a name
for himself in politics. He had gone into the House 'with a limited
armoury for a limited target',[2] namely, to promote his revised
version of the Marriage Bill, introduced there twenty years before by
Holford Knight, KC, the Labour member for South Nottingham.
That Bill had been counted out year after year by its Catholic and
lay adversaries, prominent among them Lady Astor. The Preamble
to APH's Bill defined its purposes to be 'the support of marriage,
the protection of children, the removal of hardship, the reduction
of illicit unions and unseemingly litigation, the relief of conscience
among the clergy, and the restoration of respect for the law'.

If, in steering his Bill through the maze of parliamentary
procedures, he could demonstrate the worth of the university
franchise, so much the better. That justification was always to the
fore in his mind during what he came to look back on as his
'Parliamentary episode'.

He discovered that 'public life spreads like a rash over a man',
trebling his correspondence, entangling him with committees,
diversifying his energies, reducing his earning power. The Smoking
Room was irresistible in its attraction, more so than any West End
club. The perennial topic there was 'the business of governing men',
the talk often of a kind 'to shake the world, and send Fleet Street

into a fever'. Among the supplementary benefits, the Kitchen Committee provided a five-course table d'hôte dinner for 6s. 6d.

Beyond the walls, his new public standing was variously recognized. He was cartooned by Strube in *The Daily Express* as 'Mr Punch'.
He was included in a 'gallery of fame' series of cigarette-cards issued
by the Bristol tobacco firm of W.D. & H.O. Wills. The Chief Justice
of Tasmania complimented him in writing on having 'the ear of
the public all over the English speaking world'. He was invited to
join the cerebral circus of BBC radio known as the 'Brains Trust'.
Donald McCullough, the Question Master, recalls that during one
of the sessions APH kept smiling to himself, diverted by what turned
out to be a mildly macabre private joke. He had come to the studio
from the Beefsteak Club, where he had overheard two dukes in
conversation. One asked the other: 'Is George any better?' The
other answered: 'No, his leg has gone black.' He noted, in 1936,
year of national mourning and of a fateful accession, that 'Mr
Churchill is still in the wilderness'; that it was being whispered in
Whitehall that 'Lloyd George is not the man he was'; that 'Neville
Chamberlain is not an attractive speaker'; that 'Stanley Baldwin is
master of the House, with his rugged, homely style'; that Sir John
Simon, as a speaker, was 'a beacon of lucidity'. He liked listening to
the speeches of the Scottish members: 'Geordie' Buchanan, 'with
his tales of mean streets'; James Maxton 'of the burning eyes and
compelling voice'.

'Pregnant with Bills' (his phrase), he gained useful experience
that year in drafting three, and submitting them to the Public Bill
Office, after which they could be introduced and printed, though
not necessarily debated. He tried his apprentice hand with a Bill to
reform the betting laws and abolish the football pools; a Public
Refreshment Bill to bring in the equivalent of French laws relating
to the sale of liquor; and a Marriage Bill that would 'strengthen the
institution of marriage and increase respect for the law by amending
it in relation to marriage and increase respect for the law by amending it in relation to marriage and divorce'. As part of the procedures,
he sought to revive the Preamble, a venerable practice that had
been replaced, he thought mistakenly, by an Explanatory Memorandum. 'In your Memorandum you may state in cold terms the
machinery of your Bill, but you must not be controversial. In the
Preamble you can let fly with facts and arguments.'[3] A Draft Bill
of his, not submitted to the parliamentary experts, was headed

'Spring (Arrangements) Bill', and had for Preamble: 'Whereas on every lawn and bed the plucky crocus lifts its head, and to and fro the sweet song-birds go, the names of which we do not know . . .' Proceeding through a succession of ingeniously rhymed clauses and sub-clauses, it was one of the superfluous exercises that littered his professional career, demonstrating a too-facile gift and an imperious and finally self-destructive will to finish what had been begun. When he was reproached for frittering away time and talents, he would retort with his friend E.V.'s dictum: 'Nothing is wasted.'

In May 1936 a Civil List Bill, making monetary provision for the new monarch and the royal family, was laid before the House. It also provided for the Civil List pensions traditionally paid to persons meriting the Sovereign's favour, and the public's gratitude, for services to science, literature and the arts. Catching the Speaker's eye, APH proposed that the fixed annual sum of £1,200 allotted for the purpose and disbursed in grants of £100 a year, should be doubled. The figure of £1,200 dated from the first year of Victoria's reign; even then, the old Duke of Wellington thought it 'niggardly'. APH proposed that the amount should be raised to £4,000, at which Neville Chamberlain, Chancellor of the Exchequer, was heard muttering testily: 'Say it in *Punch*! Say it in *Punch*!' Obviously, the politician shared the common delusion that a professional humorist is necessarily a playboy in public affairs. Support for the amendment came from both sides of the House, but it did not prevail. Twelve months later, 'without a word said, in private or in debate', Chamberlain increased the sum to £2,500. 'The stony ground', APH observed, 'has received the seed', which he, not unreasonably, presumed to have sown.

His instinct for reform received an odd impetus during that apprenticeship period of his in Parliament. He counted 'nineteen redundant full-stops on one page of the Order Paper'. He thought it 'a wasteful practice', and caused representations to be made on the subject to the King's Printer, who was responsible for the printing of 'many thousands of other Government publications'. That functionary listened to the argument, and 'finally yielded', leaving APH to compute what was consequently saved in 'printers' ink and effort' and, ultimately, in taxpayers' money .

In his election address he had asserted that 'whatever else is done or not done, I should abolish the cruel system of the decree *nisi*'. He also desired that his Marriage Bill should have the effect of reducing the number of judicial separations, which had been condemned by a royal commission in 1909 as a source of social harm.

On 24 April 1936 the London *Evening Standard* reported that 'Mr A. P. Herbert's Marriage Bill is third on the list of Private Members' Bills to come before the House today. It is extremely improbable that it will ever be reached.' In that atmosphere of discouragement and uncertainty he asked himself why he had deserted 'the quiet life of a man of letters to play Sisyphus in an ungrateful world', in which, for example, too many people were assuming him to be a fount of free advice on their marital problems. Elizabeth Allan (Mrs Bill O'Bryen) – then well known to stage and film audiences, later even better known to television viewers – telephoned to ask him, as a friend, to advise her on 'a certain matter'. He proposed lunch at the Café Royal. Meeting her there, he greeted her with commiseration in his tone. 'So sorry, Liz – what's gone wrong?' He had fancied that she too wished to discuss a domestic difficulty, whereas the advice she wanted had nothing to do with her private life.

He was persuaded that many MPs favoured his Bill. Mustering them into an effective body of support was another matter. 'I was frightened by the number of members who on the whole were with me but had a too dangerous proportion of Catholics in their constituencies. There are, I believe, only 2,000,000 Catholics in the kingdom, but they seemed to dominate it.'[4] He had expected bitter opposition from that quarter: 'in fact, we were much more harassed by the Anglicans'.

Some of the members he approached had their own matrimonial problems and were unwilling to identify themselves publicly with his campaign. One member who had gained a place in the ballot and had no Bill ready reacted oddly when APH sought his interest. 'Divorce? Good God, no! I was in the Royal Navy', and rushed away, leaving APH to ponder the logic of that excuse.

'Expect as much trouble from your friends as from your enemies': that, he said, was one of the lessons he learned from his political experience at that time. For instance, 'people almost cut me at the Café Royal', apparently resenting his proposed suspension of the right to divorce for three years after marriage. He did not even escape censure on the river. At the end of 'a wearing week' in the

House, much of it taken up with committees, he returned to Hammersmith in his *Water Gipsy*, enjoying a calm evening and the thought of 'no more divorce until Tuesday'. Nearing Hammersmith Bridge, he drew abreast of a tug with a string of Cory coal-lighters in tow. When he waved to a grimy figure emerging from the engine-room, a voice bellowed back at him: 'You're doin' no good, guv'nor. My mate 'ere wants to get rid of 'is old woman *now*!'

On 18 June 1936 some lines by APH, printed in *The Times* the previous day and prompted by Mussolini's defiance of the League of Nations, were read to a crowded House of Commons by Arthur Greenwood, Socialist member for Wakefield, sometime vice-chairman of the Parliamentary Labour Party. He was speaking in a debate on sanctions against Italy. 'I would like to do the honourable member for Oxford University the honour of having his poem reprinted in the Official Report' (Hansard). It was duly transmitted to posterity in that place.

> Let us be realist and face the facts,
> For peace, at any price, is more than pacts.
> The house is broke; the burglar keeps the cruet;
> Why not be wise, and say he didn't do it?
> It may be awkward to condone a crime,
> But not if it was lawful all the time.
> If humble pie be what the nations wish,
> Let them have plenty, let them lick the dish,
> Singing, 'The meek Italian left his home
> To drive the Abyssinian brute from Rome',
> Maybe that mustard[5] on the mountain tops
> Was loosed by Englishmen, disguised as Wops?

Harold Nicolson, National Labour member for West Leicester, dismissed Greenwood's speech in his diary as 'a second-rate platform performance, which included a comic poem. It is so bad that one feels actually uncomfortable at the thought that so many foreign diplomats should be in the Gallery' (18 June 1936).

Among those who sent in callers' green cards to APH at the House that summer was his election helper, Frank Pakenham, who had a tale to tell of Blackshirt roughness at a recent meeting in Oxford. 'He had been thrown down and trampled on.' APH undertook to raise the matter in Parliament. When the opportunity came he attacked Fascist techniques of deliberate public disorder, and wound up with the peroration: 'As between Blackshirts and Redshirts I cry: A plague on both your blouses!'

A. P. Herbert to Philip Agnew:[6]

> 12 Hammersmith Terrace,
> W.6.
> 12th October, 1936.

... I am having a bit of a struggle at the moment, since I became a politician, and any extra guinea is important.

NOTES ON CHAPTER 14

1 Private Members' Time is informatively discussed in *Honourable Members*, by Peter G. Richards (1959).
2 A. P. Herbert: *Independent Member* (1950).
3 A. P. Herbert: *Life and Times*.
4 A. P. Herbert: *The Ayes Have It*.
5 Mustard gas.
6 Managing Director of Bradbury, Agnew & Co., then proprietors of *Punch*.

15

The Ayes Have It

He wrote the libretto for an adaptation of Franz Lehar's *Paganini*, produced by Cochran at the Lyceum Theatre, London, in 1936. Richard Tauber, Europe's most popular tenor, was cast, some thought absurdly, in the leading role. At rehearsals, when APH suggested improvements, Tauber would rush to telephone Lehar, returning invariably with 'the master's' peremptory no. The piece came off after a short run, its last weeks financed by Tauber himself. One of its songs, for which APH wrote the words, still survives the failure – *Girls were Made to Love and Kiss*.

Before the final curtain came down, he was commissioned by Cochran to do 'the very big job of writing the entire book' of a lavish new revue designed to be part of the festivities planned for the coronation of Edward VIII. He began work in the summer of 1936, and was soon in the throes of a struggle to keep his bargain with Cochran and attend to his parliamentary obligations. His Marriage Bill was the centre of a rising tide of controversy, involving Roman Catholics, Anglo-Catholics, the Church Union, the Mothers' Union and other bodies.

With the opening of the autumn session at Westminster, he feared that he might win a place in the Unofficial Members' ballot at a time when the Cochran revue was nearing the rehearsal stages. He was apprehensive about a repetition of the nervous prostration likely to befall him from overwork. 'I should go off my head.'

Because of late sittings in the House he slept often at that time in *Water Gipsy*, anchored in Savoy Reach hard by Cleopatra's Needle. 'No one could ring me up about amendments to the Marriage Bill or Binnie Hale's songs.' He enjoyed his lonely state, watching the Embankment trams 'swimming through the lighted trees', hearing Big Ben chime the hours away, and the low-key thunder of the last trains running in and out of Charing Cross station. '*Water Gipsy* lay aloof from the world. I was lord of London', and a critical remembrancer of 'our vulgar ancestors who in 1864 dared to erect in the forefront of Wordsworth's view – "a sight so touching in its majesty" – that obscene iron-pillared, factory fashioned Charing Cross Bridge. "Earth hath not anything to show more ugly" '.

He went ashore on one of those evenings to dine with Barrie, 'just the two of us', in his handsome flat in Adelphi Terrace, overlooking the river between Charing Cross and Waterloo. During dinner host and guest were in amiable dispute over the meaning of 'some word or other'. The butler, serving the fish course, 'murmured over my shoulder the Greek origin of the word and the correct pronunciation'. In recollection, APH made the obvious comment: 'The Admirable Crichton, I suppose.' (Barrie's play of that name was written thirty-five years before.) Now the great little man's reputation was in decline. APH was 'sad to feel sorry for him', whose unhappiness was writ large on his face. As a frequenter of Adelphi Terrace in those years, I saw him often and never without being struck by his look of woe. It deepened after the resounding failure of his last play, *The Boy David*, in 1937.

APH put his name down again for the Unofficial Members' ballot, and had no better luck than before. He said that he had never drawn a winning ticket in a sweepstake; fortune rarely smiled on him in lotteries or games of chance; hence his epigraphic lines:

> Here, a dead horse, I lie in some dismay:
> I should have won, at 8–1, they say.
> My fate was sealed before I made the leap:
> One A. P. Herbert drew me in a sweep.

He was 'sorely tempted' to let the business of the Bill go by default *pro tem*. But there was a demon in him against which his inclinations rarely prevailed. With a list in his pocket of members who had drawn places in the ballot, he went to the House of Commons telephone room to try to contact them, one by one. Some were out of town or otherwise unavailable. Others were not willing to forgo their own Bills. Several feared unfavourable constituency reactions. An hour's effort yielded no promise of aid and all too little encouragement.

A last hope remained, the new Conservative member for Evesham,

Rupert de la Bere. After a series of frustrating calls, APH was able
to speak to him and put his case, that grounds for divorce should
no longer be restricted to adultery but extended to desertion, cruelty
and insanity. The new member listened carefully, mentioned that
he had been happily married for eighteen years and knew little
about the law, less about 'the tricky business of divorce'; and agreed
to sponsor the Bill. APH did not ascribe that favourable turn of
events to luck. On the contrary, he saw in it a cause for respectful
acknowledgment of 'the powers that control us all'.[1]

Not that the passage of his Bill through Parliament was yet clear
of obstructions. The crisis at Court was bringing divorce into even
greater disrepute as a subject for public sympathy. APH had
moments of 'agonising anxiety' about the possible effect on the Bill's
prospects of the new king's intimacy with the American divorcee,
Mrs Simpson. He was also riven with worry over the new revue,
which Cochran intended to produce in Manchester before Christmas under the title of *Home and Beauty*. He had scenes to devise,
lyrics to write, dialogue to invent. Superimposed on those requirements was a spate of consultations and correspondence about the
Bill. Messages awaited him at the House of Commons: 'Please ring
Mr Cochran.' 'Please ring Miss Binnie Hale', the leading lady.
'Please ring Mr Nelson Keyes', the principal comedian. 'Please ring
Mr Collins', the stage director. He had agreed to collaborate with
James Bridie in writing a new 'play with music', for which Bridie
was sending him drafts and suggestions.[2] An attack of quinsy did
not insulate him from the clamour. Over all hung the daunting
possibility that the Bill might be given a Second Reading, leading
to the critical stage of a Standing Committee, a rock against which
many legislative crusades come to grief.

'Be deadly serious,' Claud Mullins, the metropolitan magistrate,
urged him in a letter of 13 November 1936. On Friday 20 November
he travelled as usual by Underground to Westminster. It was the
day appointed for the Second Reading. 'Anxiety and fear' assailed
him as he approached the House. He was haunted by the spectre
of Lord Hugh Cecil appearing in unbending opposition to the Bill.
Lord Hugh had not spoken in the House for some time. He might
break his silence with ominous effect. APH admitted to 'joining in
Prayers' that day. Lord Hugh did not attend the Second Reading,
though he was in London, having ascertained which fact APH
concluded that chivalry had overcome principle. 'I like to think

that he did not wish to show Oxford divided. Whether or not that was the explanation, he has my respect and gratitude.'³

At the Second Reading APH put the case for his Bill, clause by clause, with a professional advocate's blend of logic and rhetoric, bringing his speech to a telling close by reading a letter picked out from the shoal: 'Please God your Bill will be passed unmutilated. I am a Roman Catholic, a happy wife and mother, but there are others in this world of ours who most grievously are not. With that anxiety they must be waiting the result of this truly great reform. We pray for you.'

A thinly attended House divided. For APH it was 'a thrilling thing' to hear the result from the lobbies: 'Ayes to the Right – seventy-eight. Noes to the Left – twelve.' On 27 November 1935, to the amusement of the House, he had made his 'impious vow' that his Bill would become law. Now it was 27 November 1936, and the parliamentary air was loud with cheers.

The time for heartfelt congratulation was not yet. The Standing Committee had to be faced, and a Third Reading in the House of Lords. He experienced what he called 'black days' in the following months; once 'a shocking disappointment'. The tensions were many and often hard to bear. The Archbishop of Canterbury and an array of Law Lords entered the battle. The *Daily Telegraph* reported 'strenuous fighting' in the House of Lords over the Bill, and noted the presence in the members' gallery of 'its anxious author, watching its fortunes' (16 July 1937). The previous day he had telephoned an indignant letter to the editor of that newspaper, answering hostile comments by a bishop. The editor's secretary, who took down the letter, would have been surprised to know that the caller was speaking to her in a state of nudity from the Turkish Baths in Northumberland Avenue.

At a late stage, law officers decided that the Bill should be renamed the Matrimonial Causes' Bill on the ground that its emphasis was on divorce rather than marriage. APH did not take kindly to the change. 'As the Marriage Bill, it had for so long been the partner of my dreams.' It was given a Third Reading in the House of Lords on 19 July. In the division, the Ayes had it by 79 votes to 28.

With a Lords' Amendment, the Bill was returned to the Commons on 23 July. APH handled his part of the proceedings with an air of authority that was noted by the Lobby correspondents. He expressed before the House his indebtedness to many helpers, first among them

Rupert de la Bere, whose generous concession had made everything possible. In private notes later, APH wrote that 'the Matrimonial Causes Act could not have been, had not Baldwin given us a whole Government day to finish the business'. In little more than an hour the Commons passed the Lords' amendment 'to a salvo of parliamentary cheers' (*The Economist*).

All that remained was the old-world formality of the Royal Assent. In the *Sunday Times*, 'A Student of Politics'[4] congratulated APH 'most heartily on a measure which will give him an abiding place in the history of our statute law. Few private members have ever succeeded in legislation so important and from its nature so contentious.' The poet of *Half-Hours at Hellas* and *The Bomber Gipsy* (rather than of *Ballads for Broadbrows*, etc., etc.), had become one of the acknowledged legislators. Shaw, in a newspaper interview, spoke of him as 'a hero'.[5] He had been instrumental in carrying through a reform that great lawyers, among them Birkenhead and Buckmaster, had failed to achieve.

'The strife is o'er, the battle done', the literary solicitor, E. S. P. Haynes, wrote to him. 'I cordially congratulate you. Without detracting from your intelligence, I think your triumph is largely due to personal charm, which so often leads to ruin!'

'Mr Herbert's Triumph' was the gist of newspaper reports all over the country; even farther afield: 'Wit's Triumph', a headline in the *Baltimore Sun* (24 July 1937). For the leader writers it was the topic of the day, their comments measurable by the yard. At 12 Hammersmith Terrace the telephone rang through all the hours with compliments from callers known and unknown. Telegrams were delivered by the bundle. A postal avalanche swamped APH's desk. 'Don't rest', J. B. Priestley urged him in a letter (25 July), and suggested that he should next give his energies to the abolition of the Entertainment Tax. APH had spoken out against it in the House ten days before.

As the congratulatory flood swirled about him, he composed a postscript to his labours of the past twelve months. 'I hope and pray that the aims of all those who have worked upon this measure with much anxiety and care may be fulfilled; that it will add not only to the sum of human happiness but to the strength of human institutions, the law, the Church, marriage itself. For myself, I have no illusions. Where there are bouquets today, there will be brickbats tomorrow.'

A hefty one was tossed at him by *G. K.'s Weekly*, not long out of mourning for its founder (G. K. Chesterton). 'No marriage is a success by its own momentum. It must be a miracle of strenuous and unceasing patience, forbearance, generosity, courage, faith, hope and sacrifice. The so-called "triumph" of Mr A. P. Herbert is therefore merely the triumph of the vandal who destroys a priceless work of art' (12 August 1937). In the previous week, he had been photographed with his wife in their riverside garden, 'looking satisfied with life' (the *Sketch*). That happy state of being was by no means chiefly derived from his success in Parliament.

A month later I wrote in my journal: 'Wholly enjoyable outing in APH's *Water Gipsy* with him and Gwen, Gwilym and Edna Lloyd George, and Angela Baddeley. One of those days that one is sure will be all right from the beginning. Perhaps the prescience of the senses is not trusted enough. Passing the Houses of Parliament on the way down river we guests genuflected elaborately, having on board one who recently made social history there.

'As usual, *Water Gipsy* was a sightseeing object for the river steamer guides, whose megaphoned comments drew attention to us with little response, I noticed, from the passengers. We have done better on other trips. We landed for drinks at the Prospect of Whitby. 'APH has adopted the House of Commons custom of murmuring " 'ear-'ear, 'ear-'ear" in conversation as a sign of approval.'

I remember our turning homeward that evening in a splendid afterglow. At Waterloo Bridge I was ordered to take over as helmsman while APH went down to join the others. 'London divides and makes way', I wrote. 'Its *parvenu* County Hall, where not long ago the Socialists voted against the appearance of an anti-aircraft gun in a recruiting drive, stands respectfully back as we pass, while Big Ben, looking a little too bland for the times, proclaims eleven o'clock and all's well, which I'm sorry not to believe'.

I recall the laughter coming up from below. APH and Angela Baddeley were rehearsing or performing a revue sketch of his in which a too inquisitive employer was engaging a domestic help called Oivy. It sounded like a private histrionic triumph.

At the end of the day, in his Hammersmith study, we discussed what we would do if war came. I mentioned that my name was on the Central Register. 'Join my crew,' he suggested. I answered that I would think about it, well knowing that the landsman would be too strong in me.

His recent parliamentary achievement had not moved him to lyrical commemoration. A chance for him to display his gift for *vers d'occasion* came shortly afterwards with the fiftieth anniversary of the first stage appearance of Julia Neilson, famous in her leading-lady years for her Rosalind in *As You Like It*.

> In '88, one golden day,
>   A lovely maiden took the stage:
> And what did Mr Gladstone say?
>   'I hear Cynisca is the rage'.
>
> Another century began,
>   Another war, another reign,
> Sir Henry Campbell-Bannerman
>   Said 'I must see that girl again'.
>
> The noise of cannon crossed the sea,
>   And 'Votes for Women' sounded shrill:
> But Mr Asquith said to me
>   'Is *As You Like It* running still?'
>
> For fifty years, serene and sure,
>   The gracious lady kept her head.
> The plays, as usual, were 'poor' –
>   The theatre, naturally, was 'dead'.
>
> But, gaily unafraid of odds,
>   One 'house', at least, preserved a style,
> Where there was joy among the 'gods',
>   And even critics forced a smile.
>
> O mistress of a hundred arts,
>   You never learned to be unkind;
> The conqueror of a thousand hearts,
>   You did not wound a single mind.
>
> Life runs, for some, beyond renown;
>   E'en angels do not get their due:
> But though the curtain may be down,
>   *We* linger still and call for *You*.

Adjusting himself to his new public prominence brought un-expected embarrassments. During the passage of his Bill through Parliament, and more particularly at the climax, the press photographers made his face familiar to every class of newspaper reader. Late one evening, he and I walked up to Piccadilly after supper at the Savoy Grill. A young woman stepped from a Haymarket shop doorway on her business of the night. We both had inhibitions about prostitution and our brusqueness offended her. Staring searchingly at APH she exclaimed: 'I've seen you somewhere – in the papers; yes, I've seen your picture in the papers!' His reaction was surprising. He darted away like a frightened hare, loping down past His Majesty's Theatre and on into the shadows of Pall Mall.

Bruce Lockhart fell in with him at Heppell's branch in Piccadilly one afternoon, 'sipping a pick-me-up (American cocktail bitter)'. They had 'a ten minutes' conversation on literature'. APH told Lockhart that his Divorce Bill had taken up 'a tremendous lot of his time with the result that he had done little writing and had earned no money' (27 October 1937).[6]

NOTES ON CHAPTER 15

1 A. P. Herbert: *The Ayes Have It.*
2 Soon it was agreed between them that the idea should be 'decently buried'.
3 A. P. Herbert: *The Ayes Have It.*
4 Herbert Sidebotham, who also wrote as 'Scrutator'.
5 *Sunday Referee*, 22 November 1936.
6 Sir Robert Bruce Lockhart wrote *Memoirs of a British Agent* (1932), and other books. He was for a time on the staff of the Beaverbrook newspapers, and served in the Political Warfare Branch of the Foreign Office in the Second World War.

16

A Row with the Buchmanites

We had arranged, he and I, to go down to Chatham to lunch with an old friend of mine who was Commander-in-Chief, The Nore, Admiral Evans – 'Evans of the Broke'. Just before the agreed day, APH telephoned me. 'Do you know what the birthrate at Roxby-cum-Risby is? Twenty-six per thousand, and no bastards. Do you know the bastardy rate for Chelsea? Nine point three per thousand. Brighton, eight point one. Maidenhead, eight point four. Cromer has eleven bastards per thousand of population'. Pause. 'Let's go to Cromer!' I reminded him of our Chatham engagement. 'Sorry, can't be there. I've a speech to make in the House. Second Reading of Kingsley Wood's Population (Statistics) Bill. It's the devil, getting the statistics right.'

The Bill was a Government measure to procure new and accurate information about the declining birthrate of the United Kingdom. It required registrars to put forty-eight questions to mothers of new-born babies and to anyone registering a death. APH considered it a bureaucratic outrage. His speech attacking it (29 November 1937) concluded with 'a memorandum in verse', which *The Times* next morning said 'convulsed his audience'.

In 1937 was rumour going round
That income Tax was soon to be six shillings in the pound
The cost of education every season seemed to swell;
And to everyone's astonishment the population fell.

They pulled down all the houses where the children used to
  crowd,
And built expensive blocks of flats where children weren't
  allowed.
So if father got a job there wasn't anywhere to dwell;
And everybody wondered why the population fell.

Five hundred brand new motorcars each morning rode the
    roads,
And flashed about like comets or sat motionless as toads;
Which ever course they took they made the public highway
    Hell:
And everybody wondered why the population fell.

The laws were very comical; to bet was voted lax,
But your betting was the only thing that nobody would tax;
You couldn't have a wine unless you'd sandwiches as well:
And everybody wondered why the population fell.

Great Science nobly laboured to increase the people's joys,
But every new invention seemed to add another noise;
One was always on the telephone or answering the bell:
And everybody wondered why the population fell.

The taverns were controlled by men who didn't want to drink,
The newspapers were run by men who hadn't time to think;
The cinema was managed by a man who couldn't spell:
And everybody wondered why the population fell.

Abroad, to show that everyone was passionate for peace,
All children under seven joined the army or police;
The babies studied musketry while mother filled a shell:
And everybody wondered why the population fell.

The world, in short, which never was extravagantly sane,
Developed all the signs of inflammation of the brain;
The past was not encouraging, the future none could tell:
And everybody wondered why the population fell.

'Mr A. P. Herbert's whimsical caricaturing of the Bill dissolved even
the ranks of Tuscany in laughter' (*The Times*, 30 November 1937).
To that newspaper's charge of 'questionable levity', APH made a
spirited reply in a letter to the editor signed 'Your servant but,
regretfully, not so obedient as usual'. The next day's headlines
were like a citation for inclusion in *The Dictionary of National
Biography*: e.g. the *Daily Mail*: 'Hansard Best Seller: Unprecedented
Demand'.

   'Wit is the last thing to make an impression in the House; the
House will laugh at anything except wit.' Whether or not the dictum
of Monckton Milnes, MP in the 1840s, was discounted in the inter-

vening years, the wit of APH, directed against the Population (Statistics) Bill in 1937, did unquestionably make an impression on the House, to the obvious discomfiture of the ill-briefed Minister in charge of the Bill, Sir Kingsley Wood. *The Times* report shows that the speech was frequently interrupted by laughter, and that the 'memorandum in verse' was received with 'loud laughter' and cheers, making it, said *Punch*, 'an astonishing occasion'. APH 'tore the Bill to pieces'.[1] What he and others did was to bring in a number of amendments that were adopted by the Government before the Bill reached the statute book in 1938. He could not resist a final dart at Kingsley Wood. 'I have had a letter from a resident of Roxby-cum-Risby who says that your statistics are wrong, because he knows four or five bastards there' (10 December 1937).

After set-backs, and the difficulty of finding an available West End theatre, Cochran's new revue, *Home and Beauty*, opened in Manchester on Christmas Eve 1937. The curtain came down to waves of applause and numerous calls. Both Cochran and APH were wary of first-night enthusiasm. Due largely to the vocal enchantment of the Hungarian soprano, Gitta Alpar, they may have been privately persuaded that all would be well. On Christmas night the singer was taken ill at the Midland Hotel. The Boxing Day matinee, fully booked, was cancelled. In the evening, with a doctor and nurse standing by, she resumed her role; a valiant but luckless performance. Transferred to the Adelphi Theatre, London, *Home and Beauty* bore with it an aura of misfortune. Bookings were heavily down as a consequence of the Abdication crisis. On the last night, five other London productions were withdrawn. Total success in the theatre still eluded APH.

One of his *Home and Beauty* lyrics, 'A Nice Cup of Tea', was retrieved from the ruins to yield 'an acceptable windfall' of royalties *via* The Performing Right Society. It was set to music by an American composer, Hank Sullivan, and given wings by Binnie Hale. Its flight into popularity is still maintained by BBC radio and over public-address systems in factories and works' canteens, at flower shows and fêtes. When 'our man in Montevideo', Sir Geoffrey Jackson, was abducted in 1971 by the Tupamaro guerillas of Uruguay, he was 'so elated' at being given his first cup of tea that he 'broke quite spontaneously' into a Spanish rendering of APH's song, 'to the vast amusement' of his guards. (Letter, 4 June 1973.)

A preposterous shadow fell across APH's desk as he worked on a commission to 'English the lyrics' of Johann Strauss's *Die Fledermaus* for a film in 1937. His version of the celebrated Champagne Song expressed his dislike of that beverage:

> This wine is full of gases,
>   Which are to me offensive,
> It pleases all you asses
>   Because it is expensive.

The producer of the film, 'a huge and commanding German', named Fellner, visited APH at Hammersmith to hear the new lyrics. APH sang the Champagne Song to his own piano accompaniment. The German groaned as if in pain. 'Out! Cut!' he ordered. 'We must not speak so of champagne!' APH had forgotten what everybody knew, that Ribbentrop, the Nazi Foreign Minister, was a former champagne salesman.

As an Independent in Parliament, APH was vexed by 'the horrid business' of making up his mind; unlike the Party men, he had no one to make it up for him. He was 'not ashamed to confess', he wrote, that on occasions he was 'firmly inclined to the Right'. He insisted that when the Parties raged furiously together, as at the time of Munich, Independent members had a duty to consult their consciences with care, showing the Party leaders 'which way the pure air of free opinion blows'.

He knew the 'agonies of mind suffered not by feeble Independents alone' in 1938, when Europe was nearing the brink. He had never liked Neville Chamberlain, but he would not deny respect for him 'as a Christian gentleman who was seeking peace'. A self-accused 'wobbler', he was 'very unhappy' during those September days when it seemed that catastrophe must come. The revival of German power stirred memories of the horrors that haunted his dreams twenty years before. 'The whole thing made me sick.' On 3 November 1938 he enrolled in the newly formed River Emergency Service of the Port of London Authority. A month later he was formally notified that 'the duty allotted to you in the event of mobilisation is Master of *Water Gipsy*'.

Lord Hugh Cecil having retired from Parliament to become Provost of Eton College, Sir Arthur (later Lord) Salter, whose family name was well known on the upper reaches of the Thames, took his place as an Oxford University member. 'Very proudly', in consequence, APH assumed the mantle of Senior Burgess. A remark made by a bishop was passed on to him: 'Oxford University is now represented in Parliament by a boat builder and a buffoon.' Coming from that quarter, he thought it 'not very Christian' but amusing enough to be quoted in a speech to the House.

He forced himself to speak there on a number of occasions during the following year. 'I badgered poor Mr Burgin', the Minister of Transport, about the Thames and the canals, demanding that they be integrated in a national waterways plan in readiness for what might be dire emergency. He continued to be baffled by the Londoners' sublime indifference to their great river.

There had lately come into prominence an owl-faced Lutheran pastor from Pennsylvania named Frank Buchman, bearing the banner of 'moral rearmament'. He was the founder of a religious movement that began as A First Century Christian Fellowship and became in or about 1929 The Oxford Group. The assumption of affinity with Oxford University affronted many, none more than its Senior Burgess. He had sent a warmly approving telegram to Margaret Rawlings, then playing in *Black Limelight* at the Duke of York's Theatre, after her speech at a Foyle's Literary Luncheon, which some of Buchman's men made the occasion of a publicity campaign. It was deflated by Miss Rawlings's reference to their 'psychic exhibitionism'. To his congratulations, APH added the comment: 'If anyone writes a history of the "Oxford Group" it will have a pre- and post- Rawlings period.'

His indignation flared when in 1939 the Buchmanites sought official sanction for their identification with Oxford. The governing authority of the university, the Hebdomadal Council, issued a public protest. Buchman's young men dashed into the fray with rugger-playing zest to organize their defences against APH's onslaughts in *The Times* and in Parliament. 'Since when', he asked them, 'was there "moral armament"?'

He checked Buchman's career as recorded in various reference books, including *Who's Who*. There were curious discrepancies. A letter from S. K. Ratcliffe, formerly of the *Daily News* and the *New Republic* (USA), referred to 'the many dishonesties of the Buchmanites', citing in particular 'their flagrant claims that the movement began in Oxford in 1921'.

At a debate at the Oxford Union 'a resolution was unanimously passed' supporting the Senior Burgess's endeavours to prevent the name 'Oxford Group' being appropriated by the Buchman movement. The letter conveying the sense of the meeting to APH was signed 'E. R. G. Heath, President of the Union' (23 February 1939). The Registrar of the University wrote to him that 'Council felt the greatest sympathy with the efforts you are making in this matter and respect for your energy' (1 May 1939). The Warden of New College, H. A. L. Fisher, insisted in a letter to APH that 'the title assumed by these Buchman people is clearly misleading, because in fact it misleads'. He had heard of 'a gentleman in Toronto' who threatened Buchman with an action on the ground that he paid for admission to a Group meeting 'in anticipation of hearing the Oxford accent and was disappointed'. The Warden thought it 'intolerable that Oxford should be saddled with the responsibility for this Salvation Army for snobs' (5 June 1939).

APH went to Oxford that spring to engage in controversy on a wider issue, the occasion a debate at the Union on the motion: 'That this House is in favour of conscription.' It took place on the day of the introduction of a peace-time conscription Bill in the House of Commons. Preferring to hear 'what the young men had to say', he arranged a 'pair' in the Commons and attended the Union debate. The motion was carried, a result that received far less public attention than the notorious 'King and Country' affair of a few months before.

Concerning APH's anti-Buchman sentiments, his *Punch* colleague, Anthony Armstrong (A.A.) recalls an afternoon when they adjourned to an out-of-hours club in King Street, Covent Garden, much frequented by journalists from adjacent publishing houses in Long Acre and Southampton Street. Approaching it *via* Maiden Lane, APH changed places with A.A., to walk the rest of the way with one foot in the gutter 'He bobbed up and down along the length of the street like a cripple, making conversation difficult.' Within minutes of their arrival at the club a mild-looking man on a bar-stool mentioned Buchman. APH brought the life of the place to a standstill by raging at the man as if he were an offensive heckler at a public meeting. The poor fellow was utterly subdued by the onslaught which, says Tony Armstrong, was continued for 'a good twenty minutes, by which time I left', cheated of his hope of a companionable interlude with an admired contemporary.

The decision of the President of the Board of Trade, Oliver

Patrick and Beatrice Herbert, APH's parents.

APH with his brothers
Owen (killed at Mons 191.
and Sidney (lost in HMS
Hood 1941).

Harry Quilter, APH's
father-in-law, with his wife
and daughters.
By courtesy of Lady Herbert.

APH in 1918.

(*Above*) Master and crew of HMS *Water Gipsy*.

(*Below left*) Thames Conservator and a Freeman of the Company of Watermen and Lightermen, APH surveys the Thames from his Hammersmith garden.
(*Right*) Petty Officer A P Herbert MP in the Second World War.

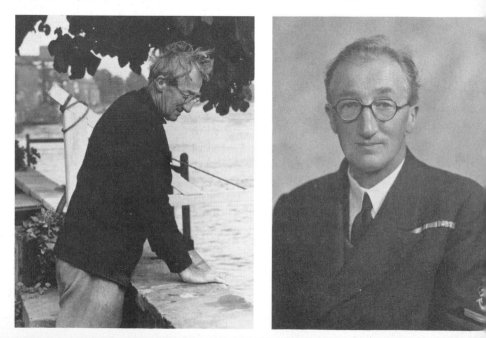

As broadcaster of
Sunday Night
'Postscripts' for the BBC
in 1941.

Rehearsing for *Big Ben* (1946) with Vivian Ellis (left), C B Cochran, and Carole Lynne.

National-and-Grindlays unflappability.

(Or, the cheque that didn't bounce.)

The late (and sadly missed) A. P. Herbert liked keeping our bank on its toes.

Hence the decidedly eccentric cheques he presented from time to time—written on wine bottles, on napkins, on eggs, or even in verse.

We never failed him, which, we feel, makes the point that for National and Grindlays, private customers are still to be treated as individuals rather than as mere numbers on the computer.

We look after them through a network that includes branches and subsidiaries in London, in Jersey (of special interest to non-U.K. residents who qualify for tax privileges there), France, Switzerland, South Asia, Africa, the Middle East and Hong Kong.

And we offer them all the services

you expect of a major bank; current and deposit accounts, personal finance, a fully-qualified Trust Department and expert advice of all kinds.

(As well as a few more unusual services, like those of our subsidiary the Cox & Kings Group who are travel agents and shipping and forwarding agents).

If you—like us—think that personal banking should still mean personal service, why not contact us to find out more about what we can offer you?

 NATIONAL
AND
GRINDLAYS
BANK GROUP

Head Office: 23 Fenchurch Street, EC3M 3DD. Tel: 01-626 0545

An APH cheque drawn on a wine bottle and duly honoured by the bank.

APH with his daughter Crystal in the garden at 12 Hammersmith Terrace.

(*Above*) Sir Alan and Lady Herbert, photographed during the river voyage to Greenwich organised by the Society of Authors in 1970 to mark APH's eightieth birthday.

Training Sail Barge ceremonially re-named *Sir Alan Herbert* in April 1974 as a memorial tribute from the East Coast Sailing Trust.— *Photograph by courtesy of Lieut-Commander G A Jones.*

Stanley, to allow Buchman to register his movement under the Oxford name brought APH a new wave of protesting letters, one of them from an illustrious personage in cricket annals, 'Plum' Warner, who was 'furious'. Going into action against a spiritual movement, however dubious its antecedents, was unpopular work. As the chief political representative of his university, APH was held by many to be its official spokesman, thus putting him in the false position of seeming to be conducting a personal vendetta. It was no mere matter of *amour-propre* for him as an Oxford man. Nor would he concede that the challenge to the Buchmanite movement was another of Oxford's lost causes. To him it was 'a question whether naked humbug should triumph in public life – one of the matters which principally moved me to enter Parliament' (Letter to Lady Corcoran, 26 June 1939). 'So, all alone, I was defeated all along the line. And seldom, I am sure, was I so right.'[2]

> It gives me shy but sharp delight
> To think how often I am right.
>
> How often, and, alas, how long
> The world insists on being wrong.
>
> In pub and press the fools dissent
> From what I find self-evident,
>
> And end the maddening debate
> Reluctantly – perhaps too late.
>
> It can be comforting, I know,
> To say at last 'I told you so',
>
> But in the public interest
> A quick decision would be best;
>
> For while they dicker and delay
> The mischief's done – and it will stay.
>
> How different the world would be
> If all, *at once*, agreed with me!
>
> But still it gives me shy delight
> To recollect that I was right.[3]

His three years in Parliament had taken toll of his earning power outside, where *Punch* was still his tower of strength. He could show a healthy balance in public services rendered. Leaving aside his Matrimonial Causes Act, which was lifting a heavy burden of unhappiness from many hearts and homes, he had been strenuously active in other causes: libel law reform; the reduction of entertainment tax; a Thames passenger transport service; organizing from his sickbed opposition to aerial advertising; challenging local licensing justices on their refusal to permit 'innocent and lawful games' in public houses; planning a betting tax bill, concerning which he made a speech during the Budget debate of 1939. Coincidentally, as he told a correspondent, 'I was preparing myself, my boat, and my friends for emergency service on the river'.

The House adjourned on 4 August 1939. On the night of the last debate of the session, APH joined a Smoking Room group gathered round Winston Churchill. Someone asked Churchill: 'Do you think there will be a war?' Without hesitation he answered 'Yes', and then said: 'I think we may have to abandon the Thames.' APH was startled by what to him was a *non sequitur*. Springing mentally to attention, he announced: 'I belong to a Service that means to see we don't!' It was an impulsive utterance with an ingratiating undertone that made him feel uncomfortable afterwards; 'a puny and pompous pronouncement'.

The Port of London Authority was well prepared with plans for the defence of its realm of sixty-nine miles of tideway that included navigation systems, deep water quays, docks, wharves, warehouses. Its River Emergency Service, in which APH was enrolled, had carried out exercises during the summer designed to ensure wartime efficiency. He practised semaphore all over again after twenty-five years, and Morse signalling, and learnt to read the flag signals of the International Code. 'All that summer we were organised and drilled and instructed.' He took part in exercises involving lifting dummy bodies from the river as simulated air-raid casualties, clambering over lighters to deliver them to the ambulance steamers. Elizabeth Allan remembers as a visitor aboard *Water Gipsy* in those pre war months that one of the 'mocked up' casualties consisted of a tightly stuffed pillow-case known to APH and his crew as 'Lady Astor'.

In the last days of August 1939 APH took to his bed, a victim of what appeared to be nervous exhaustion. The doctors diagnosed intercostal neuritis. Gwen Herbert still believes that the underlying cause was an upsurge of the old dreads of 1918 and after. On

September 1 he made his will, leaving her 'everything absolutely'. From his sick-bed he protested in *Punch* against the term 'evacuation', current jargon for the dispersal of mothers and children from the cities. 'Scattering', he insisted, should be the word.

That week the sixty small ships of the River Emergency Service reported to their war stations between Hammersmith and Southend. *Water .Gipsy* had recently been painted white and dark blue for a peaceful family excursion to Oxford. Considering her in the light of the ominous new situation, APH agreed that she looked 'a queer, comical, uncommon craft', laughed at by the lightermen in the first weeks of her service on the Thames.

He had mustered as his temporary crew Darcy Braddell, vice-president of the Royal Institute of British Architects; Victor Pasmore, artist; Magnus Pyke, DSc, chief chemist of Bemax Limited (who nicknamed himself 'Priority' Pyke, having received his call-up telegram in advance of his colleagues); and John Pudney, poet and BBC producer, his son-in-law. APH, wearing a peaked yachting cap with a blue blazer and grey flannel trousers, preferred but did not require his crew similarly to conform. Punctilio was reserved for saluting. He perfected his own style; as one of his superior officers later observed, it was 'most certainly not in the Admiralty Manual of Seamanship'.

Receiving the secret order, *Proceed to your appointed station*, he took *Water Gipsy* down to Lambeth Pier, 'remembering sadly' that it was twenty-five years almost to the day that he had enlisted there in the Royal Naval Volunteer Reserve. Parliament was recalled. He was crossing New Palace Yard when the first air-raid warning sounded over London; a false but momentarily real alarm. He had ordered his crew to anchor off the Speaker's Steps by Westminster Bridge. The pram dinghy was waiting for him as he doubled back along the Terrace to go aboard *Water Gipsy*. At the sounding of the sirens, John Pudney has recalled, 'crowds of MPs came out of the House on to the Terrace to watch the destruction of the capital. Being the only unit of His Majesty's Services in sight, we were the focus of their whole attention. They cheered at the sight of the gallant Senior Burgess of Oxford University being frantically rowed towards his command'. Briskly saluting, and being saluted, he embarked on six years' continuous and devoted war service on the river that he . loved.

'This is a little river', he wrote, 'as they measure them in Europe or America, a mere 200 miles or so from Thameshead to the Nore. But it is mighty in our minds and history. Few other waterways can claim such names of fame as Oxford, Windsor, Westminster, Greenwich, Tilbury, Chatham and the Nore. Francis Drake – the first Virginian settlers – the Mayflower – went the same way as our tugs and sailing-barges go today. The meridian of Greenwich is still the honoured line by which the navigators of the world determine their position.'

'What about you?' he asked when we next met at the Savage Club a week or two later, meaning had I been successful in my efforts to obtain a war job. I told him I had importuned various Government departments and many individuals with the offer of my services, all with no result; presumably because I was the recipient of a life pension from the First World War. 'I now have to accept the possibility of England saving the world without any help from me.' During lunch he left to make a telephone call. He came back to the table with the news that he had 'fixed an appointment' for us both at the Admiralty that afternoon.

The appointment was with an assistant to the Director of Naval Intelligence, a tall, lean-faced, rather supercilious lieutenant introduced as 'my friend Ian'. APH was eloquent and generous in his commendation of me for unspecified duties. His friend made notes and finally said: 'We will see what can be done.' I did not know then that I had met Ian Fleming. More important, here was further proof of APH's positive view of friendship. For him, in my experience, it was always more than lip service.

NOTES ON CHAPTER 16

1   Sir Dingle Foot: *Punch*, 23 September 1970.
2   A. P. Herbert: *Independent Member*.
3   A. P. Herbert: *Calendar for Every Day*.

17

Master of HMS Water Gipsy

'He put all his enthusiasm into performing his duties. He took the whole thing extremely seriously. As a skipper, he was unique.' Victor Pasmore also recalls 'the tense and magical moonlight patrols from Westminster to Wapping, tying up next to an old wharf or Thames barge for a snack, and night watching, and waiting for the bombs that, up to that time, never came' (Letter, 10 October 1973).

Magnus Pyke went ashore from Savoy Reach to practise semaphore signalling with APH aboard *Water Gipsy*. Pyke had proposed for transmission some bawdy lines attributed to Belloc. The exercise had hardly begun when APH stopped it. A young member of the Women's Royal Naval Service, walking along the Embankment, had paused by Cleopatra's Needle and appeared to be reading the signals. He resumed them only after she had passed beyond range.

He divided his time, 'a little unfairly', he thought, between Westminster and the tidal Thames, spending more hours afloat than in his place in the House of Commons, where attendance too often had little more than token value. Early in the first wartime session he spoke forcibly against a new proposal to abolish Private Members' Time which he had so spectacularly justified two years before. In spite of the gravity of the hour, he would not accept the assumption that 'the stock of creative legislative wisdom' was confined to the Treasury Bench. In taking that stand he was supported by 114 other members, to no avail. There was to be no more Private Members' Time during the next eight years.

Water Gipsy, officially reprieved after a threat of superannuation, liable to ungovernable behaviour in gale force winds, her cockpit for 'ard, her wheel aft with no protection for the helmsman, traversed 20,000 miles (her skipper's estimate) up and down the Thames on her lawful business. For off watch purposes her crew had been allotted a room in Lambeth Palace, cherishing a wayward hope that if bombs fell the contents of the archiepiscopal wine cellar would be an added amenity. Meanwhile, the palace butler was considered neglectful of the black-out regulations. Seeing the archbishop, Dr Cosmo Gordon Lang, walking wearily home from the House of Lords one evening, APH leapt ashore to speak to him about the black-out difficulty. As an afterthought, he asked the archbishop whether 'anything has happened in the House'. His Grace, for whom those were years of enervating anti-climax, answered in terms that may have reflected his own state of mind. 'Everything', he said, 'seems vague.'

By the spring of 1940 APH's crew of accomplished professional men had dispersed to wider spheres of national service. More than once he went out on patrol alone. At the time of Dunkirk, the Admiralty decreed that the River Emergency Service vessels should remain at their stations 'for the safety of the river'. For their officers and crews it was a frustration hard to bear. APH had been engaged by the Ministry of Information to lecture to naval 'personnel' – one of his hated jargon words – at Portsmouth, a duty he discharged with something less than enthusiasm. 'I was bored but they seemed to like it.' It bored him more to be asked: 'Weren't you at Dunkirk?' His lecture, revised and extended under the title *Let there be Liberty*, was published as a Macmillan War Pamphlet in September 1940. In it he made the point that 'few things that are free, alive and natural, are perfect. The tendency is to emphasise the imperfections of the two great institutions which make free expression in England a real thing – Parliament and Press.'

He was visited late one night by two naval captains with the confidential news that the River Emergency Service was being replaced by a new formation, the Royal Naval Auxiliary Patrol. They hoped he would join it for whole-time duty. It would give him the right to fly the White Ensign and to be known as Master of HMS *Water Gipsy*. His veneration of the Senior Service was such that he still carried in his pocket-book a tattered cutting from *The Times* in the First World War reporting the tribute of the US Admiral Sims: 'The Royal Navy is the foundation-stone of the cause of the whole of the Allies.'

Having passed at fifty the prescribed medical tests, he went to Chatham Barracks to be 'kitted up' as a Petty Officer, RN, at seven shillings a day, and proud to show off his crown and two anchors.

He telegraphed to a colleague in the House of Commons: *Passed A1 for Navy please tell Nancy.* Nancy was Lady Astor, MP, who had recently rounded on him when he told her that he 'always found it hard to say "No" to a cocktail party invitation'. She replied by return: *Must be something wrong with Navy.* Like an over-eager subaltern putting up a second 'pip', he lost no time in repainting *Water Gipsy* battleship grey.

He signed on a new mate, Eric Udale, who held a Royal Navy commission in the First World War and saw much sea service after. *Water Gipsy's* crew was drawn from the patrol Service headquarters at Lowestoft, men mostly from the fishing fleets and minesweepers. He constantly marvelled at his little ship's capability in fair times and foul. With her two 9 h.p. 'Handy Billies' by Thornycroft, she covered 45 miles daily on thirty successive days during the London blitz, calling at stations between Westminster and Canvey Island to deliver stores and ammunition. He wrote in some unpublished notes: 'It was a great education in seamanship and everything else. We learned more of the river every day. We became adept at "cheating the tide", creeping up inshore against the strong ebb, but not so close as to go aground. That gave us about 5 knots "over the tide"; without our artful "cheating" we were lucky to make 4. Soon we could boast that we knew every buoy and barge-road, every wharf and dolphin, every useful eddy or stretch of slack water, all the short cuts inside the lighter moorings, and every wreck that made them dangerous. We became so confident that we steamed on, sometimes in thick fog (but against the tide), when all the tugs with their tows had to give up, and every steamer lay at anchor, ringing her bell. From Hole Haven to Tilbury (10 miles) I had compass courses from buoy to buoy; and two or three times we steamed successfully for an hour and a half without seeing the shore, a thing you would not think could be done on the Thames.'

He spoke of having had 'a wonderful view' of the Battle of Britain, though much of the action took place to the south, over the Channel. He saw Big Ben hit by incendiary bombs, the docks ablaze, the walls of St Thomas's Hospital crumbling, Charing Cross and Waterloo Bridges burning simultaneously, petrol tanks shrouded in dense black smoke clouds at Thameshaven, the Sea Reach at Gravesend bubbling with burning oil.

He wrote a memorably vivid account of those early wartime nights on the river. 'Due south at Chatham, seven miles away, began one of those terrible, brilliant bombardments, a concentration of flash and fireworks, the more frightful because, unless the wind was right, it made no noise. It was like seeing the silhouette of a murder behind a suburban blind. Which flash was bomb – and which was gun? We knew not. But many a night we wondered if anything could be left of Chatham. Still, far off, let us confess, it was exciting, almost enjoyable . . . When the bombers began to roar over us for London, we were in the front row of the stalls. Tall tents of light were erected all about us. The din was outrageous. The "shrapnel" clattered on the deck, or hissed as it hit the water . . . From Sea Reach we could see the whole vile show. We saw the procession of searchlights march up to London, and, far off, over London, the flicker of the shells . . . The "All Clear" came, a thin, reedy pipe, far off, across the water. All was over; and again we were alone in the dark. Something shining and beautiful and stimulating had gone away. That is perhaps the worst of war: it can be beautiful – and, far enough away, you can enjoy it.'[1]

On 18 June he went ashore to hear Churchill speak in the House of Commons, the first of his resounding wartime calls to the nation as Prime Minister. 'Let us therefore brace ourselves to our duty and so bear ourselves that if the British Commonwealth and Empire lasts a thousand years, men will still say: "This was their finest hour".' APH described the effect the words had on him as 'a glow of the soul'. He was overcome by a less exalted emotion when, returning to duty, he learned that a bomb had fallen so near *Water Gipsy* that shore watchers thought she had received a direct hit. Her acting master, Eric Udale, was struck on the head by a piece of bomb-casing that fractured a vertebrae. APH felt cheated of a long-awaited chance to engage low-flying enemy aircraft with his two Lewis guns. *Water Gipsy*'s armament was completed by a miniature rifle, three revolvers, a dozen hand-grenades and two cutlasses. When one of the Lewis guns went into action from Lambeth Bridge during a late night raid, local observers inaccurately reported that it had shot down a captive balloon. APH was rebuked by a harassed commander for permitting the Lewis gun to be fired. 'Don't you know that there's no war above Dagenham?' he demanded. APH replied: 'Does Hitler?'

At Hole Haven in the last week of June 1940 he wrote in his ship's log: '11.15. Searchlights. Wrote letter to *The Times* about purchase tax on books. Blowing hard from N.W. Air raid warning.' His letter to the editor, drafted in the log book, which also contained scraps of libretti and notes for his 'Little Talks' series in *Punch*, was in protest against the plan of the Chancellor of the Exchequer, Sir Kingsley Wood, to include books in a list of items selected for purchase tax at 33⅓ per cent, along with newspapers and periodicals, domestic hollow-ware, brooms and brushes. 'The Treasury notion', he wrote, 'that there can be no distinction for the purposes of taxation between books and boots, Shakespeare and soap, is only to be stated to be scorned by any civilised person' (26 June).

The Chancellor was prepared to hear the case for exempting newspapers and periodicals; books stirred him to dogged resistance. APH wrote: 'He was not much to look at, and nothing to hear. He had a voice which tended towards the alto, and a maddening habit of beginning each new section of a speech with the phrase, "So far as so-and-so is concerned . . ." I used to count them.'

Speaking in the House on 25 July, he said that Kingsley Wood's progress from one ministry to another reminded him of 'some cheery reveller staggering from pub to pub, emerging from each with such a radiant smile that no one has the heart to stop him'. It put the House in a humour for the philippic that followed. 'It is a sad and shocking thing that at this time in this truly titanic conflict, when we are saying, and saying truly, that there are arrayed on one side the spirit of force and, on the other, the forces of the spirit, we should have sunk so low as to be seeking to put a tax upon learning and literature in the same way as we treat brooms or something that is kept under the bed.' He invoked the shades of Caxton, Milton, Dickens, in denunciation of 'a Chancellor of the Exchequer who at this hour of civilisation sees no important distinction between boots and books'.

> Domestic hollow-ware and books,
> The tools of teachers, chars, and cooks,
> And petticoats, and skirts, and stays,
> And mustard pots, and Shakespeare's plays,
> Goloshes, socks, and Holy writ
> (For Bibles too must do their bit),
> Macaulay, Dickens, Scott, and Lamb,
> And things in which you put the jam—
> All those impartially you pass
> Into the selfsame class;
> And in the scale of Ways and Means
> Weigh Wells and Shaw with soup-tureens.

You drive the scholars from their seats,
For Euclid pays as well as Keats;
Nor may they knit the boyish brow
O'er *Deeds that Won the Empire* now.
All knowledge, I suppose, is doomed,
For knowledge must not be 'consumed'.
But least of all we need what's new,
And last year's calendar must do.
You're even putting 12 *per cent*
On the reports of Parliament;
And we'll be paying through the nose
For reading your delicious prose.
In fact, as far as I can see,
A betting book alone is free.

Sir Kingsley, when your star is set,
You will, no doubt, go higher yet;
And England's men of letters there
Will greet you with a stony stare.
But I should like to hear that day
What Dr Johnson has to say.[2]

Three weeks later Wood relented and removed books from his new tax schedule – 'at least, for the time being', the parting shot of a Chancellor not utterly lacking in self-esteem. APH considered that 'no mean victory was won that day'. He was glad to share the credit with two fellow members who had taken up arms with him, Kenneth Lindsay (Combined Universities), and George Isaacs (Southwark North), a respected printing trades union leader who became Minister of Labour.

The Thames lightermen and tugboat crews no longer looked on *Water Gipsy* as an oddity, though under her new official designation of Mail and Store-boat she might have been mistaken for a floating pantechnicon. They recognized that she was being capably handled, and that her famous skipper knew more than a thing or two about their river. They sometimes cheered him on his way; more often, they gave him the thumbs-up sign and a fraternal grin.[3] He became so intimately acquainted with their habitat that he could boast: 'Sitting in the cabin and catching a glimpse of the skyline through a port, a chimney, some cranes, a warehouse roof, I could say at once where we were in our sixty miles of river.'

On 9 September 1940, after the heaviest night raid so far on London's dockland, he went ashore at Blackwall Pier and wandered round the battered streets. It impressed and pleased him to see that the pubs were open long before the regulation hours, whether voluntarily or by some emergency decree no one seemed to know. 'There the veterans of that awful night', he wrote, 'exchanged adventures and gathered courage for the next.' He had always regarded the public house as one of England's meritorious institutions (adjective his). From that grim morning he saw it in a new and hallowed light. It did not matter whether or not drinks were being served. 'The pub was the natural and proper place for common counsel and moral refreshment on such a morning. It was the finest and truest tribute to the pub that I remember', and it was in no spirit of deference to publicans or brewers that he preached eloquently in print against the impoverishment by prejudice and taxation of that ancient amenity of the people.

The boarded-up windows at 12 Hammersmith Terrace were symbolic of its shattered home life. APH rarely slept there more than two nights a month. When Gwen, his wife, was not driving through the bombings for the London Ambulance Service, 'with screaming casualties behind', she was firewatching and growing vegetables in the little garden where only flowers had grown before. He was amused, admiringly, to be told that when incendiary bombs fell on the roof, and one through a drawing-room window, she answered a neighbour's frantic knocking at the door: 'Yes, I know the house is on fire. Won't you come in?' He wrote: 'She lost all her windows time and again, and lived in the dark behind cardboard, and in the cold when the cardboard went. She would not go away, as many did; but stayed like a lighthouse of faith and fortitude among poorer neighbours who could not go.'[4] Her enfolding sympathy was not found wanting on the day in 1942 when Dylan Thomas, homeless and all but penniless, arrived on her doorstep with his wife and child, asking for shelter like orphans of the storm.

It is remembered that on those intermittent home visits during the war APH repeatedly played to himself on the piano Handel's *Largo*, for him the music of consolation. One night during a raid, calling on Hammersmith friends, he played it in three different houses.

John, his son and heir, wore the uniform of the Royal Navy, as much to his father's satisfaction as to his own. Crystal, Jocelyn, and Lavender, the daughters, were variously engaged in war avocations. To the alternating currents of family anxiety was added a shock for APH when HMS *Hood* was sunk in 1941. His brother Sidney was lost in her. Only a few weeks earlier Petty Officer A. P. Herbert had gravely saluted Captain S. J. Herbert on landing him at Greenwich during his last leave in London.

APH explained his sedulous observance of the ritual of the salute as an expression of 'the almost mystical feeling I had for the Navy'. He was gratified, he wrote, to salute his son's superior rank. Passing midshipmen in the streets, he would salute them with a deference that brought blushes to their cheeks. He was offended when, having ordered his crew to attention while he saluted the quarter-deck of a damaged destroyer steaming slowly up river, her officers waved cheerily in reply. 'Most improper!' he exclaimed with clouded brow. His sometime commanding officer, Lieutenant-Commander L. M. Bates, RNVR, has recalled APH's 'most punctilious' relations with the higher ranks. 'A meeting was invariably accompanied by a fearful clash of heels and a sweeping naval salute, even if it was followed by an invitation to lunch at the House.'[5] Many of his postwar letters were subscribed: 'With salutes, APH.'

His scrupulous performance of the salute brought him to a halt one morning in Jermyn Street, when a captain RN accosted him with the peremptory inquiry 'You're Herbert, aren't you? You – er – wrote those – er – verses?' The implication was awkwardly clear. 'Standing severely to attention', APH listened to his superior officer's recitation of lines 'composed by some of us on the China Station', taking the form of 'a reply from the women's point of view'. They did not make music in APH's ear.

> . . . You may agree to differ and make learned dissertations
>   on the relative importance of a name,
> But we women know that when it comes to intimate relations,
>   then your acts are essentially the same . . .

APH thought it 'the strangest literary episode in the history of Jermyn Street'; an amiable supposition. A stone's throw away was Rosa Lewis's Cavendish Hotel, where probably more famous literary names were deliberately omitted from the register than appeared in it.

1941 was *Punch*'s centenary year; because of the war, an occasion
for muted clebration only: a cartoon of past editors at the Table by
E. H. Shepard; a perfunctory letter from APH; otherwise no more
than a pious raising of glasses at the weekly editorial meeting on
16 July. It was also a milestone year in Cochran's career, rounding
off his half-century in 'show business'. APH saluted him with a
lyrical fanfare.

FIFTY YEARS

13 August, 1941
(To C. B. Cochran)

For fifty years, with pleasures grave and gay,
    You have invited all the world inside
To see the playhouse in its right array–
    A thing of beauty and a place of pride.

And what a fine mixed feast you had to show –
    Ibsen and Coward, Shakespeare, Shaw and all,
Ballet and boxing, Robey and Rodeo,
    Cowboy and Circus – and the Albert Hall!

Reinhardt and Hackenschmidt were one to you;
    Carpentier, Bernhardt, Duse, did your will;
Helen of Troy and Jessie of Revue,
    Barrie and Pirandello filled a bill.

Nothing was done because it was 'the thing',
    Nothing was done in avarice or haste.
Beauty was Queen, Efficiency was King,
    And over all these ruled the god of Taste.

How much you spent on that Young Lady's shoe
    Was not a worry – if the shoe was right:
How much you made – or lost – you hardly knew,
    If only London loved it on 'the night'.

Alas, how little can the actor keep
    Of all the joy he lavishly distils!
Some faded programmes in the scrapbooks sleep –
    A few old photographs – and many bills.

'Who was the man in that delightful play?'
    'Who was the girl who took the leading part?'
Well, never mind. For she has had her day,
    And lives in lodgings with a broken heart.

To men like you we pay no living wage,
And all their work is swept away like snow.
Yet you have left your footprints on the stage:
The world is richer for the 'Cochran show'.

Harold Nicolson, APH's guest on a trip down to Woolwich in *Water Gipsy*, told his wife, Vita Sackville-West, in a letter (11 September 1941) that 'Herbert knows the river blindfold', and that though the blackout was complete, with not a light to be seen anywhere, 'he hit off each post with miraculous ease. "Post number thirty-one?" he shouts. "Okay, sir!' comes the answer, and off we chug to another dim post among the docks and wharves', which by then were exposed to the new enemy tactic of dropping parachute mines on the Port of London. *Water Gipsy* was seconded to the Thames Mine-watching and Mine Clearance Service, formed to combat that latest menance. The job entailed not only more navigational complexities but a new set of operational hazards. Lieutenant-Commander Bates, APH's commanding officer, has stated that APH 'assisted considerably' in the setting up of the organization that finally nullified the parachute mine danger. 'It is in the matter of minewatching exercises that he made his greatest contribution to the defence of the Thames.'[6]

He was ordered to investigate a parachute mine alleged to have been dropped near Hammersmith Bridge. All the thousands of members of the mine-watching organization had been warned of the extreme sensitivity of the new mines. APH's report: 'I prodded the whole area with a boathook and found nothing', became a standing joke. The humour of it was savoured less appreciatively by his superior officer, Lieutenant-Commander Bates, who had been seriously injured in a mine explosion a few months before. He suggested that APH should 'take more care to avoid a by-election at Oxford'.

Bates recalls *Water Gipsy* as 'probably the untidiest ship in HM's service'. In the recollection of Commander S. R. Brown, in charge of minesweeping in the Thames, APH's personal appearance conformed closely to that description. He considered APH to be 'the most conscientious man serving out of London'. The commander also pays tribute to his extraordinary knowledge of the river. 'He could smell his way downstream with a signal for a ship in the port when nothing else moved.'

Both Brown and Bates were present when APH stepped forward as a request-man with a complaint to the officer commanding the river defences, Commander Stewart Lockhart, RN. The Admiralty had directed that the qualifications of all ratings promoted early in the war to petty officer rank should be re-examined. Henceforth those 'hostilities only' petty officers who were serving in seagoing ships above a certain size were to be known as Petty Officers Patrol Service (POPS). Those serving ashore or in small ships were to become Petty Officers Small Craft Only (POSCO). All POSCOs were to appear before a board to be passed out as POPS within six months, or revert to ordinary seaman rank. APH was classed a POSCO.

The morning after the promulgation of the Admiralty order, he left a slip of paper on Lieutenant-Commander Bates's cabin table. It bore the lines:

> Oh, why do they call me a POSCO?
> It makes me feel like the Wops.
> I'd seem like something from Moscow;
> If only they'd call me POPS.
> Why this invidious gradation?
> We're not real sailors, we know,
> But we do what we can for the nation;
> Oh, why can't I simply be PO?

He was examined on his fitness to be rated POPS by a board of two captains, one Royal Navy, the other Royal Naval Reserve. He easily passed the tests, and was given a form to sign acknowledging that he had been 'properly examined'. Studying the form with a lawyer's scrupulosity, he regretted 'with respect' that he could not put his name to it; he had not been 'properly examined'. The two captains were astonished. 'But you've passed. What's the problem?'

He pointed out several flaws; one of them that when he was asked how many fathoms there are to a shackel of anchor cable, the examiners themselves disagreed about the answer. Again, he was shown models of two vessels, one crossing the other's course, the question being: What action should be taken in such circumstances? What *were* the circumstances? he asked. No indication was given whether the ships were operating in enclosed waters like the Thames or in the open sea. Further, the syllabus insisted on proficiency in signalling. He considered himself proficient but was asked no question on the subject.

Finally, the examiners ordered him to sign the form. Courteously but firmly he refused; he had not, he maintained, been 'properly examined'. He had in mind the hundreds of POSCOs who might be failed for inadequate reasons. He would have been aware of the gravity of refusing an order by superior officers; in the Navy, a serious offence. He was conscientious about not asserting his status as a Member of Parliament to gain advantage for himself, especially during the war. When the choleric Commander Lockhart ordered his attendance as a defaulter, counsels of moderation warned that 'unfortunate' publicity might follow. Instead, APH was briefed to appear before the commander to state a complaint. Here is Commander S. R. Brown's account of the proceedings:

'One Thursday morning found Commander Lockhart standing behind a table, flanked by Lieutenant-Commander Bates and myself (both lieutenants then). In marched APH, untidy as always, badly needing a haircut, the strap of his gasmask case twisted a hundred times into a thick cord. He whipped off a salute and stood at attention, waiting. Commander Lockhart said: "You wish to see me, Herbert." "On the contrary, sir, you sent for me," said APH. "However, I am delighted to be here." The commander went red to the gills. "You wish to complain that you were ordered to sign a form with which you did not agree?" "Oh, no, sir. If I have a complaint, and to be frank I have not, it would be that such a form was prepared for signature in the first place."

'The dialogue went on to the joy of us two RNVR. officers, standing behind the Commander, R.N. APH quoted common law, statute law, and his rights as an Englishman to exercise his conscientious objection against doing what he deemed to be wrong. The Commander blustered a bit; APH remained calm, courteous, and at attention; the battle was one-sided; established authority hadn't a hope.

'Finally, APH was dismissed with the promise that his so-called complaint would be forwarded to higher authority. It was; the Admiralty order was withdrawn and one to which closer thought was given was substituted.'[7]

Lieutenant-Commander Bates remembers an episode in which APH figured to the amusement of many in the London Command. 'A very sour and unpopular' Paymaster Commander was in the habit of changing into civilian rig and snooping round the little ships of the Service refitting at various Thames-side yards, intent on catching ratings in the act of smuggling duty-free rum and tobacco ashore. Boarding *Water Gipsy* in Tough's Yard, Teddington he ordered her White Ensign to be struck; improperly, as she was still in commission. APH sent a note of protest to the Flag Officer i/c Thames, Admiral Sir Martin Dunbar-Nasmith, VC. 'Sir, During my absence from the warship I have the honour to command, a person purporting to be Paymaster Commander X—, but not dressed as a naval officer, boarded the vessel and ordered my crew to strike the White Ensign. It is of course understood that this distinguished and gallant officer would have known better than to issue such a palpably erroneous order, and it is requested that the matter be put before the Director of Naval Intelligence with a view to the arrest of the impostor.' The boatyards were troubled with no further spying visitations.

Amid the difficulties, the distractions, the imponderables, he continued writing regularly for *Punch*, his main source of wartime income. One of his articles consisted of a series of tabulated examples of classically rooted words taken from a new book by H. G. Wells who despised Greek and Latin as 'dead and eviscerated' languages. He delivered a series of Sunday night 'Postscripts' for BBC radio, in the wake of J. B. Priestley whose *basso profondo* style had made him one of the foremost broadcasters of the war. From the evidence of surviving correspondence, APH's lighter tone was welcomed by some listeners; and his Easter Sunday 1941 broadcast in rhyming couplets, *Let Us Be Gay*, struck a resounding chord of appreciation in numerous homes:

> Let us be gay. It's Easter Day;
> And spring at last is on the way.
> It's Hitler's habit, in the spring,
> To do some dark, disgusting thing;
> But you and I may still decline
> To sign on Hitler's dotty line.
> So let's be gay. Yes, grim but gay.
> It is the Resurrection Day,
> The feast of life, the first of spring,
> When all, except the wicked, sing.
> And all the ranting, all the row,
> Can't kill the blossom on the bough.

The bees, whatever Hitler does,
Refuse to stop their happy buzz.
The birds, not in their usual form,
Are trying to pretend it's warm.
The crocuses come out once more
Although they're useless in the war.
The little lambs, the little larks,
Are making seasonable remarks.

Let us be gay. It is the spring;
And even Postscripts have to sing.

. . . .

In all the stories ever told
Of all the valiant Greeks of old,
Is there a poem, or a play,
To touch the tale of Greece today?
The star of Hellas shines as bright
As when the Persians forced a fight.
And drowsy schoolboys, hard to please,
With Homer and Thucydides,
Will think a little more, maybe,
Of all those dull affairs BC.,
And when they come to Persia's name,
Write 'Prussia' – and the tale's the same.

Let us be gay. For, come what may.
The war will not be won today;
So nothing matters in the news
For those who hold the longest views.
Napoleon died at fifty-two;
And, Adolf Hitler, so may you!

. . . .

He had agreed to supply 'a piece of verse or two' every week to
the *Sunday Graphic*, 'to cheer, comfort, or chide my fellow citizens'.
Topicality was the keynote. Striving for it, he lapsed too often into
cheap rhetoric, as when Hitler, threatening invasion, was denounced
in verse as 'a low land-rat'. A more authentic sentiment impelled
him to write:

These are the boys of whom we said
    'They are not what their fathers were;
They have no heart and little head;
    They slouch and do not cut their hair'.

> Yet these like falcons live and die;
>   These every night have new renown;
> And while we heave a single sigh
>   They shoot a brace of bombers down.

Too often the discipline that would have been better applied to his talent was concentrated on the business of delivering the fruits of it to the market place. His weekly verse was frequently shouted over the telephone syllable by syllable late on Friday night to the *Sunday Graphic* offices in Grays Inn Road from a waterside pub loud with drunken disputation and song. At times, going ashore to grope his way in the blackout to a telephone kiosk, he found the lines down after an air raid. 'Somehow, the stuff got through', bringing with the editorial cheques the satisfaction of knowing that his public reputation was being sustained and with it his income. The *Sunday Graphic* paid him £40 a week. 'I have never pretended to be a "serious" poet', he wrote in the 'Foreword, Preface, Apology, etc.,' to *Siren Song* (1940), a selection of his newspaper verse that preserves evidence of deeper feeling than the brisk topicality often suggests.

> The secret is clothed in tender green,
> And there is made Trinitrotoluene . . .
>   Be of good cheer –
>   Is not the tulip here,
>   Fair phosgene too, in bloom,
>   A non-persistent fume
>   Smelling of hay?

A cartoon by Low in the *Evening Standard* seemed to him to be offensive to the Polish patriots. His indignation, echoing eighteenth-century invective without the malice, was as heroic as the couplets in which he chose to express it.

> Honour the Poles. They fought the bully first.
> When some said die, they shouted 'Do your worst!'
> They fought him well; they gave him blow for blow
> While bigger men made treaties with the foe.
> They yielded only to the front attack
> When someone smugly stabbed them in the back.
> They fight him still; he cannot quench the flame:
> There is no Quisling with a Polish name.
> They fight beside us; and it seems too soon

To kill a comrade with a low cartoon.
A 'little sensitive'? Are we surprised?
Four times 'partitioned' – murdered – robbed – despised!
'A hundred miles or so! Why all the fuss?'
Those hundred miles did not belong to us.
We can of course, be calmer, cooler men:
We're not 'partitioned' every now and then.
No one has taken Oxford from us, yet.
No man says 'Give us Scotland – and forget'.
But if he did, I fancy we would strike
The same proud pose that you dislike.
Maybe we cannot help those loyal souls.
But let us not insult them. Honour the Poles.

One of his down-river points of call was Brunswick Wharf, where Mrs J. M. Patterson, now secretary of the Royal Society of Literature, had a wartime job as superintendent of stores from which medical and other supplies were drawn for vessels of the Patrol and Mine-watching Services. APH used her telephone for his professional purposes, and her typewriter for his letters to *The Times*. He asked her to type a letter to the Hammersmith Borough Council, to which he had applied for planning permission to build steps from his garden wall down to the river foreshore. The Council asked him to submit a plan of the proposed work. Replying, he 'begged to enclose' a photograph of the steps, already built.

A minor mishap on board *Water Gipsy* involved his seeing a chiropodist. Mrs Patterson suggested tactfully that he ought to wash his feet before the consultation. He returned from it in a mirthful mood. 'I washed my bad foot', he said. 'The man insisted on seeing the other one – and I didn't wash that!'

A favourite off-duty resort of his in the lower reaches was the Lobster Smack Inn on Canvey Island, where there was an old upright piano at which he presided over noisy sing-songs with sailors, anti-aircraft gunners, and bargemen as chorus. His friend Bill O'Bryen, who had been awarded two bars to his Military Cross in the First World War, was now a major in command of an anti-aircraft battery. He remembers the agitation of the Lobster Smack landlord, Percy Went, when APH at the piano ignored the warning, 'Time, gentlemen, please'. To his plaintive appeal, 'Remember the law, Mr Herbert – remember the law', APH retorted through the haze and noise: 'I *am* the law!'

Bill O'Bryen was on board *Water Gipsy* when APH decided to investigate a large riverside area of apparently deserted land that was heavily encompassed by barbed wire defences. 'I've been curious about it for some time', he said. 'Let's go and have a look.' Surmounting the wire was not easy. Doggedly undeterred as always, he found a way through. They had trespassed on a vast underground munitions depot, seemingly unguarded. Wandering about, they came to the main gates, where they were challenged for the first time. When the civilian in charge demanded to know why they had not used 'the proper entrance', APH replied jauntily: 'Because I couldn't get my boat up your drive.'

During his river service APH often talked with Francis Chichester, then working on maps and charts for the Admiralty. That subsequently famous navigator recalled in writing 'our very pleasant and interesting discussions together' in the mid-war years. They had a common interest in sundials. APH could discourse learnedly about cross-staffs and back-staffs, cursors and transomes.

Relaxing during his 'forty-eight hours off' he liked to go to the Savage Club in Carlton House Terrace, very much his milieu, the condition of membership being achievement in the arts and science combined with social acceptability. The club appears under its rightful name in *Holy Deadlock*, and as The Martyrs in his later novel, *The Singing Swan*. 'We are, we say proudly, the active rank and file of the arts, though we have among us some of the greatest in their line. Our members, whatever their craft or calling, are gallant and gay, generous and loyal, shrewd critics, and stout friends, good company always.'

He often arrived at the club with members of his crew in tow, as Stan Atkins, who joined *Water Gipsy* from a Grimsby minesweeper, well remembers. 'We went with him to the Savage Club many times on our off days. He introduced us to some wonderful people', once to the victor of El Alamein. At one of the club's famous Saturday Night dinners, when APH was in the chair, he was flanked by two rear-admirals, a captain, a lieutenant-commander, and a sub-lieutenant; his guests. 'It is not every Petty Officer', he said, briefly introducing them, 'who achieves the dream of all of his kind – to have his officers exactly where he wants them'.

At another of those mostly memorable occasions Alfred Reynolds, the composer, brought as his guest an air commodore who was in civilian clothes. APH asked him in a severe tone: 'Why aren't you in uniform?' For the rest of the evening Reynolds had to apply himself to the entertainment of a guest who had been deeply affronted and could not get over it.

APH himself wore uniform on any and every occasion throughout the war years, proud, he said, to be the only non-commissioned officer in the House of Commons, where he hoped to advance the interests of the lower deck. Attempts to persuade him to apply for a commission were wasted effort. Once, early on, he was pressured into appearing before a selection board. 'Ah, Mr Herbert,' the presiding officer greeted him genially, 'we understand you wish to apply for a commission.' Standing at attention, APH replied: 'On the contrary, sir', and waited, amid expostulations, to be dismissed. A commission meant constraints. The same consideration applied when, over lunch at Downing Street, Churchill asked him: 'Would you like a job?' APH's prompt response inhibited discussion of the nature of what was proposed. 'No, thank you, sir. I'm quite happy where I am.' He might not have cared to risk being a public misfit. Conceivably, his 'no' to Churchill proceeded from a private conviction that all governments are a confession of human failure.

Buchman's young men came back to the front pages with an appeal to the Minister of Labour, Ernest Bevin, for the exemption of some of their 'lay evangelists' from military service. In the House of Commons Bevin gave examples of the methods used by the Group to try to influence his decision. He advised them to be 'a little more careful'. APH made a speech in which he said, finally: 'I know very well how many people point at me the finger of scorn and say "King Charles Head, Bees in the Bonnet, Bats in the Belfry", and all the other epithets which these super-Christians have cast upon me, but the pursuit of humbug and, if I may be pardoned for mentioning it, the good great name of Oxford, these are bees and bats and King Charles's heads which I will gaily carry about with me till I die.'

A leading propagandist for the Group, Peter Howard, formerly a Fleet Street political writer, replied with an attack on him in a pamphlet, *Fighters Ever*. APH was comforted in his opposition by a letter marked 'Secret' from an intelligence department in Whitehall. 'You will be interested to know that everybody I have seen who has had the opportunity of watching Buchman, in this country, on the

Continent, and in the United States, is of the opinion that he is working for Germany. A number believe that he has been subsidised by Dr Goebbels. At the moment proof is wanting.'

APH's Celtic temper was roused afresh when a Clydeside MP, John McGovern, used obstructive tactics to prevent Charles Taylor (Conservative Member for Eastbourne) taking part in a debate. APH was 'shocked and outraged'. He rushed from the Chamber to overtake McGovern in the Members' lobby, where he denounced him as a bastard. 'Say that again', said McGovern, 'and I'll knock your block off.' APH said it again, at which point two officers of the House intervened with polite entreaties. 'My only parliamentary brawl', APH said afterwards, excusing it as his 'defence of a friend and of the principles of free speech and fair play.'

His 'little volcano' had been activated in the first place by resentment at the hostility shown towards his avowed hero, Churchill, by McGovern and Aneurin Bevan. Bevan and APH had been on amiable terms for some years in the House of Commons and at the Café Royal, where Bevan was as familiar a figure in the early thirties as he was on the back benches at Westminster. APH had signed the register at Bevan's wedding to Jennie Lee. He believed that Bevan's antipathy to Churchill was more than political; that there was personal animus. Challenged by APH, Bevan denied it. APH passed on the denial to Churchill and received the orotund reply: 'All I can say is that when I look across the Chamber I see in those eyes the fires of implacable hatred.'

That APH's pugnacity of temper was demonstrable physically was unsuspected by most of his friends, including myself. Lance Sieveking had a story of APH hailing a taxi outside the Gargoyle Club late one night and being brushed aside by a couple of Soho roughs when he was instructing the driver. According to Sieveking, he emerged from a melée of flying fists having sent one of the men to the pavement with 'a terrific blow in the eye, and then dived into the taxi and hauled the other out'. Whether or not he was fortified by wine on that occasion, he was not an intemperate man; far from it, in spite of Sir Martin Lindsay's recollection of his 'intervening in a debate when he was drunk' (Letter, 12 May 1973). In many years I never saw him the worse for drink. He was inclined to look with silent pity on drunkenness in others.

The *News Chronicle* had published in 1940 a poem entitled *The RAF* by Sylvia Lynd. It included the lines:

> Instead of Bear or Wain or Plough,
> Splendid to see in night's great dome,
> Give to those stars a new name now,
> Call them the Squadron Flying Home.

Whether or not there was inspiration in them for APH, not long afterwards he told me over drinks at the Carlton that his latest literary preoccupation was a book on his plan to rename the stars. He had been studying works on astronomy and could now claim to have in his head 'a clear map of the whole heavens'. He wanted a Battle of Britain galaxy, to include the names of prototype aircraft and of pilots who won renown in the battle. Churchill, Roosevelt and Stalin were to be commemorated in the heavens above as in the earth beneath. His Tyrants' constellation would bear the names of Attila, Tamburlaine, Robespierre, Hitler and Mussolini. Canopus, Arcturus, the Pleiades (to which Ulysses set his helm) were to become – I forget what. As he talked, his ideas unfolded in a grand design. 'I would divide the middle sky into two great sections' – and so on. His imaginative grasp, his far-stretched power of comprehension, was most impressive. He seemed to have no awe of the immensities. One can imagine him saying, with an accompanying bout of head jerking; 'The only immensity that frightens me is human stupidity.'

The *Illustrated London News* published across its 'middle spread' his chart of the whole revolutionary concept. He wrote as part of the accompanying text: 'We honour the work of the Arab and the Roman who went before us, but those old names are hindering the spread of knowledge and hiding the glory of the stars. They are perhaps the most stupendous work of God, and it is not fitting that they should be named after the beaks of hens, the claws of scorpions, the mouths of fish. We could very well describe the stars by nothing but alphabetical and arithmetical signs, but if we are going to relate them by names to the things of this planet, these things should not be the limbs of animals but the mind and spirit of man, which are a work of God more wonderful still.'[8]

The widow of a master mariner had sent him her husband's sextant, an instrument of which APH had little knowledge and no experience. It led him to the study of celestial navigation, his word for which was 'fascinating'. He had become concerned to 'make things easier', he said, for seamen cast adrift in open boats and had invented a device enabling them to determine longitude. He was submitting it to the Admiralty.[9]

His single-minded pursuit of any theme to which he was attracted, however casually, remained a source of wonder to those who knew him; a source of concern to those around him who felt that he should be putting his powers to better use. His *Punch* colleague, H. F. Ellis, thought it 'most astonishing' that, following an argument at the Table over an astronomical technicality, APH wrote him 'pages about the moon'. In the grip of his quixotic demon he sent an elaborate chart of his renamed firmament to the Royal Astronomical Society, receiving 'a nice reply' and an invitation to meet 'some of the Fellows' at dinner. 'It was, for me', he wrote, 'a memorable meal. Eddington, Jeans, and the Astronomer Royal were among the thirty or so present. He was invited to state his reasons for abandoning the classical star identities. During his dissertation, Sir James Jeans rose in silence and walked out. When, afterwards, APH asked him to write a foreword to his book *A Better Sky*, Sir James declined on the ground that there was 'quite enough international ill-feeling already'. Reviewing the book in the *Sunday Times*, the Astronomer Royal, Sir Harold Spencer Jones, commended APH for 'fighting for a principle'. In that unending battle he carried the lance and shield of a champion.

In 1943 the Performing Right Society, of which he was a member, won a notable victory in the courts in respect of copyright infringements by the BBC in its wartime broadcasts of 'Music While You Work'. APH entered the lists with a *Punch* article (10 March) in which he stated the case for the composers with telling logic. 'Is there any proposal to waive the fees due to holders of patents in use in the munitions factories? Are newspapers and cigarettes to be distributed gratis in the factories?' It was one of the first salvoes in his campaign to secure justice not only for composers but for his fellow authors, the victims of 'public plunder', whose cause he was to uphold with unswerving firmness through the next twenty years and more.

NOTES ON CHAPTER 17

1   A. P. Herbert: *Independent Member*.
2   A. P. Herbert: *Siren Song* (1940).
3   Later they made him a freeman of their Company of Watermen and Lightermen.
4   A. P. Herbert: *Independent Member*.
5   L. M. Bates: *The Londoner's River* (1949).
6   L. M. Bates: *The Londoner's River*. In 1942 APH was twice commended by the Flag Officer in Charge, London, for his services to the minewatching organization.
7   Letter, 13 May 1973.
8   26 December 1942.
9   'Duly turned down.' APH.

18

To the Navy, a Sad Farewell

On a June day in 1943, Winston Churchill, just back from addressing Congress at Washington, entered the Smoking Room of the House of Commons and sat down next to APH. 'Where did you get the metre for that verse you were kind enough to write for my birthday?' he inquired. APH explained that 'it started with "Many happy returns of the day" and seemed to go on from there'. Churchill said: 'I thought I recognized the metre. I went to a shelf and found it.' He then gave a sonorous rendering of what APH said was 'a kind of *ballade* with some French in it'. There were several stanzas. 'He began a little haltingly but the last lines flowed as smoothly as a Head Boy's recitation on Speech Day.' It was astonishing to think that, 'in the midst of his mighty cares', he had time to memorize 'all that verse'.

Divested by time of its contemporary sentiment, APH's birthday tribute to Churchill in 1943 hardly bears reprinting today. Worthier of recall are his *Less Nonsense* lines, challenging the 'excessive adulators' of Joseph Stalin and the foolish clamour for a Second Front that recurringly frightened the pigeons in Trafalgar Square.

> Let's have less nonsense from the friends of Joe,
> We laud, we love him, but nonsense NO.
> In 1940 when we bore the brunt
> *We* could have done, boys, with a second front.
> A continent went down a cataract
> But Russia did not think it right to act.
> Not ready? No. And who shall call her wrong?
> Far better not to strike till you are strong.
> Better perhaps, though this was not our fate,
> To make new treaties with the man you hate.
> Alas! These sly manouevres had to end

When Hitler leaped upon his largest friend.
(And if he'd not, I wonder, by the way,
If Russia would be in the war today.)
But who rushed out to aid the giant then,
A giant rich in corn, and oil, and men,
Long, long prepared and having, so they say,
The most enlightened ruler of the day?
This tiny island, antiquated, tired,
Effete, capitalistic, and uninspired.
This tiny island, wounded in the war
Through taking tyrants on two years before.
This tiny island of muddles and mistakes,
Having a front on every wave that breaks.
We might have said 'Our shipping's on the stretch,
You shall have all that you can fetch'.
But this is not the way we fight this war,
We give them tanks and take them to the door.
And now we will not hear from anyone
That it's for us to show we hate the Hun.
It does not profit much to sing this tune,
But those who 'prod' can not be quite immune,
And those who itch to conquer and to kill
Should waste less breath on tubs on Tower Hill.
Honour the Kremlin, boys, but now and then
Admit some signs of grace at Number 10.[1]

Once again he was the unofficial laureate of wardrooms and messes round the world. The circulation of *Less Nonsense* was far in excess of that of the weekly paper *Truth*, in which it first appeared; for instance, Commander L. K. A. Block, then navigator in HMS *Duke of York*, received a typed copy of it from his opposite number in HMS *Sheffield*. Professor D. L. Savory, MP, of Queen's College, Belfast, wrote of its being 'clandestinely passed from one group to another; it was so true, as well as brilliantly clever'.[2] APH met a Canadian whose copy of it came from a friend in Australia. Elsewhere, its reception was less cordial. Shop stewards at Short's works at Rochester threatened a protest strike and sent a telegram, denouncing the poem, to APH's fellow Wykehamist, Sir Stafford Cripps, Minister for Aircraft Production. In the House of Commons, another old Wykehamist, who was also a Marxist, D. N. Pritt, KC, MP for Hammersmith North, asked the Secretary of State for War whether he was aware that 'over two hundred copies of a piece of verse entitled "Less Nonsense", which is offensive to the Soviet Union and calculated to injure our friendship towards that country', were being circulated among units of a certain command. The Secretary of State for War, who was 'careful to express no opinion on the merits of the verses', promised to make inquiries 'in this matter'. APH drew the House's attention to the point that *Less Nonsense* was written 'not against Russia at all, but against certain British citizens who are never happy unless they are running down their own country'.

Privately, APH believed, but did not claim, that another of his topical poems, *Bring Back the Bells*, influenced the Government's decision that year to end the silence imposed on the belfries of England's parish churches. He was well pleased when Admiral Dunbar-Nasmith asked him to appeal 'in verse' to naval ratings on leave in London to look to their personal appearance. 'You have seen them yourself, overcoats wide open, slouching along. They bring discredit on the Service'. APH agreed to 'write something' on condition that his anonymity was preserved. 'Any lecture from me about personal tidiness might cause more laughter than loyalty.' His Dibdenesque *Jack Ashore* was therefore signed 'British Sailor'. It was distributed to naval establishments up and down the country.

> Cap flat-aback, too Jolly Jack,
>   You yaw about the street,
> And who would guess, to see your dress,
>   How well you rig the Fleet?
> You wouldn't show a foreign foe
>   A single yarn adrift:
> You'd never sail in half a gale
>   With half a topping lift.
> On every coast the Fleet can boast
>   Your rig is her renown:
> And Lord knows why you let it fly
>   At home in London Town.
> There isn't one would stint your fun
>   Safe back from storm or boarding:
> But fight or fling, you serve the King,
>   So set your sails according.

In the late summer of 1943 the Deputy Prime Minister, Clement Attlee, who was also Secretary of State for the Dominions, named

APH as one of three back-benchers comprising a goodwill mission to Newfoundland; the others, Sir Derrick Gunston, Bt. (Conservative), and Charles Ammon (Labour). Newfoundland's self-governing powers had been suspended in 1933. Since then the country had been run by Crown Commissioners. The war had given it a large measure of self-sufficiency. 'Our job', APH wrote, 'was to find out, informally, the facts of the situation, and the mind of the people.' Did they want an independent future or confederacy with Canada?

APH was shocked (his word) by finding that the parliament building at St John's no longer contained the furniture of Parliament. 'The Speaker's chair and the Bar of the House had been stored away in a loft.' As a consequence of meetings with local people he became a great admirer of the Newfoundlanders and a profound sympathiser with their problems. 'What charming folk they are! They are the best-tempered, the best-mannered people walking; politically maddening but the salt of the earth.' He noted how 'intensely English' they were. 'Their names are English still. The great go-getting, twanging continent next-door has not got the Newfoundlander yet',[3] an allusive jibe that may have seemed unworthy to readers of *Punch* in Grosvenor Square.

Typically, after several weeks' investigation with his colleagues – 'how we worked!' – he chose to stay behind in Labrador while they flew back to Newfoundland. 'I dislike going about in a gang, however friendly'. He was absent sixteen days, 'incurring displeasure'. He believed that the Government was not giving enough attention to 'this remote, extraordinary part of the British Commonwealth and Empire'. He wanted to see 'more of the human side of life in Labrador'. Returning to Newfoundland by sailing ship, he and the Newfoundland crew were fogbound 'in a tiny cove' for nine days, living on salt cod and seagulls. A nagging tooth inclined him to ponder the situation of toothache sufferers marooned in those remote parts by the winter snows. He was told of 'half a dozen men all looking for a doctor to "haul" a tooth'.

Before leaving Newfoundland, he wrote a 'pompous and enormous' report, 30,000 words of it, for the official masters in Whitehall. Having been bored on the outward flight across the Atlantic, with 'only the starboard wing to look at', he contrived a passage for Derrick Gunston and himself in HMS *Orwell*, one of the destroyers supplying the mid-ocean escort for HMS *Renown*, in which Winston

Churchill, with his wife and daughter, were returning to England after the Quebec Conference. The rendezvous with *Renown* was made the second day out.

'It was an exciting encounter – late on a dark and ugly afternoon, low, purple clouds, not a gleam of sun, driving rain and a dirty sea. Suddenly, converging through the rain, we saw two cruisers, and the *Renown*, with four destroyers about her. All were steaming at twenty-six knots; all were winking Morse at a fantastic rate. Perhaps I am a sentimental old thing, but I must say it stirred my soul to see that punctual meeting of the ships, the British Fleet defying the enemy in mid-Atlantic and carrying the great leader safely home. The speed of the evolution was astonishing'.[4]

Commander I. A. Scrymgeour-Wedderburn, RN (Retd), then a lieutenant in HMS *Orwell*, remembers APH's keenness to send a personal greeting to Churchill, and his doubt about the wisdom and propriety of doing so. 'Who knows', he asked himself, 'what periscope may read our salute?' He consulted *Orwell's* captain, Lieutenant-Commander J. M. Hodges, DSO, RN, 'himself no mean poet', about sending a signal in rhyme. The security problem was overcome by APH's suggestion that Churchill should be designated Ulysses, comparing the present voyage with that hero's adventurous return to Ithaca from Troy. Two questions momentarily defeated the classics scholar of Winchester and Oxford: had Ulysses a daughter, and what was the name of his son? 'Their lordships had failed to provide HMS *Orwell* with a classical dictionary'. Finally, a message was composed and flashed to *Renown*. It read:

'Return Ulysses soon to show the secrets of your splendid bow. Return and make all riddles plain to anxious Ithaca again. And you Penelope the true who have begun to wander too we're glad to meet you on the foam and hope to see you safely home'.

The signal was acknowledged; then silence. APH wondered if he had 'done the wrong thing', his worry for the next twenty-four hours. Then came word: 'A message for you from *Renown*.' He dashed up to the signal bridge. 'Ulysses and Penelope too return their compliments to you . . .' continuing through seven couplets, the last: 'To chide these simple lines be wary. They are the first attempt by Mary', added by Churchill himself. 'All very childish, no doubt', APH wrote afterwards, 'but could it have happened with Hitler or Stalin?'

'The trouble with h-h-Herbert is that h-he h-has no d-d-discipline.'

Sir Derrick Gunston's stammered comment stays in the recollection of Commander Wedderburn *apropos* APH's resolve to continue on passage in HMS *Orwell* to Scapa Flow from Lough Foyle, Londonderry, where she put in to refuel. His determination finally had to be undermined by a concocted message ordering him back to London forthwith.

In the correspondence awaiting his return was a reminder from the secretary of the Society of Authors that his subscription was 'somewhat in arrears'; in fact, nine years.

Back on the river, he missed 'the whales and icebergs' but there was much else to engage his interest; not least, the mustering of the ships and landing-craft for the coming invasion of Europe. He had acquired, proudly, another good conduct badge, and was a trifle put out when Churchill asked him: 'Have you been promoted – or vaccinated?' He thought the joke unworthy of his hero; it had been made to him by another member the day before. 'Sir', he said, as dismissively as he dared, 'you've been First Lord of the Admiralty. You must be familiar by now with the badges of Petty Officers of the Royal Navy', and turned aside.

In a minor blitz that spring, *Water Gipsy* made fast alongside Captain Scott's famous ship *Discovery*. A fire glow hung over Essex Street, where Methuen, his publishers, had their offices and stockrooms. With Seamen Atkins and Cheesman, APH went ashore to investigate. Water was rising fast in the basement store-room, where there were shelves full of books from floor to ceiling. He saw only one book of his, *Uncommon Law*; out of print. Rows of Belloc volumes invited rescue. He gathered an armful, lost his torch, and stumbled helplessly about in the darkness, the water level still rising. He was 'conscious of a slight unease'. It would have been sensible to forget the Belloc books; in deference to 'that great man' he held on to them. 'Where are you, Skip?' Seaman Atkins shouted from above, adding in a tone of good cheer: 'It's all right – firewatcher says whole lot's insured!' By the light of the seaman's torch he spotted a book by his *Punch* colleague, Anthony Armstrong, floating by. Insured or not, it was returned to its author some days later inscribed as having been salvaged 'with amazing bravery, and in preference to the works of certain other authors', by the crew of HMS *Water Gipsy* 'on night patrol'.

Unknown to the mass of Londoners, their lower river was crowded with ships preparing for the invasion of Europe. 'There have never been so many ships in London River before; there will never be so many ships in London River again. There were not enough berths in the river for all the ships. They anchored them in long lines down the middle of the lower reaches, in the Northfleet Hope, in Gravesend Reach, in Sea Reach – all the way. Looking down Sea Reach from Hole Haven, one saw an endless forest of ships – transports, hospital ships, landing ships, tankers, and barges. They lay quiet with their distinguishing flags and the pilots flags flying, waiting to go.'[5] *Water Gipsy* plodded stubbornly about her business as a unit of the Royal Naval Auxiliary Patrol, a humble assistant in the task of servicing the preparations for the great liberation drama about to be enacted across the Channel.

Then came the V1s, the flying bombs, the doodle-bugs. He logged one of the earliest arrivals: '0020. Fifth Mysterious Episode – white light moving target; 0030 something (plane or secret weapon) came over river from S. Great bombardment from all sides. Passed over us, came down N. and exploded. Cheesman thought he saw a parachute. Fred thought it was a Dornier 217. Activity continued all night. Explosions as late as 0745.' A few days after:

'One of the Things came roaring and glowing up from Tilbury towards us. We all waited on the bridge to see it go over. But, some way short of us, the monster's light went out and the engine stopped. "Boys," I yelled, "it's a by-election!" We all scrambled below and lay on our stomachs, expecting the worst. Nothing happened; and presently, incredulous, I heard the noise of an engine again. I clambered out on to the bridge, and there, astern of us now, was the Thing in full flight again, light and all, as if it had taken a good look at *Water Gipsy* and decided to go for bigger game. It roared away and came down about two miles off in the Barking area.'

From that time his 'by-election drill' became a feature of life in *Water Gipsy*. Every day a number of 'those fiendish contrivances' (APH) evaded the RAF fighter attacks, the anti-aircraft defences, the barrage balloons. Every citizen had his ears cocked for the warning throb in the sky. Nerves were strung up to a point at which 'the common sounds of the city set the mind alert – a car being started in the street below, a lorry ticking over, a vacuum cleaner next door; even the sound that certain types of refrigerator made. Conversation, work, continued, but each man knew what the other was thinking.'

When *Water Gipsy* was under orders, the clatter of her eighteen horse-power engines blotted out the sound of the Vis approaching. He compared his situation with that of the London bus drivers, enveloped in traffic noise. 'They just drove on, in peril always.' He thought of his friends in the theatre, on stage perhaps, hearing the dreaded 'cut-out' that heralded 'the Thing's' descent. Gertie Lawrence told him about Dame Lillian Braithwaite, playing in the long run of *Arsenic and Old Lace*. The daily takings were a matter of constant concern, whether they were up or down. Dame Lillian lived alone on a top floor. During the flying bomb raids she used her bathroom as a shelter, and often slept there. One morning her household help arrived looking *distrait*. 'Oh, dear,' she said, 'what a terrible night it's been!' 'Not at all,' said Dame Lillian. 'We were thirty pounds up.'

Domestic cares never lay heavily on APH. He admitted to 'fussing outrageously' when, during that stressful time, Jocelyn, his second daughter (then Mrs Anthony Lousada), waited at 12 Hammersmith Terrace for the event that made him the grandfather of twins. Every flying-bomb that seemed to be set for West London became for him an object of anxiety and of intense observation. He judged its course by *Water Gipsy*'s compass, making allowance for deflections caused by iron bridges and piers. He worked out intricate stop-watch calculations for estimating the distance of the explosions. 'The result of all this scientific work, as a rule, was that Hammersmith Terrace was destroyed three or four times every night.'

In his diary for 29 November 1943, Sir Alan Lascelles, private secretary to the King, complained that 'owing to the unexplained absence of A. P. Herbert', his place at lunch with the Belgian ambassador that day was 'switched'. He was made to sit between Lady Cunard and Mrs Corrigan, 'and wished myself elsewhere'. He wrote to APH: 'Just think what you missed'.

A request for a copy of *Less Nonsense* on notepaper headed TAC Headquarters, 21 Army Group was accompanied by the information that 'the weather is not too good but a very great number of Germans are being killed and otherwise "written off"'; signed B. L. Montgomery (15 July 1944). Two weeks later APH was invited to 'come over to Normandy' as the guest of the newly promoted field-marshal, 'for a night or two'. Air transport would be provided.

He did not expect to find Tactical Headquarters in a setting 'that would have been perfect for *A Midsummer Night's Dream*'. The Bois de Cerisy was a French Arden of 'tall trees reaching to the sun'. Three or four camouflaged caravans disposed about a clearing gave remarkably few signs of being the nerve-centre of a great military campaign. A tame rabbit loped among the bracken clumps. A canary was in full song in the field-marshal's caravan. 'It might have been a gipsy encampment.' APH's account of his visit in *Independent Member* emphasized the contrast between that sylvan scene and the destructive operations that were directed from it. As for his host, he saw him in a light that diminished the stature of his detractors.

A news item torn from *The Times* of 29 December 1944 is retained in APH's pocket diary for that year. Headed 'The Miraculous Hitler', it gives extracts from an article written by Goebbels, the Nazi Party's arch-propagandist, in the latest issue of *Das Reich*. 'If only the world knew how much the Führer's love extended beyond his own people towards the universe they would forswear their false God and turn to worship him, the greatest personality history has known', etc. Germany's new Jove was meanwhile hurling his thunderbolts of wrath, the V2 rockets, on London.

Further elaborate calculations with sextant and compass convinced APH that his home territory was in the direct line of attack from the launching sites in Holland. What is more, his prediction was uncomfortably accurate. On the thirtieth anniversary of his wedding at Bethnal Green a rocket fell three hundred yards from Hammersmith Terrace, on the river bank opposite. Number 12 not only lost its window-glass again, but this time the frames too.

Far away in a Japanese prisoner-of-war camp on Haroekoe, an island in the Moluccas, a disintegrated copy of *The Water Gipsies*, from a Chinese pirated edition, was being passed round, page by page, among the survivors, Dutch and British, of a ruthless system of forced labour. Of 2,000 men 650 had died. Dr F. R. Philps, now of Hailsham, Sussex, has written: 'Books were scarce with us. We spent a memorable day in 1944 reading *The Water Gipsies*, each man handing the page, when he had read it, to his neighbour, and so on through the camp. To me it represented an oasis of calm and decency in our sordid and troubled situation.' Unaware that APH knew of his existence, Dr Philps was surprised, and much touched, to receive, after his release, a letter from him asking: 'Is there anything I can do for you?'

The end of the war was near. Post-war rehabilitation was becoming a matter for bureaucratic concern. The Admiralty wanted to know: What was your occupation before the war? APH replied: 'Author and member of Parliament.' Briefly describe the character of your work. 'Good.' *Water Gipsy* was paid off in March 1945. Proud of his good conduct badges, her master said 'a sad farewell' to her last war-time crew, Tom Cheesman and Dan O'Connor, who were returning to their respective peacetime jobs of deep-sea fisherman and plumber.

A chance to go to sea after the years of confinement in so-called 'sheltered waters' could not be resisted. He agreed to sign on as mate in an MFV (Motor Fishing Vessel) that was being sent up to the Clyde for eventual delivery to the Far East on harbour service. Within a day or two of committing himself to that enterprise he received another invitation from his friend Montgomery, whose armies were sweeping across Germany towards the grand climax of the war. 'If I had gone I would have seen the surrender of the German generals.' He had given his word and would not make an excuse that in the circumstances might have been accepted. ' "Duty!" I said, poor fool, and off we went to Brightlingsea.'

An inordinately slow, uncomfortable trip at four knots up the east coast became more bearable when he was put in charge from Lowestoft onward. 'I was very proud to have a sea command under the Admiralty after five years on the river', the more so as war risks had not been entirely eliminated. German E-boats still ranged the North Sea. A look-out had to be kept for floating mines. In the 'rough and raging Wash' the vessel was reduced to one knot, 'rolling like a sinner in Hell'. At Cromer the order came from the signal station to return to Yarmouth. From there, on Admiralty instructions, the MFV was taken in tow to the Forth by a minesweeper bound for Scapa Flow.

The voyage over the remaining three hundred miles was a miserably uncomfortable one. After three weeks they put in at Leith. 'It was Sunday, and the pubs were shut.' They moved up to Grangemouth. 'It was Monday, and the pubs were shut.' When he was asked if he would carry on in command of his 'ridiculous charge' through the canal to the Clyde, he decided that he had more than kept his word, and that in future he could speak of tenacity as 'one of my major vices'.

He flew to Paris with the friend who signed his letter of invitation 'Monty'. The occasion was the field-marshal's investiture with the Grand Cross of the Legion of Honour by General de Gaulle. 'In the Champs Elysée the car could move no faster than my Motor Fishing Vessel. He could have walked for miles on the adoring heads.' The enormous crowd would not leave the British Embassy until 'Montee' had shown himself again and again on the balcony. *'Merci'*, he said at last. *'Et maintenant – allez-vous-en'* – his imperative tone leaving no doubt that he meant 'shove off'. It was conveyed to him that he had said 'the wrong thing'. He consulted APH. 'Alan, what should I have said? *Allez-vous-en* means go away, doesn't it?' 'Yes, sir.' 'Well, that's what they did. I think my French must be pretty good.'

He went on with the field-marshal to Luneberg Heath, where the act of surrender had been made by the Germans. In the guest's caravan, between flights over Hamburg and the Kiel Canal, he wrote his address to his Oxford University constituents in preparation for the general election of 1945. It confessed his sin in ignoring correspondence and not keeping in touch with Oxford. He hoped 'to be forgiven' in the light of the 'modest part' he had played 'in the great story of London River at war'. It was a long and discursive document and may not have been closely studied by every one of the thirty thousand voters who received it. He had a case to make against income tax that bore 'harshly on the artist and professional man.' He agreed that teachers 'can scarcely be paid too much'. He proposed to keep an eye on Buchman, 'this usurper of a noble name', and would 'continue to watch the *language* of Government departments'.

The general election was necessary, 'and with so much synthetic venom about the sooner the better'. He deplored 'the bitterness, the unfairness, the intolerance (of which the Yellow Books are a good example[6]) recently imparted into our public life. This is no time for intellectual arrogance or class warfare. Some of the Socialists seem to be bursting with the one and bent on the other.'

Parliament had no attraction for his host, who told him that there had been overtures to him from 'all the political parties'. APH believed that 'Monty' would have preferred a sequestered future as head of an Oxford college – 'with a garden'.

APH's demobilization at Chatham Barracks, where he had been 'kitted up' six years before, was the occasion of an hilarious comedy involving him in an embarrassing public performance with the indelicate object medically known as a 'specimen' glass. Finally, 'when I walked out in my "demob suit" with a gratuity[7] and a great envelope of papers to assist me back to civil life, I said goodbye with sadness to the Navy'.[8] It was a small but welcome consolation that he was free to go hatless again.

He was 'almost sorry' that he was returned to Parliament in the general election of 1945. Rightly or wrongly, he believed that the defeat of G. D. H. Cole, chairman of the Fabian Society, who – with C. R. Attlee as his chief sponsor – stood against him and Sir Arthur Salter at Oxford, was a reverse that the victorious Labour Party avenged by abolishing the university seats.

On 10 August he had a letter from Churchill. 'My dear A.P., I have been granted the privilege of sending in my Resignation Honours List.' The fallen leader hoped that APH would allow him to include his name among the recommendations for knighthoods.

He had 'thought twice' about standing for Parliament a second time. About the knighthood, he hesitated again, largely in deference to his wife, who had no interest in social advancement and especially not in being exalted above friends and neighbours. He did not want to be regarded as 'a literary knight', and neither was he impressed by the official announcement that he was being rewarded for 'political and public services'. He can have had no doubt about the widespread approval of the honour bestowed on him.

'Congratulations to the sanest man in England. – Karsavina.' The *prima ballerina*'s sentiment was echoed in the 'rejoicings' of Rose Macaulay; in the avowed satisfaction of Sir Robert Vansittart, late of the Foreign Office; in the 'great pleasure' of the Printer of *Punch*; in the goodwill messages showered on him by unknown admirers from near and far. Welcome reassurance came from Sir Richard Livingstone, writing from The President's Lodgings, Corpus Christi College, Oxford: 'The honour will give pleasure to many in the University besides your parliamentary supporters' (14 August 1945). To take a slight liberty with Pope's well-known line, he gained a title but lost no friend.

He did not like the prospect of losing his public identity in 'Sir Alan'. Garter Principal King-at-Arms set his mind at rest. 'You can call yourself "Sir A. P. Herbert" if you wish.'

NOTES ON CHAPTER 18

1   Included in the *New Oxford Book of English Verse:* ed. P. A. Larkin, MA.
2   Field-Marshal Lord Wavell wrote a ballad about the Second Front clamour.
    Hearing it read at a dinner-party at Dalmeny in 1943, Professor Dover Wilson,
    the Shakespearean scholar, thought it 'highly entertaining and that it was by
    A. P. Herbert'.
3   *Punch*, 17 November 1943.
4   *Life and Times of A.P.H.*
5   A. P. Herbert: *Independent Member.*
6   Presumably a reference to the yellow-jacketed publications of the Left Book
    Club.
7   £50.
8   A. P. Herbert: *Independent Member.*

19

The Hampden of Hammersmith

At 55, in a post-war world in which the victory sign of Churchill had been replaced by the scowl of Demos, APH hoped for rather than dreamed of high success in the theatre as the crown of his professional career. He had written nothing for the stage during the war, and said that he 'could not see how a member of Parliament could write a novel worth reading', in view of the incessant demands on his time and attention.

Cochran wrote to him on 5 July 1945: 'At last the opportunity has come for me to do a musical play, if I can get a libretto which I think is worth while, and you are the only person, I believe, who can supply me with what I want.' What he wanted was 'a thoroughly English play, with the past, present and future of our people specifically in mind'. He wished APH to understand that he would not be asked 'to write one line without your being paid a reasonable sum in advance'. The show Cochran had in mind was to be 'your, and my, *chef d'oeuvre*'.

In a follow-up letter Cochran discussed the possibility of William Walton writing the music. 'I should like to make a big effort to get him.' *En passant*, 'Evelyn [his wife] and I were tickled to death that you have been honoured. You should have had it for the Divorce Bill' (15 August). Still undecided about a composer, he wrote again: 'As to Walton, I think it is a question whether you and he can work together. I think he might be "tuney". I am keen on getting somebody new to opera, musical comedy, or whatever you like to call it, and I think my second choice would be Eric Coates, who is decidedly tuneful. Benjamin Britten, having given a new start to Opera in English with something very heavy,[1] why shouldn't it be followed by something light?' He reminded APH that 'Donizetti, Offenbach, and even Puccini, wrote some tuneful scores to amusing stories, to say nothing of Rossini. Anyway,' he concluded, 'my main wish is that you should be fancy-free' (14 September 1945).

'The surge of Socialism into the House of Commons was something to see.' APH was referring to the Parliament that assembled in the autumn of 1945. Its tone was voiced by a prosperous Socialist KC, MP, Hartley Shawcross, who in a moment of reckless euphoria announced: 'We are the masters now.' The noble impatience of the best Radical thought was overwhelmed by the ignoble impetuosity of the massed new supporters of the victorious Government. They set the House in a roar by responding with the 'Red Flag' when Churchill's name was invoked. They scribbled graffiti where none was seen before. They sneered at Opposition speakers and jeered at APH, the Independent, when in a debate on a Supplies and Services Bill he declared himself non-partisan. He observed 'their friends and relations' crowding into the precincts for tea and gallery tickets. 'Arrogance, I am sorry to say, remained. There was such a *concerto* of nastiness and hate and imbecile yelling, that I thanked God, many times, that I was an Independent and could be silent without disloyalty.'

His political temper corresponded with the 'animated moderation' of Bagehot, for whom it was the clue, 'in a certain sense, to England's success in the world'. For APH there was no virtue in the assumption that all established institutions are ripe for demolition, and little in exaggerated postures of any kind. In that scene of embittered ascendancy he stood for the civilized man who has a classicist's respect for balance and proportion, and a humanist's disinclination to believe that his opponents are unregenerate. It pleased him to record that later 'there was a mellowing of manners', and that 'even compliments' were exchanged across the floor of the House. He made friends among the Labour men but 'it took longer than in my first Parliament'.

The first post-war Government was necessarily committed to an exceptional legislative programme. Private Members' time was once more at risk from a largely unheeding administration preoccupied with massive reconstruction measures. In rising to its defence again, APH secured the support of such parliamentary stalwarts as Churchill, Eden, and Lord Winterton, 'the father of the House'. He was determined that the several hundred newcomers to Westminster should be made aware of the significance of private members' time in the history of Parliament and of free opinion. Important legislation had reached the Statute Book by the exercise of the private members' prerogative; he instanced, in particular,

Samuel Plimsoll's Act of 1876, with all that it implied for the safety of those going down to the sea in merchant ships.

With Olympian detachment from other demands on his time and services, he prepared a cluster of Bills dealing with a variety of proposed enactments, among them the abolition of the decree *nisi*; Sunday entertainments; legal aid for the poor; a fairer voting system; aerial advertising; betting reform; eleven Bills in all, each fully drafted with the usual Explanatory Memorandum (or Preamble), and an appended array of clauses and sub-clauses. It was a task obviously involving intensive thought and labour that might have been profitably employed on the new 'musical' that he was to write for Cochran. But a parliamentary right was under threat, and his private interest was subordinate to the need for challenging the 'despotic power' (his words) that would trample it under.

His melodramatic gesture in flinging the bundle of Bills on to the floor of the House during his speech of protest roused no excitement. Instead, there was a disconcerting silence, relieved by friendly words from Herbert Morrison, then Lord President of the Council: 'A very interesting, witty, eloquent, and quite relevant speech.'

The battle for private members' time was to be renewed through several further sessions before it was restored to the parliamentary calendar. The climax counted as one more of the Hammersmith Hampden's tangential victories as a champion of English liberties.

On 13 January 1946, the *New York Herald-Tribune* published his valedictory lines to the American soldiers departing from England's shores after war service in Europe. 'This poem has been printed po on postcards and mailed to thousands of Americans. Written by England's famed author and member of Parliament, A. P. Herbert, it first appeared in the London *Sunday Graphic*.'

GOOD-BYE, GI[2]

Good-bye, GI – Good-bye, big-hearted Joe.
We're glad you came. We hope you're sad to go.
Say what you can for this old-fashioned isle,
And when you can't – well, say it with a smile.

Good-bye, GI – and, now you know the way,
Come back and see us in a brighter day,
When England's free, and Scotch is cheap but strong,
And you can bring your pretty wives along.

Good-bye, GI; don't leave us quite alone,
Somewhere in England we must write a stone:
'Here Britain was invaded by the Yanks',
And under that a big and brilliant 'Thanks'.

Cochran's desire for 'a thoroughly English' show suggested that
he still had faith in the *Cavalcade* formula that had made money for
him in the early thirties. APH, who had his own fortunes to repair
after the long interruption of his earning capacity, 'worked like a
madman' on the 'book' and lyrics for 'a musical show' set in the
Palace of Westminster, which had been the scene of his pre-war
Streamline burlesque of Gilbert and Sullivan.

The new 'musical' was to be called *Big Ben*; and APH seemed to
take a mildly perverse pleasure in recalling that 'feeble old Gilbert'
in *Iolanthe* 'never got beyond Palace Yard'. For *Big Ben*, he devised
episodes on the Terrace and in the Chamber. His legal clash with
the Kitchen Committee ten years before gave him qualms about the
privilege question. They merged into alarm when, during the dress
rehearsal, Cochran suddenly said: 'My God! I've forgotten to send
the script to the Lord Chamberlain!' APH said: 'My blood ran cold.'
Forty-eight hours' suspense was ended, 'to the great relief of our
feelings', when the script was returned with only a minor dialogue
excision. In the debate on the Censorship of Plays (Repeal) Bill
four years later he was a strong upholder of the office and powers
of the Lord Chamberlain.

Cochran had decided that Vivian Ellis should be his composer for
Big Ben. The rightness of his choice was confirmed by the reception
given to the show on its protracted opening tour of the provinces,
during which Cochran had to battle with his worsening infirmities,
the problem of making money out of small theatres, and the
temperaments of certain members of the cast. 'Don't tell anybody',
he bade APH, writing from the Caledonian Hotel, Edinburgh,
'but I have had a little recurrence of the old trouble' (25 May 1940).
As for the temperaments, 'I wouldn't have remained in the business
all these years if I didn't feel capable of coping with them'.

Big Ben opened at the Adelphi Theatre, London, on 17 July 1946,
one of those theatrical occasions customarily evoking the flashy
adjective 'brilliant'. Except for Cochran, who in a shakily pencilled
note addressing APH as 'My dear, kind friend', confided that he
was not well enough to be present, 'everybody' was there, including

Winston Churchill, 'very sleepy' (APH), and Field Marshal Montgomery. The Establishment prestige that *Cavalcade* had brought
Cochran was renewed and, it seemed, enhanced. Allegedly it was
the first time that members of the royal family attended an opening
night. They saw a show that artfully combined the best of both
political worlds, with a general election in the first act, and a
Labour heroine married to a Tory. By APH's personal invitation,
the Prime Minister and some of his Cabinet were in the stalls,
highly appreciative of his 'Wheels of the World' song but showing
no disposition to adopt it in place of the official dirge of the Labour
Party, which Shaw said might have been composed as a funeral
march for a fried eel.

> March, brothers, march – ever freer and faster!
>   We are the bridge, and the ship, and the plough!
> We are the engine, the gun, and the steeple,
> We are the voice and the might of the People –
> Left, Right, Left – the bully must bow.
> We are the makers. We must be master,
>   For we are the Wheels of the World.
> Wheels of the World, roll on to glory,
>   Carry mankind to a nobler day.
> Wheels of the World, roar a new story –
>   Carry us all on the one good way.
> Over the frontiers, over the seas,
>   When the bad old flags have gone,
> The Banner of Man shall ride on the breeze!
>   Wheels of the World, roll on!

Perhaps in reaction from recent unseemly demonstrations in the
Commons, a Tory ex-Minister was seen to be in tears as the curtain
fell on the final scene in which the entire company stood gazing
raptly up at Big Ben chiming the midnight hour.

As the last of a succession of curtain calls was taken, APH,
escorted by Vivian Ellis, emerged from the wings to explain
Cochran's absence. Cochran had counselled him: 'When you
return thanks for me you might tell the audience that I am laid
up – nothing very alarming.' He hoped that APH would 'kill the
report' that he had been ordered to rest 'by saying that I was at
every rehearsal this week'. He added: 'God bless you. Many, many
thanks for your lovely play and all you have done to help to get it

to tonight.' Within the next few days he was hurried off to the London Clinic for a grim kidney operation.

The pick of APH's lyrics was considered to be his mildly satirical defence of the Upper House, sung by Eric Fort as Lord Lavender:

> We don't represent anybody, it's true,
>   But that's not a thing to regret:
> We can say what we think – and I know one or two
>   Who've never said anything yet.
> While the Commons must bray like an ass every day
>   To appease their electoral hordes,
> We don't say a thing till we've something to say –
>   There's a lot to be said for the Lords.
>
>   · · · · ·
>
> From father to son our high offices run:
>   What a sensible way to proceed!
> It's not any old horse you support on the course –
>   You go for a creature with breed.
> I'd very much rather succeed a good father,
>   Who wore a top hat and a sword,
> Than be chosen by masses of ignorant asses –
>   There's a lot to be said for a Lord.
>
>   · · · · ·

'It's getting round that funny things are said on the stage but not heard', Cochran told APH in a letter from his sickbed. Peter Fleming had complained about the 'poor diction', so had an old friend, Pulvermacher, of the *Daily Telegraph*. 'He wrote to me to the same effect about Carole [Lynn] and others of the cast. Please jog them up every time you see them.' He regretted that, having begun work on the production, 'God denied me the strength to carry it through'. And, as a postscript: 'Please tell the boys and girls again and again that unless your words are heard their looks and acting don't count enough.'

During its first three months, *Big Ben* took an average of £4,000 a week at the box office. Running costs were high, and there was to be no fortune for Cochran. He wrote to APH on 6 August 1946: 'I wish I could hear of more people like Rab who cried (uncharacteristically) all through. I visualised people streaming out of the theatre with tears in their eyes after the finale. Alas, Stewart, my manager, tells me that the majority grab their hats and cloaks and are out of the theatre before the curtain is down. If that is the case, I fear we must look on the present good box office as a lucky flash in the pan.' He was 'beginning to feel alive' after his surgical ordeal, and his main worry was his wife's health. He confided in APH: 'She has lived through a nightmare and wrings my heart whenever I see her. It is tragic that a woman should centre her life in the being of one man and such a man! My only ambition now is to give her some happiness and peace for the rest of her life. I can't see the road clear.'

In a formal statement dealing with events at that time, drafted for possible affidavit use, APH recalled that 'C.B.C. was old and infirm and worried about his position in old age and his widow's, if he died. We knew that his "finances" were shaky. Like Vivian Ellis, I felt a deep respect and affection for him. I think we were willing to do anything for the old man.' With the co-operation of Chappells, the music publishers, Ellis and APH conceded certain subsidiary rights in *Big Ben* and other works to Cochran through the Performing Right Society. Their gesture of friendship was to have a sequel of unhappy legalistic complications.

On a hot August afternoon, APH and Ellis sat beside Cochran's bed at the Clinic. He was still weak and in pain. To their astonishment, he said: 'I want you two to write me another play.'

The weekly editorial dinner in Bouverie Street, that for so long made Wednesday a day of obligation for APH, had been replaced by a lunch-time repast. Quite often he prefaced it by a sherry session at El Vino in Fleet Street, with Ivor Brown from the *Observer* and James Bone and Gerard Fay from the London office of the then *Manchester Guardian*, close by. In Bouverie Street, he was an elder of the Table to the newcomers in the post-war swim. They were heralds of change whose responses had been quickened by ITMA and other radio incursions into the domain of the comic, and by the contagious satire of the *New Yorker*. They cried down the importance of the long-dominant political cartoon, and disclaimed the wit that was class-conscious at the expense of the poor and humble. 'Short-sighted old lady' was not a figure of fun to them; and discouragement awaited those comic artists who fancied that 'hen-pecked husbands' and 'late revellers' were an inexhaustible source of humorous inspiration.

APH was critical of the new generation of *Punch* artists who, it seemed to him, could only draw figures 'facing west', who worked in angles rather than curves, who appeared to him to despise the need for apprenticeship to drawing. Their nihilistic style impelled him to ask:

> What is the matter with the comic draftsmen?
> They do not seem to like the human race.
> They may be funny; they may be good craftsmen,
> But can't they draw an ordinary face?

'The trouble is, public standards and taste have gone down' H. M. Bateman wrote to him. 'The young artists mostly won't study. They adopt a few hackneyed tricks to hang their weak jokes on. It is a sort of standardisation – a result of the Socialist State.'

APH applied his astringent logic to the cartoonists who depicted public men with invented physical deformities. Supposing a political gossip-writer wrote of a Leader of the Opposition as 'pot-bellied and long-nosed' when he was neither, the legal pundits would dismiss it as 'vulgar abuse' and non-actionable. They had even less to say to the victims of the cartoonists' distortions. He knew 'four different statesmen' who had been 'fitted with funny noses that grew longer every month'. To his sardonic amusement, they were identifiable only by name tags.

> Our ancestors who also drew for money,
> Did not see man so ugly or so mean;
> Perhaps they weren't so very, very funny,
> But they were mirrors of the human scene.
> They did not only labour for derision;
> Old folk were gracious and the young were fine.
> At all events, we knew with some precision
> What men were like in 1869.

His initials, as familiar to *Punch* readers as the archetypal nose on the front cover, stood for the comic spirit harnessed to sanity and the public good. His maturity of opinion, even in his more eccentric judgments, offset the undergraduate attitudes that were characteristic of much that appeared in the paper between the wars, e.g. 'that distressing page entitled *Charivaria*.[3] As a contributor under contract, he was sure of his £50 a week; less sure of the extra benefit from the arrangement with Seaman in 1924 by which he was paid 'at our usual rate' for additional material supplied. It had brought his basic earnings up to £3,000 a year. Now he was running into a period in which his 'additional material' would often be rejected. A freshening wind was blowing down Bouverie Street, bearing rumours of editorial superannuations, policy revisions, new directions, new faces. The circulation of *Punch*, inflated by the organized idleness that is a large part of modern war, was falling back to a more realistic level, with adverse effects on advertising revenues.

APH held on doggedly to his participation in the outings and special dinners with which some of the editorial men and chief contributors occasionally regaled themselves before and after the war. On those convivial occasions, including the Christmas dinners to which wives were invited, he appointed himself master of ceremonies as if by right, not from a sense of self-importance; rather from a naïve belief in his ability to induce others to enter into any project that appealed to him, trivial or otherwise, with an enjoyment matching his own.

He was one of seven members of the Table who, in the late forties, crossed the Channel on a gourmets' outing to Le Cygne, a Michelin Guide-starred eating-place between Dieppe and Rouen. As Humphrey Ellis and Bernard Hollowood remember, APH was in his element, assuming from the start that he was the unanimously approved overlord of the proceedings. Within minutes of stepping on board the Channel ferry he was on the bridge, exchanging nautical talk with the captain. At Le Cygne, he introduced E. V. Knox to the proprietor with a sweeping gesture and the announcement: 'Voila, M. Knox – er – grand redacteur – du magasin – no, dammit – journal – Poonch.' The morning after, he was the first afoot, the others 'nursing hangovers in varying stages of collapse'. Consulting local maps but not his companions, he re-routed the return journey to Dieppe in order to call on 'a grande dame of his acquaintance', who received them in her 'formidably elegant salon' where, again quoting Humphrey Ellis, they 'sat miserably erect on gilded chairs', drinking 'an unsuitable liqueur'. Their unease was accentuated by a feeling that they were unwanted visitors, that APH had summarily imposed himself and them on the hostess.

Cochran wrote to tell him that he was 'dead keen on the Victorian light opera', and sketched out a cast in an invalid's hand. 'For the leading soprano I should prefer a more mature woman than Carole

Lynn or Lizbeth Webb. The others would depend on the characters you write. A comedian who can sing well would be useful. I have one in mind. I have also a robust woman who would make a big hit in the right part. She is jolly looking, a bit common, and Welsh. She can look smart if necessary.' He urged the avoidance of crinolines: 'They're costly and take up too much room'. He would like 'an excuse' for a good party scene, 'with a rollicking polka'. And if APH could also 'find an excuse to go to Trouville for one scene, it would make a nice change'. He stressed the importance of 'a good chorus and orchestra'.

Victorian *Punch* was a prime reference source for APH as the writer of the 'book' of the new Cochran show which, in draft, was given three different titles before *Bless the Bride* became the final choice. Thematically, it followed the fortunes of an English family during the Franco-Prussian war of 1870. In *Punch* APH found 'the whole sweet scene; there was everybody's dress in detail; there was the Archdeacon in his gaiters playing croquet with the girls. Du Maurier's tall young ladies were perhaps not very sexy; but they are good to look at and are recognizable human beings'.[4]

Putting words to music was 'a fascinating but tricky task. You are confined not only by the tune but by the character of each note, and the speed and spacing of all of them – quavers, crotchets, long notes, dotted notes. The thing you most want to say may not fit in anywhere.' Words, he insisted, must have point and sense, 'even in a sentimental song. There must be strong rhymes, and on the high notes good singable vowels.'

Discussing his collaboration with Vivian Ellis in *Bless the Bride*, he said: 'I think we earned our money.' Band calls, when producer, cast, composer and librettist assembled to hear the orchestral part of the production, were a 'battle of words'. Sitting at the back of the stalls, APH would call out with more than a hint of sarcasm in his tone:'I can hear some of my lines quite well.' Vivian Ellis remembers 'the heart-breaks of chorus auditions'. APH, 'ever warm-hearted, would have liked to engage all who came'.

After reading APH's *Bless the Bride* scenario, Cochran wrote: 'The atmosphere is delightful.' Regarding the cast, he 'wouldn't despair' of finding a French actor who could sing well in English. 'We must think of diction.' Going on to consider, in a long, instructive letter, other casting possibilities: 'Trefor Jones is romantic and cannot be comic. Let's face it. Although he is a delightful singer, his personality, so far from appealing to our audiences [*Big Ben*] has, from the commencement in Manchester, right through to London, been generally disliked. Some find him an unsympathetic personality. *I don't*.[5] Cochran insisted: 'A Sid Field must be found. I have a "possible" in mind.' Concerning his health, he was 'getting along fairly well', but was finding that 'it takes longer than I expected to get properly on my feet'. He hoped that APH, who was on holiday at the Ferryboat Inn, Helford Passage, near Falmouth, was 'having a good time and lots of lovely lobsters' (29 August 1946).

Jean Nicol, the 'tiny and twinkling' young public relations officer of the Savoy Hotel, has told in a book[6] that, on first meeting APH, during the run of *Big Ben*, she exclaimed in a fluster: 'My grandmother used to read *The Water Gipsies* every six months!' His response was: 'I could do with a little less of the grandmother', and took her aboard *Water Gipsy* for a cocktail. When he had no time for his Turkish Bath in Northumberland Avenue, he arranged with her to borrow a Savoy bathroom, where he could luxuriate in his own steam. She forgot that she had lent him the bathroom key when, one evening, she and her husband, Derek Tangye, entertained 'some important Americans' in a suite at the hotel. While the drinks were going round a door opened, filling the room with a billowing cloud of rose-geranium scented steam, from which APH emerged in a bath-towel, his hair 'shampooed to a downy fluff'. He stood blinking at the astonished guests, then retired, mumuring: 'The Tangyes use a most superior brand of soap.'

It was true that he had a preference for being seen with presentable young women rather than with their grandmothers, but not as a maudlin middle-aged man in search of his youth. He formed sentimental attachments that never led to emotional entanglements; his affection was given with reserve. Jean Nicol made just about the truest statement on his relationship with both sexes: 'He was the ideal companion.' His concern to avoid suspicion of moral obliquity was comically illustrated when, sleeping late after an overnight party, he tried to conceal from his wife, who never shared his liking for bohemian revels, a pair of pink frilly garters on his bedside table. His hostess at the party, Naomi Royde-Smith (Mrs Ernest Milton), had noticed that his silk socks were falling over his shoe-tops. 'You can't go through the evening like that', she told him, and lent him the garters. As described by his wife, his fumbling concern to avert misunderstanding was as funny as an incident in French farce.

Big Ben came off towards the end of 1946, after 172 performances that showed a small production loss. In default of unanimous critical acclaim, he retained in his files two letters, one from the spokesman of the Gallery First Nighters' Club, who thought *Big Ben* 'one of the most brilliant productions' seen in the West End for some time, and who assured him: 'You are needed in the Theatre'; the other from the then editor of the *Daily Express*, Arthur Christiansen, for whom *Big Ben* seems to have been the theatrical experience of a lifetime. APH's royalty cheques from the production showed no more than a modest return on his capital expenditure of mental effort and energy.

In 1946 his parliamentary expenses, not onerous compared with those of members for territorial constituencies, were more than covered by the latest rise in MPs' pay to £1,000 a year. Not because the food was poor, he seldom had guests to lunch or dinner at the House; they inhibited his freedom of movement among colleagues who were not to be met collectively elsewhere. John Pudney, his son-in-law, would have liked to be invited; he never was.

APH received lecture agency offers of well-paid engagements but he rarely accepted them, preferring to earn fees as an after-dinner speaker, a role in which he had long since attained professional status. At the annual banquet of the National Paint Federation, at Grosvenor House, London, in November 1946, he delivered a speech consisting of sixty-five rhyming couplets, mostly memorized; a remarkable performance. To be flattered with eighteenth-century wit and delicacy, to be reminded that their business was with Watteau as well as with Welfare State windows and front doors, may have been a new experience for his audience. Their applause was loud enough to be heartfelt.

> . . . though my knowledge, I repeat, is faint,
> It must be fun to manufacture paint.
> Who else does nothing but distribute charm
> Gives so much pleasure, does so little harm?
> (You're not responsible, I think, for those
> Who paint their faces and – my hat! – their toes.)
> Let's praise the painter too, who toils all day,
> Makes our home beautiful and goes away,
> Happy, I hope, as painters ought to be,
> For they do something that the world can see.
> And here's a fact that never should be hid:
> House painting came before the houses did.

Primitive man, who could not build at all,
Could paint good pictures on his cavern wall.
(And, by the way, if present trends remain,
We'll soon be living in the caves again.
But when we dwell in holes beneath the hill
You folk at least will do some business still.)
Meanwhile, I wish that I could set you free
To make old England what she ought to be.
There should be much more colour in this Isle;
The streets should glitter and the houses smile.
Look at old London, drabber every day:
How you could serve her if you had your way!

. . . . .

So to the end, kind folks, I now advance.
Pray charge your glasses – if you have the chance.
The Toast is you – and those who work with you
To bring more colour to the people's view.
To make more gay the houses of the town –
And, by the way, to stop them falling down!
Rise then, good people – even if you fall.
Let there be colour – I salute you all.

APH was named one of the 'neo-Tories' by George Orwell, writing on current forms of nationalism in the autumn 1946 issue of an intellectually impressive, obscure, and short-lived new journal called *Polemic*. Orwell's new breed of Tory was a super-bigot, identifying himself 'with a single nation, or other unit, placing it beyond good or evil, and recognising only the duty of advancing its interests'. Others on Orwell's charge-sheet were G. M. Young, Lord Elton, Kenneth Pickthorn and the Tory Reform Committee, with T. S. Eliot, Wyndham Lewis, Evelyn Waugh and Hugh Kingsmill listed as suspicious characters. Kinsgmill dismissed a 'nonsensical charge' with the observation that Orwell was 'disgusted with all existing parties . . . but still involved in the collective mania of the age, and determined to implicate everyone else in his own predicament'.[7]

APH would have rejected the Tory affiliation, though his inclinations were with the Right. Essentially he remained an Independent, whose chief purpose in Parliament was to ensure as respectful a hearing for the voice of reason as for *Land of Hope and Glory*.

NOTES ON CHAPTER 19

1   *Peter Grimes.*
2   A recollection, possibly, of *Good-bye, Australians*, published in *Punch* just after the First World War.
3   Harold Nicolson: *The English Sense of Humour* (1946).
4   A. P. Herbert: Unpublished article.
5   Neither did I, who enjoyed his friendship.—R.P.
6   Jean Nicol: *Meet Me at the Savoy* (1955).
7   Hugh Kingsmill: *The Progress of a Biographer* (1949).

20

His Last 'Who Goes Home?'

Rising to speak in the House of Commons during the fuel crisis of 1947, APH 'could not miss the opportunity of attacking on behalf of thousands of citizens the principle of summer time'. Readers of *Punch* had long been aware of his objection to it; 'single or double', to him 'summer time' was an abomination of the law, 'the most frightful confession of weakness of which the human race has ever been guilty'. Moreover, it had been arbitrarily inflicted on many who, like him, had no use for it.

His conviction was deep and abiding. As always, he had a firm grasp of his case. His research had sent him back to 1884, when there were thirteen different meridian lines of longitude. In that year a Washington conference of 'the assembled seafarers of the world' recommended that Greenwich should be the prime meridian, superseding all others; in APH's view, 'a cosmic compliment, a universal trust', a matter for patriotic pride. 'There are too few of us who realize what a bright and enduring honour it is that the navigators of all nations should reckon their time and fix their position by reference to an invisible line through a London suburb.'[1]

Nor was he being facetious in asking why it was 'not possible for us to get up an hour earlier', instead of 'mucking about with the clock'. He suggested that 'it would be the simplest thing in the world for the Government to say that all Government offices would begin work an hour earlier', with the reasonable expectation that industry would follow suit. It was all of a piece with his mission to invigorate a timorous society that bowed to the powers that be as grass to the harrow.

Shivering in his rooms at St James's Court, Cochran viewed with misgivings the outlook for *Bless the Bride*, due to open at the Adelphi Theatre, London, in April. 'If writing is illegible', he told APH in a scrawl, 'you must put it down to the fuel restrictions.' Official regulation of lighting and heating in public places had 'a frightening aspect'. His letter went at some length into the problems of theatre management and production in the adverse conditions then prevailing.

He wrote again on 8 March 1947, informative as before about current theatre economics. A Government order that matinées should start at 4 p.m., 'or later', seriously prejudiced a position in which receipts from them meant the difference between profit and loss. Without matinées, 'production becomes an economic impossibility. Theatre burdens are already excessive.' He rejoiced to see that APH had denounced the iniquity of entertainment tax in yet 'another admirable letter to *The Times*'.

Bless the Bride, opening at the Adelphi Theatre on 26 April 1947, ran for two and a quarter years, Cochran's greatest success with a 'musical', and for APH the source of 'an accretion of cash' beyond anything that had come to him from the ten productions in which he had previously collaborated. On his income for 1949–50 he paid £8,383 in tax. At last he could look Noël Coward and Ivor Novello in the eye, and regard with equanimity the West End advent of two raucously high-spirited productions from the New York stage, *Oklahoma* and *Annie Get Your Gun*. 'By 1948', Vivian Ellis recalled in his autobiography, *I'm on a See-Saw*, 'we were all floating on a cloud with a silver lining.' After a hesitant start, advance bookings at the Adelphi rose to more than £5,000 a week.

Three 'numbers' in the show were successful with the public, their popularity vastly extended by the dance bands and broadcasting. 'They are still singing our songs', APH proudly noted twenty years later. He had convinced himself that one of them, 'This is my lovely day', would be sung 'long after the last Beatles number is dead'. When in 1949 Cochran went to Buckingham Palace to be knighted by George VI, the Coldstream Guards' band in the forecourt played 'Selections from *Bless the Bride*' as one of the compliments of the day. Cochran, to whom it pleased APH to defer as 'the Master', had done more for the theatre than produce revues and musical comedies. He had brought the plays of Ibsen and Rostand, Brieux and Pirandello, O'Neill and O'Casey, before English audiences.

In the first weeks of *Bless the Bride*, APH professed to be 'worried about the acoustics' at the Adelphi Theatre. He was receiving letters with a monotonously common theme: 'We loved the show – what we could hear of it.' I sat with him in different parts of the house during five successive performances, by the last of which we concluded that seat-holders in the back rows of the stalls were not getting their money's worth of his lines and lyrics or of Vivian Ellis's music. It was Laurence Irving's experience, communicated to me perhaps not more than half seriously later, that 'APH never tired of hearing his musical shows, and expected his friends not to tire of them either'. It may therefore have been that those serial attendances of ours were 'nothing scientific'. After my fifth visit to the Adelphi I felt as one might from over-indulgence in the confectionery department at Harrods.

Like so much that APH did, not only in the theatre, *Bless the Bride* strengthened one's conviction that he had opted for today's acclaim rather than tomorrow's remembrance. His imagination took in more than it gave out. It was not subject to eruptive passions or tormenting fantasies. Beset by no neurosis more disabling than an underlying anxiety about his health, he was comparatively free in mind and will to cultivate the art of being 'a miscellaneous person', his self-ascription in later years. He was hardly asserting affinity with Renaissance man. A claim to it might not unjustly be made for him.

Not even 'the Master' could prevail on him to sign a contract at the expense of whatever public cause he had on hand; usually more than one. Life was real, but not all that earnest; and the spirit of community service implanted in him as an undergraduate in the 'mean streets' of Arthur Morrison's tales had become a justifying corollary of less noble endeavours. He counterpointed the frivolities of musical comedy by the solemnities of the Supreme Court Committee on Practice and Procedures on which he served under Sir Raymond Evershed; the committee was inquiring into the cost of litigation, a subject that APH had tried to bring before Parliament in his first year there. He was chairman of the Literary Sub-Committee of the XIVth Olympiad, London, 1948. Besides helping to judge 'the literary compositions of twenty-nine nations in their own languages', he wrote a poem, *Let Us Be Glad*, as part of the grand finale of the Games at Wembley. It was sung to the tune of *A Londonderry Air* by the massed choirs, conducted by Malcolm Sargent. Lord Burghley wrote to thank him: 'I have never seen so many tough old gentlemen unashamedly weeping!' He had accepted an invitation to serve on the 'large and distinguished' Council of the

Festival of Britain, 1951, and considered himself an 'exceptionally faithful' member of it.

Those were supernumary commitments; he was already a member of the Thames Conservancy Board, a trustee of the National Maritime Museum at Greenwich; president of the Inland Waterways Association; a vice-president of The Pedestrians' Association for Road Safety. That was by no means the sum of his voluntary efforts; sufficient assurance, though, that he had qualified for the approval, perhaps at last the respect, of that older Wykehamist generation for whom the appearance of his name 'in lights' in the Strand was no shining compliment to their Alma Mater. He was never received *Ad portas* by the College, the ceremony with which it honours its famous alumni.

He saluted, in *Independent Member*, 'the great army of citizens who in this age of "something for nothing" think only to be of service to the people': members of royal commissions, advisory councils, committees of inquiry. He suggested that it would be 'a good thing' if they went on token strike – 'say, for one week'. He imagined them marching through London with bands and banners. 'It would be no mean procession', a great parade of 'unpaid, incorruptible, independent amateurs', representatives of 'a fine old English thing', voluntary public service.

His commendation of members of royal commissions, 'who receive not a penny' for their often long-extended labours, did not imply approval of their function. It provoked him to satirical utterance in verse:

> I saw an old man in the Park:
>   I asked the old man why
> He watched the couples after dark;
>   He made this strange reply:
> 'I am the Royal Commission on Kissing,
>   Appointed by Gladstone in '74.
> The rest of my colleagues are buried or missing;
>   Our Minutes were lost in the last Great War.
> But still I'm a Royal Commission,
>   My task I intend to see through,
> Though I know as an old politician
>   Nothing will be done if I do.'

He used the verse as preface to his critical study of royal commissions issued under the imprint of the Institute of Economic Affairs.

'Had it included graphs and tables and been written in a heavy style it would have been accepted as a major contribution to the practice of sound administration.'[2] The light touch was considered inappropriate. APH was unlikely to have had second thoughts on that account. Much of his life's effort was spent in dissolving the ghastly earnestness of all forms of officialdom, and in puncturing the gravity of institutional man.

'I was infuriated.'[3] He was not a high blood-pressure case; otherwise, the abolition of the university franchise by the Labour Government of 1945–50 might have gone hard with him: fortunately, too, he had channels of release for his *saeva indignatio*: letters to *The Times* and the *Manchester Guardian*. Nor was he unprepared for what he denounced as 'a stupid and spiteful Act', the first pressures of which had been applied by D. N. Pritt in 1944, moving an amendment attacking the university seats. It was defeated by 152 to 16. The Speaker's Conference that year decided that 'the university representation shall be retained'.

In the next four years the climate changed, and Churchill's amendment to the Representation of the People Act 1948, that the university franchise should be preserved, was defeated. 'The debates', APH wrote, 'were able, obstinate, and bitter', the result one more manifestation of frenzied egalitarianism. The note of Party civility was sustained by the Prime Minister, C. R. Attlee, who wished to take his family to *Bless the Bride*. 'It seems rather impudence on my part to ask you for seats when we have just deprived you of yours' (23 March 1948).

Appeased by an understanding that the mischief would be undone by the next Conservative Government, APH looked forward to visiting the Argentine, as a delegate to the Fifteenth Congress of the International Confederation of Authors' and Composers' Societies. As a speaker at the preceding congress, held in London, he had received the plaudits of delegates from twenty-four countries for his speech to them in alternating English and French couplets. The reception of that *tour de force* was encouragement to even more ambitious effort at the Buenos Aires assembly.

Before leaving, he was briefly but intensively embroiled again in 'the affairs of Newfoundland'. He had cause to fear that Whitehall was secretly committed to federation with Canada as the next and final stage in Newfoundland's advance to the future. It was a decision that he insisted the people should be free to make for themselves, and he went vigorously to work in and out of Parliament on their behalf. When, in September 1948, he sailed for South America in the Royal Mail liner *Highland Brigade*, he could fairly claim to have earned the restorative rest and change of the four weeks' voyage to come.

In Buenos Aires, having listened to a thunderously cheered speech by Peron, addressing an enormous public holiday crowd, APH achieved his own triumph in a minor key by delivering to a gathering of Argentine writers an 'oracion' in twenty-five rhyming couplets, each with its equivalent in Spanish learned from Hugo textbooks on the outward trip.

> We do not labour to destroy our sons
> With bombs, torpedoes, hand-grenades or guns.
> *No fabricamos nada destructivo –*
> *Bombas, canones, o alto explosivo.*
> It is our happy, honourable place
> To fashion gladness for the human race.
> *Nuestra gloria, nuestra gana*
> *Es de deleitar la raza humana.*
> A little tune, a simple word or two,
> May do what Parliament can never do.
> *Arlas pequenas, verso de sentimiento,*
> *Hardn, tal vez, mas que el Parlamento . . .*

and for peroration, turning to the chairman:

> Good Sir, good friends we must for ever be.
> In *vino veritas* – so drink with me.
> *Senor, llamame siempre su amigo.*
> *In vino veritas – Bebed commigo.*

No one ever saw a 'Do Not Disturb' notice on his study door. The disciplined regularity, the dedicated solitude of authorship, was not for him. He was a more immediately obedient servant of his will as a writer of letters to *The Times*, or as a champion of public causes, than as a novelist or poet. Disturbance of any kind produced in him the psychological reflex of a prisoner hearing the key of release being turned. He had been back in London a week when 'three fighting Newfoundlanders' arrived with a Petition to Parliament to restore self-government to their island. At once he pushed aside his work on the libretto of the new show that was to replace *Bless the Bride*, and gave his undivided attention to 'a great bag of signatures' backing the Petition, 50,000 in all, set out on sheet after sheet bearing the address as well as the name of every signatory. For him who had been among the Newfoundlanders, 'it was a moving thing to see those thousands of simple scrawls, many of them the names of old England'. There were Pilgrims, Grenfells, and Loders; Blakes and Drakes; Tarrants and Turpins; a Samuel Butler, and a Churchill who could not write his name and so 'made his mark'.

Having satisfied himself that the Petition was 'respectful, decorous, and temperate in language', in accordance with the rules of Parliament, APH himself presented it to the House of Commons on 24 November 1948; that is to say, he carried the finely engrossed document to the Table and handed it to the Clerk who, at the Speaker's bidding, read it to the assembled members. The presenter than proceeded to 'drop it into the bag behind the Speaker's Chair'. He thought it a proud proceeding. 'It showed once more what strength and soundness there is in some of the ancient customs we take for granted, or disregard, or even belittle.'

The visiting Newfoundlanders, by his testimony, were in tune with that sentiment. But the dignified parliamentary charade was virtually the end of the affair for them. He had been affronted by the refusal of the Secretary of State for Commonwealth Relations, Philip Noel-Baker, to receive the delegation. The Minister's mind was changed by a hint if not by a command from 10 Downing Street, where, during lunch, APH contrived to 'slip a remark' to the Prime Minister. Conceding that it may have been a coincidence that the Commonwealth Secretary relented a day or two later, he reflected that it was in keeping with 'the queer kind of way in which things get done in this queer world of government'.[4]

With the departure of the Newfoundland delegation, APH felt that 'there was nothing left to do but surrender – or fight'. His combative spirit took charge, to the detriment of his professional liabilities. He addressed the Conservatives' Imperial Affairs Committee. He 'harangued Chatham House for fifty minutes'. He wrote articles and more letters to *The Times*, exposing himself to the rebuke: 'The Editor would be glad if in future when you are engaged in a correspondence in the columns of *The Times* on any topic you did not simultaneously write letters on the same subject to another paper' (26 January 1949). He replied expressing gratitude 'to *The*

Times for their hospitality and support' and promising 'always to bear the rule in mind' (January 29). He made a long and forceful speech in the House, putting the case 'in no half-hearted or scanty manner'. He secured backing in the House of Lords. He suffered all over again, as in 1937, the disheartening process of soliciting the favour of colleagues of both Parties who had drawn places in the Private Members' ballot; this time with no good fortune.

His unstinted efforts were all in vain. The modern mania for conglomeration prevailed. The *Daily Mail* reported that on the day of the inauguration of Newfoundland as a province of Canada, 1 April 1949, there were no public rejoicings at St John's, the capital. 'A few flags were flying at half-mast, and some Newfoundlanders wore black ties.' To him, who had fought a good fight for the cause of self-determination, those were emblems of mourning for what he intemperately defined as the 'murder of a Dominion'. He imagined, with an uncharacteristic touch of bitterness, a hearty celebration at the office of the Commonwealth Relations Secretary – 'a happy bonfire of files and papers', coupled with the toast: 'No more bother with Newfoundland!'

'I felt it severely,' he said, pondering the failure of his Newfoundland crusade. Resuming work on the new light opera for Cochran, he wrote lines that might have been composed as an epitaph on his recent labours:

This is not the end: this is but a beginning:
When the fight is lost, there's a fight worth winning . . .

A colleague of APH's in the House of Commons, Sir Martin Lindsay, Bt, then Conservative member for Solihull, Warwickshire, did not 'regard him as any kind of hero. In the 1945 Parliament he played no part and rarely came to the House. In fact, for the rest of his Parliamentary career he continued to trade on the great reputation he had made at the beginning with his Marriage Bill but really did nothing except enjoy the status and draw the salary' (Letter, 12 May 1973).

APH's rejoinder might have been less polite than the commendation: 'See my book, *Independent Member*, page 387, *et seq*.' There he consoled himself for the demolition of the university seats, his defeat over Newfoundland, the arrogance of Ministers and his weariness of Party strife, by listing his 'small causes' that had 'ripened, or flowered at least', in the life of his last Parliament. He counted among them the virtual abolition of the Decree *Nisi*; the report of the Porter Committee on the Law of Defamation; a Betting Tax; the reduction of Entertainment Tax; the Legal Aid Advice Act; the report of the Supreme Court Committee on Practice and Procedure: changes in the licensing laws. 'It was better, I thought, for those of us who have neither the power of supermen nor the position of dictators to try to get a few small things done than to vapour about the woes of mankind.' Reviewing his legislative efforts, he did not forget that for those that came to fruition in the 1945–50 Parliament, Labour ministers and members deserved the credit; 'but I felt that my years of chattering and scribbling had, perhaps, assisted'. There are many still who would murmur an earnest parliamentary *'ear, 'ear*, to that.

If his attendances as a Member were less devoted than those of a political hack courting the Whips' esteem; and if certain of his later parliamentary performances gave cause for doubting whether he was animated by public spirit or the spirit of publicity, he had resoundingly re-established the worth of the Private Member, a type that a Liberal statesman of the recent past, Lord Morley (1838–1923), had lamented as lost to the House in his time. 'He imprinted on the records of the House of Commons the fact that the social laws of the nation could be appreciably modified by a wholly independent Member of gaiety, wit, perseverance and guile'; to which compliment *The Times Literary Supplement* appended the regret 'that the rigours of party politics would exclude his like today' (12 November 1971).

Facing parliamentary extinction, he went cheerfully into action against the Spelling Reform Bill, introduced to the House in March 1949, considering it 'a proper fight for a University Member'. The purpose of the Bill was 'to eliminate unnecessary drudgery and waste of time at school, to lighten the task of Civil Servants and others writing the English language, and to make English a world language'. His speech against the Bill at its Second Reading contained wittily apposite allusions to anomalies in French and Spanish. As always, he could not be faulted in his grasp of the business in hand, and his was probably the strongest influence in bringing about the marginal defeat of the Bill. Afterwards, he was hailed as 'this great contemporary of ours' by one of the proponents of the Bill in the House, Professor Savory (Queen's University, Belfast).

Following the defeat of the Bill, George Bernard Shaw re-entered what for him was an old controversy with a letter to *The Times* denouncing 'the stale tomfooleries and poppycock customary when spelling reform is discussed by novices and amateurs'. APH replied with an expansiveness permitted to few others debating the issue in the correspondence columns. 'From Mr Shaw we get nothing but dogmatic assertion and vague invective. He should be almost old enough to know that you prove no case by shouting words like "tomfooleries" and "poppycock".' The reformers, he had noticed, wished to represent the 'aw' sound in 'paw' by the letters 'oo'. He was 'tempted simply to say "Pw! Mr Shoo!" ' He expected that 'a thunderbolt would fall in reply from the great intellectual tyrant of the day'. For once Shaw kept his silence.

Attending one of the post-war Commemoration Days at Oxford as a Burgess with a prominent place in the waddling procession of dons and dignitaries, APH walked immediately ahead of Churchill, who led the Doctors. The Latin speech of the Public Orator was in what APH dismissed as 'the horrid new pronunciation'. His heart warmed to his old hero when he heard Churchill remark: 'I was so glad Edward' – Lord Halifax, the Chancellor – 'refused to talk this Dago talk. We should pronounce Latin as we pronounce it every day in our own language. After all, we don't teach the young that the month of August is named after the Emperor Owggostoos'. APH turned to tell him that he had been denouncing the new pronunciation for years. 'We had an animated discussion all the way to All Souls, myself walking sideways, and Churchill punctuating every sentence with the V-sign.'

The Encaenia of 1949 was the last APH would attend as an MP. Marking the occasion, the Burgesses were given pride of place behind the Vice-Chancellor and ahead of the High Steward; 'a very Christian thing for the university to do'. In future, 'this ancient, unique, and enlightened tradition' of Commemoration would be deprived of the Burgesses, 'whether for party pique or a mathematical formula, it seemed a pity'. Recording the occasion in print, he added bitterly: 'Two of the chief murderers, in robes of honour, marched behind us.' They were Lord Jowitt and Sir Stafford Cripps, both members of the iconoclastic Government.

Bless the Bride's profitable run of 886 performances came to its end in June 1949. Cochran took it off at the flood rather than risk an ebb-tide. APH noted as the curtain fell for the last time: 'Receipts for the day, £642. Entertainment Tax £116', the latter deducted before royalties. From 1937, in *Punch*, in *The Times*, and in Parliament he had fought against 'that wicked imposition, the barbarous tax on turnover which couples blindly the plays of Shakespeare and the exhibition of performing seals, the music of Beethoven and the racing of dogs'. In 1948 he had headed a delegation of theatre managers to the Treasury. Some months later the tax was reduced by fifty per cent, for which he was entitled to at least fifty per cent of the credit.

With the closure of *Bless the Bride* Cochran's luck ran out; so did APH's as a man of the theatre, though both had great expectations of *Tough at the Top* which followed at the Adelphi in a heat-wave that was not conducive to theatre-going. Writing the 'book' of the new show, APH trespassed hopefully into the domain of Ivor Novello, who was establishing developer's rights in Ruritanian territory.

By September 1949 Cochran was reporting a decline in the takings at the Adelphi. 'Join me in my prayers for a bit of luck,' he asked APH in a letter (October 27). APH responded by offering to forgo a percentage of his royalties from the show. Cochran returned thanks for 'a most generous gesture'. It was agreed that APH should receive 'a flat £50 a week' for the remainder of the run. 'I hope this will help you in your troubles', he wrote to Cochran on November 9. 'I wish there was some other way in which we could get those terrible weekly bills down.' One day during the last weeks, APH and Vivian Ellis lunched together 'rather gloomily' at the Savoy Grill. Passing their table, 'Gertie' Lawrence asked: 'How's the show going?' APH replied that it was not going very well. 'Wonderful,' she murmured in the self-absorbed manner of her kind, and went her way.

Novello diagnosed the weakness of *Tough at the Top* when he told Vivian Ellis: 'I think perhaps one was not sufficiently interested in the two leading people.' That was Cochran's misjudgment, ignoring APH's advice. APH himself was criticized for not providing a happy ending and a more compelling title. He claimed originality for the phrase, 'tough at the top', counting it another of his contributions to fashionable jargon. 'I wish I had a pound for every time it had been used in the papers, especially in sporting headlines.'

He described the end of a run in the theatre as if it was an event rather than an incident in his emotional life. 'When the fortnight's "notices" go up at last, and the play is under sentence of death, we are moved by more than loss of money or employment. It is like the breaking-up of a happy family or regiment. We have shared many toils and trials and emotions. The painted scenery has become a common home. The costumes and characters have taken on a kind of reality. . . . The living unity that we built up together is to die, and tomorrow we shall be sixty or seventy separate individuals again, sharing nothing but memories. So we are inclined to weep a little. But there are still the songs and the music, and we can gather round the family piano, and croak the tunes again and wistfully revive the old days.'[5]

At that reference to 'gathering round the family piano', there springs vividly and poignantly to one's mind an image of APH in the post-war years, repeating a scene familiar to so many of us from the twenties and thirties, when the L-shaped drawing-room at 12 Hammersmith Terrace was a setting in which was preserved the authentic charm of a once-popular form of domestic entertainment. The Herbert musical evenings were never programmed, always artlessly improvised, and joyfully recorded, one has no doubt, in unpublished diaries of both periods. I myself noted in 1929: '12 Hammersmith Terrace for the evening. Michael Arlen and I sang 'Where e'er you walk . . .' in rather dismal unison, APH accompanying and joining in'. One recalls that his piano technique had hardly advanced from the 'strumming' of his Oxford time, and that his accompaniments seemed to consist in the main of chords impressively struck in appropriate passages. His best performance was Handel's *Largo*.

The musical evenings of our forebears have more often been caricatured than faithfully reproduced, especially by radio and television, substituting passivity for participation. Their comic possibilities were exhausted by *Punch* artists, whose drooping-moustached tenors and simpering sopranos are enshrined in a century of bound volumes. None the less, those home-generated entertainments, so delightful a feature of the family ethos at 12 Hammersmith Terrace, have a title to remembrance as an embellishment of the civilized life.

Unforgettably associated with them in that house for all seasons was the lovable presence of Gwen Herbert, an artist by instinct and unadopted profession, who suffered the often demanding social propinquities imposed on her in the years of APH's prominence with a grace that drew its refreshment from the solitudes of the South Downs or some unfrequented shore where she could paint in peace. Often unavoidably at the centre of clusters of distinguished talents, she achieved her own memorable status by being herself, 'a gentle lady, sweet and kind'. APH extolled her supreme virtue in print: 'She nearly kills herself with kindness.' It is a kindness above all of the understanding, an innate sympathy that draws her to those whose energies are not primarily dedicated to success. At the famous Boat Race parties, resumed with all the old gaiety after the last war, it was not she who appeared at an upper window with the Prime Minister of the day. She was happier in the company of the inconspicuous and the distracted, provided that their obsessive interests were not politics, diseases, or diets. If they could talk intelligently about contemporary art they had in her a wholly engaged listener; even more intimately so if their passion was chess. She still travels to the tournaments and congresses, an ardent and authoritative observer and critic of the moves of the masters.

In November 1949 APH made a speech in Parliament that was received with 'loud cheers' (*The Times*). He was supporting a Bill to provide additional facilities for the forthcoming Festival of Britain, among them a water-bus service, one of the 'small causes' that he had kept alive for many years. He was not to know that it would be his swan song as 'a member of the faithful Commons of His Majesty the King', the phrase with which he had proudly concluded his maiden speech in that place fourteen years before. He was unwell, and had no intention of taking part in the debate. 'They wanted me to make a speech about fun and games, when all I wanted was a Turkish bath.' He was unusually nervous and wished that, as of old, he could prescribe himself a tonic at Heppells in the Strand. When he was called by the Deputy Speaker, he spoke for nine minutes, commending the Bill in terms that the Lord President of the Council, Herbert Morrison, told him had 'changed the whole course of the debate'.

He heard the cry, 'Who goes home?' echoing down the corridors of the Palace of Westminster for the last time. Parliament was dissolved two months later, a general election following in February 1950. The university franchise passed into history; a petty political triumph turned into folly by the campus events to come.

NOTES ON CHAPTER 20

1   A. P. Herbert: *The Singing Swan.*
2   *The Times Literary Supplement* (18 September 1970).
3   A. P. Herbert: *Independent Member.*
4   A. P. Herbert: *Independent Member.*
5   A. P. Herbert: *Independent Member.*

21

Prospect of a Peerage

A Labour MP, well known to APH and me, lost his seat in Parliament and was so dispirited by his unexpected severance from a milieu highly congenial to his ego that he went into a health decline and died. I chanced to see him after his electoral eclipse, leaning on the parapet of Westminster Bridge gazing down on the empty Terrace below. Of his own situation, APH wrote: 'I was sad when I was abolished and had to go. I missed it.' To me he admitted: 'I miss the smoking room gin and gossip at six o'clock.'

There was a vacuum too in his theatre ambit. *Tough at the Top* had failed after five months. Good judges thought well of it. He himself considered it 'a worthier work' than *Bless the Bride*. Holding a private inquest, 'the show lost I know not how much money'. Cochran wrote to him with a palsied hand: 'I miss you very much' (3 May 1950). He wrote again a month later: 'I've established another record – the smallest receipts I've ever played to at any one night, or in any one week, in London' (2 June).[1]

APH looked back to that period as one of bleakness in his professional career. 'I had lost my seat; I had lost the great battle of Newfoundland; I had written no book; and my new play had been, comparatively, a failure.' In fact, a new novel of his, *Number Nine*, was published in 1951. It was dedicated to 'our long-suffering Civil Service', and was mildly sardonic about the advent of psychiatrists into the processes of selecting men for official appointments. Omitting *Number Nine* from that doleful review of his position in the early fifties was symptomatic. The writing of fiction did not meet his greatest need, self-justification.

For instance, he was at last free to finish the long-postponed novel of life among the Thames sailing bargemen that was to be called *The Sea Gipsies*. He had collected material for it years before from his friend Frank Carr, director of the National Maritime Museum and author of *Sailing Barges* (1931). APH's family, and doubtless his publishers, hoped that he might repeat the success of *The Water Gipsies*. Instead, to the dismay of some and specially of his wife, who protested that he was wasting time, energy, and talent, he gave months of effort to studying and analysing the football pools.

In 1938 he had tried to bring about their abolition through Parliament. Since the war they had become a solemn weekly observance by the masses. 'The proletariat', he wrote in a light-hearted elitist mood, 'are getting an unfair share of the big prizes.' He set out to make the pools acceptable to the 'cultured classes', e.g. the readers of *Punch*, who might be expected to conduct themselves with more dignity and responsibility in the crisis of a sudden windfall than some of the publicized winners, among them the milkman who precipitately abandoned the customers on his round on hearing of his good fortune.

The chief interest here of APH's not very aptly titled textbook, *Pools Pilot* (1953), is its evidence of his undiminished mental tenacity. His lively exposition of the subtleties of pools permutations and combinations did not conceal the exceptional power of application needed to master them. He gave weight to, but did not wholly share, the expert opinion of his old fellow-member of The Midwives at Oxford, Hubert Phillips, who asserted that the pools are a lottery, involving no element of skill. APH pronounced his verdict: 'We are not convinced.' He resumed the coupon-filling routine and in due course won £800. His luck did not hold when he sought tax-relief in respect of the £100 he claimed to have spent in pools 'investments' while writing his book.

He marked his sixtieth birthday in September 1950 with the reflective lines:

> . . . if I could have my time again,
> I do not think I'd choose another reign –
> If I may muster, when my journey ends
> The same fine family, the same good friends.
> And see old England splendid in the van,
> Foot-sore but fighting, of the March of Man.

In October he sailed for Australia, a return visit after twenty-five years. He went as an unpaid lecturer for the British Council, which presumably provided for his expenses. The tour took him to distant townships with names like Toowoomba and Mildura, 'green oases of flowers and fruit trees snatched from the desert'. He was glad 'not to have missed the three-days train journey' across the arid Nullabor Plain, 'a hot, dusty, but worthy experience'. In Brisbane an audience of 3,000 assembled to hear him speak on the English sense of humour. 'We all needed it. There was a tram strike and it was raining.' He fancied that the local sentiment for England was 'even warmer' than when he was there in 1925. The fine reception given him at the Commonwealth Club of Adelaide endorsed that conviction.

Returning home in the P & O liner *Himalaya*, he heard by ship's radio of the tragic death of Cochran in the last week of January 1951. To APH it may have seemed more than the end of a friendship. He composed an elegiac tribute that was cabled to London. Inspiration failed him.

> Dear master, this blue sea is sad today,
> That Fate should finish you in such a way! . . .

Felicity was regained when the *Himalaya* met her sister-ship the *Chusan* in the Indian Ocean at 21.00 on Sunday, 4 February 1951. He was moved to write a commemorative ode 'for Captain H. C. C. Forsyth with respectful salutes'.

> Ah, yes, the distant stranger in the night
> May leave no memory but one red light.
> But you should see two sisters pass in style,
> No farther than a fraction of a mile,
> The latest, swiftest of a splendid Line,
> As like as bottles of a noble wine.
> The house-flag flutters in a flood of light,
> Salute of sirens shocks the velvet night.
> Here are no strangers. Officer and man
> Are life-long members of a loyal clan.
> We crowd the rails, mere passengers, and yell,
> Tonight proud owners of the Line as well.
> Such vessels, for a century and more,
> Have made the sea as solid as the shore.
> Such ships have made all Capricorn a friend,
> And Sydney not much farther than Southend.
> (And may we whisper, every vessel flies
> The ancient flag of Private Enterprise.)
> The lights, the signals, die. The sisters part

But something bright long lingers in the heart:
And British breasts may be allowed to swell,
For here's a thing we still do rather well.

He had paid £36,000 in income tax and surtax over the previous
six years and was resentful when, soon after his return from
Australia, he received a demand for more surtax. He wrote to the
Solicitor of Inland Revenue: 'I hope you will write no more such
letters to one who has so good a record as I think I have as a
taxpayer, and, to some extent, as a public servant. The only effect
of peremptory letters to me is to upset me and disturb myself and
my secretary from the urgent work upon which we are engaged, the
completion of which work is necessary to enable me to meet the
almost impossible and certainly unjust demands of the State' (5
April 1951).

What specially irritated him was the official attitude to his share,
amounting to £1,200, of the proceeds of the sale by Cochran of the
amateur production rights in *Bless the Bride*. A possibly unwise
transaction was treated by the Inland Revenue as the income of one
year, and taxed accordingly; it meant that APH would be left with
about £160. 'This cannot be right', he protested; 'this cannot be
just.' He cited to the authorities his book, *Independent Member* (1950).
'It took me more than three years to write, but the income from it,
I gather, will be treated as the income for a single year for the
payment of income tax and surtax. This is the sort of thing that
makes us unfortunate authors feel a great sense of injustice, and puts
us into such difficulties.'

The authors' predicament was brought before the public that
year by John Brophy, sometime editor of a popular literary weekly,
John o' London's. He proposed that authors should receive a penny
for each borrowing of their books from the public libraries. APH
noted that the total of borrowings in 1950 was 340,000,000, yielding
nothing to the authors. Brophy's 'penny a loan' plan was the
opening of the first phase in a long campaign of which APH later
assumed the leadership. For the time being, he was more concerned
about the taxation problem. 'We work for three years or more on a
book; but the royalties are taxed as if they have all been earned
in a single year, and we soar into surtax regions.' A letter of his to
The Times, 19 April 1951, produced a rush of endorsements from
representatives of other arts that were similarly penalized.

A yachting cruise in the Mediterranean with his friends John and Violet Astor gave him the opportunity to visit Venice 'without going into St Mark's'; likewise Athens, 'without going up to the Acropolis. Is this a record?' His grand moment came when he set foot on Ithaca, the island of Ulysses. It stirred old war memories, 'and excited me much more than the cathedrals and architectural ruins'.

Still smarting from the Labour Government's destruction of the university constituencies, he retorted pertinently in *The Times* when Attlee dismissed them as 'pocket boroughs'. 'I should be grateful if the Prime Minister would explain whose pocket I was in. Would not the description, "pocket boroughs", be more appropriate to members who are chosen and financed by wealthy trade unions, and bound, more or less, to do their will?' (15 June 1951). He seemed to take pleasure in noting that 'there was no reply'.

His standing with *The Times* was such that he had acquired almost a right to the last word. 'God bless *The Times*!' he exclaimed when that newspaper crowned, with a first leader, the correspcnd-ence on aircraft noise that he had initiated. Typically, he gave weight to his views with his own set of observations, carried out with a bubble sextant, and his self-taught trigonometry. Hours of recording and checking the altitudes of aircraft over Hammersmith brought him to the conclusion that the existing thousand-feet limit was 'too low'.

One remembers the sextant, and a chronometer, on the mantel-piece of a room that a *Times* interviewer described as 'more like a rock garden than a study'. One would suggest, more like a museum of APH's decent fads and fancies and of his life style as a 'miscel-laneous person'. An inventory would have itemized a medley of framed theatre photographs, cartoons, and illustrated dinner menus; shelves of books in general disarray; a palpably home-made sundial; the radiogram for more or less instant *Tristan*; the old-fashioned wooden filing-cabinets cumbersome with the correspondence of his many-sided life; and the latest batch of Durrants' press-cuttings scattered about as if blown in by the wind. A room entirely expressive of APH's Byronic disdain of routine and the settled habits of convention.

An invitation to lecture to the Anglo-Danish Society in Copenhagen on the English sense of humour sprang him as from a trap. The morning after the lecture, seeing his name in headlines and asking for a translation, he discovered that he was being credited with the escapades of the celebrated practical joker, Horace de Vere Cole. 'Every one of his jokes, including roping off Piccadilly, was put down to me. I left the country at once.'

Sir Max Beerbohm's eightieth birthday in 1952 drew from him a spontaneous metrical salute that was printed in *Truth*. Not every reader may have been sensitive to the sublime oversight in the final stanza:

> Some birds can swim, some fish can fly,
>   Some folk at many arts excel,
> But testy fellows still reply:
>   'They do not do it very well'.
>
>   . . . . .
>
> God cried: 'Be silent – if you can!
>   Let crowd and critics all relax:
> For I will make the perfect man'.
>   He clapped His hands – and there was MAX!

In 1937 he had tried, as a Member of Parliament, with unattributed success, to make life easier for Civil List pensioners. In 1952 a new Civil List Bill came before the House, a consequence of the accession of the present Queen. 'She will reign, we hope, for fifty years. Costs are rising all the time. The pensions should be raised again.' His representations did not fall on deaf ears. The amount allocated to pensions in the Bill was increased to £5,000.

He lapsed no less readily into the parenthetical activities of trying to procure a Civil List Pension for Sylvia Lynd and promoting consideration for his old friend Belloc as a candidate for admission to the Order of Merit. Sylvia Lynd, widow of Robert Lynd, the accomplished literary journalist, had written him 'a sad letter', telling of hard times since her husband's death. As for Belloc, consulting a Court personage, APH was informed that he had 'incontinently refused' the dignity of Companion of Honour offered him some years before. It was put to APH that Walter de la Mare was 'as much, if not more', deserving of the OM.

A new honour for APH himself was evidently in the mind of Churchill, who had returned to power in 1951. One day in the following summer APH's eldest daughter, Crystal, was at Chartwell with her children to meet those of the Soames' family. She was sitting by the swimming-pool when Churchill came down from the house in his swimming garb, plus a wide-brimmed straw hat and cigar. He asked after APH's health, said that APH was 'greatly missed in the House'; then, using a quaint turn of phrase, inquired: 'Would your Papa like to be a nobleman?' Presumably, Churchill was posing the possibility of a life peerage for APH. Crystal replied that 'he would probably rather go back to the Commons'. Churchill nodded understanding and remarked: 'We must see what can be done.'

APH was still fighting his 'Word War', the first fusillade in which he had fired nearly thirty years before in *Punch*. Reading a newspaper comment on a play 'currently running' in the West End, he objected: 'There is nothing whatever to be said for "currently". It is a wasteful, ignorant way of saying "now", employed by people who like to show that they read the New York newspapers. I suppose we shall all have to sing presently: "Currently the day is over . . ." and say "Currently let us praise famous men". What an improvement – "currently or never"!'

Sloppy thinking, too, had to be exposed; for example, simplifying the race problem into terms of black and white. That *reductio ad absurdum* ignored 'how the Indians love their brown brothers, the Pakistanis, how the islanders of Ceylon love the Tamil Indians, how the Indonesian loves the Malay. What general goodwill prevails in Ghana, what fraternity in the Congo!'

He secured an impressive new public hearing for 'the grim theme of authors' taxes' in *The Times* and the *Daily Telegraph* in 1952. Editorial latitude was generous. The distinguished historian, Arthur Bryant, instanced Compton Mackenzie's experience in selling the copyrights in twenty-one of his books, representing many years' work, for £10,000, and being charged tax on that sum as if it were the earnings of a single year. APH was disconcerted when A. A. Milne, writing as an affluent playwright, would not concede that authors were 'a special case'. He accused Milne of 'creeping out of his comfortable tent to stab us in the back', and asked readers of *The Times* to believe that 'the only work that gives me any real hope now is my weekly toil for the football pools'. He added: 'I am the only man living who has tried to abolish the Pools (in Parliament). I am glad I failed!'

He was doubtless the only author that Christmas who was

transfixed by the innocent question of a grandchild: 'Which was the star in the East – the one the shepherds saw?' All other business was brought to a standstill while Middle East maps, a star globe, and the sextant, were consulted. 'This was a question I had never seriously considered.' He advanced, and abandoned, theories in favour of Venus, Sirius, and Canopus. Obviously the search was engrossing. 'Just when goodwill is glorified on Earth we see in the South the most dramatic, deep and wide assembly of grand stars that can be found in the heavens: Orion and his fine flankguards, Aldebaran and Procyon, Castor and Pollux, the many coloured Capella above; the Pleiades to the West, and Sirius, the brightest star in the sky, who comes up from the South to see us now and now only, below. It really does seem to be a Christmas celebration; for Orion sprawls across the meridian just before midnight on Christmas Eve, and Sirius stands over Greenwich at midnight, or near it, on New Year's night.' The point had to be considered whether the Wise Men lived in a valley, on a plain bordered by mountains, 'or in a misty region'. Finally, 'I decided to refer the question to the Wise Man of Greenwich', the Astronomer Royal. That authority cited 'three main conjectures': that the Star in the East was a nova; that it was a bright comet; that it was not a single star but a close conjunction of Jupiter and Saturn. 'No grandfather', APH concluded, 'need be ashamed to admit that he does not know.'

His position at *Punch* was 'deteriorating', his word. He had lost the privilege of sending his 'copy' straight to the printer. His work was no longer appearing in the paper as by prescriptive right. He often appeared to be baffled, and was at times upset, by the changed attitude to him at the Table. He could hardly have been unaware of proprietorial stresses. Circulation and advertising were still in a down phase. E. V. Knox had retired as editor in 1949 and was succeeded by a staff man, Kenneth Bird. A break with tradition was about to be made by the appointment, in 1953, of a new editor who had never sat at the Table. He was Malcolm Muggeridge, from the *Daily Telegraph*.

Despite intimations of impending *emeritus* status, and perhaps of unspoken hopes that he would resign his *Punch* contract to become an occasional contributor, APH seemed no more concerned than he ever was to take thought for the morrow, though he had a growing overdraft and little collateral to support it. He was accepting too many invitations to lunches, dinners, banquets, increasingly with a sequel of anti-social somnolence.

One such occasion is recalled by Ian Watt, then at the Colonial Office. APH was a member of a deputation that went to the Home Secretary to propose an experiment in Proportional Representation in the United Kingdom and the Colonies. The meeting was late in the afternoon. 'It was patently clear that he had lunched well, and to start with he was more or less comatose.' He joined the discussions with a rambling account of his recent experience of a general election in Ceylon. He insisted that the voters did not know who or what they were voting for. 'Each side had a symbol.' People voted for the symbol that took their fancy. 'One side had an elephant symbol. The other party had a teacup. I was not surprised that the winning symbol was the teacup. The world price of tea had recently risen.' He went on to urge that 'we should not try to inflict our ideas about elections on places like Ceylon'. Persisting in that vein, he reached a stage at which the patience of another prominent member of the deputation, Lady Violet Bonham Carter, ran out. Interrupting his flow, she said: 'You have just referred, Sir Alan, to the market price for tea. Can you quote the market price for elephants?'

Robert Aickman, who launched the Inland Waterways Association in 1946, has not forgotten an annual dinner at which APH, as president, was in the chair. After the formal speeches, he rose and confounded the company of two hundred by announcing that after the customary break he would call on individuals at random to make an impromptu speech or recite a poem; the choice was theirs. Instead of enlivening what remained of the evening, he deadened it and, incidentally, protracted the interval unduly. He then embarrassed a succession of diners by picking them out to perform. Finally, he called on an attractive young actress whom he had brought as his guest. 'She delivered a perfect little piece, palpably written by him in advance; and indeed it was the object of the whole tiresome exercise.'[2]

Early in their collaboration as inland waterways' propagandists, Robert Aickman decided that at heart APH was a pessimist, 'a deeply unhappy man'. That places him as a self-conscious if not self-pitying humorist, smiling through his tears. But the keynote of APH's humour was nothing so positive as defiance; rather it had reflective good-nature as its well-spring. His infrequent *farouche* outbursts cannot be said to have seriously marred a personality so engaging to so many. His general tone and temper, wonderfully civil and humane, strengthened the view that the three Christian graces should have humour added unto them.

He was reverting more often, if not with divine afflatus, fine frenzy, or with Coventry Patmore's *curiosa felicitas* (borrowed surely from Petronius), to the common poetic measure of an earlier age as a vehicle for his humour. The couplets of *The Sign* (1953) have the snap of a fine-fashioned clasp. The whole poem illustrates a growing mood of mistrust of a social development that has since provoked more violent forms of expression.

> Planning! There is some honour in the name:
> But why must planners cover it with shame?
>
> Beside a river stands an ancient inn,
> A humble place that's hardly heard of gin.
> Here sit the labourers and talk of oats,
> Here come the men who mess about in boats.
> *The Barge Aground* – a name that's fair and fit –
> Though I'm half afraid to mention it!
> I'll tell you why. Since 1869
> The little tavern's had a tavern sign.
> The sign is painted with an artful hand,
> An old barge perched upon a bank of sand –
> Seagulls – a red sun sets behind a wood!
> It may not be a Turner, but it's good.
> At least, it tells the navigator 'Here
> Is rest, refreshment, bonhomie and beer.'
> And, oh, what lectures we have had to stand
> About the lack of colour in the land!
> Poets, reformers, bellowed 'on the air'
> 'There should be light and brightness everywhere.'
> And black rebukes were muttered, I recall,
> About the inns that had no sign at all.
> Here was the artist starving for a job:
> And here was art demanded for the mob.
> Enlightened brewers handsomely obeyed,
> And called platoons of painters to their aid.
> Hope came to Bloomsbury, *The Barley Mow*,
> *Green Men*, *Red Lions*, filled the studio;
> And A.R.A.s were not ashamed to rub
> Artistic shoulders with the lowly pub.
> Bright new *King's Heads*, *Lord Nelsons* by the mile,

Old Ships and *Spanish Captains* decked the isle.
Alas, how often in the tale of Man
Must Poetry surrender to the Plan!
See the canals, where in their private day
The painted boats were beautiful and gay!
Gone is the Heart, the Castle and the Rose:
The solemn State does not approve of those.
They say that since the nation ran the line
The locomotive does not look so fine.
And now grey councillors are circling round
(With hostile cameras) *The Barge Aground*.
Well, have you guessed? The sign is to be sacked
Under the Town and Country Planning Act!
It's an 'advertisement', and it must class
With hideous hoardings in a field of grass.
(That is the peril of the planning kind;
Their logic leads to feebleness of mind.
They cannot, like the children of the light,
Admit exceptions which are wrong, but right.)
But other men disclose the things they sell:
One wonders what will have to go as well.
The chemist's bottles and the barber's pole.
The three gold balls, are clearly for control.
The jolly flags the shipping fellows fly
Are mere advertisements and shame the sky.
The flag that shows that Parliament's on view –
What is its purpose but to cause a queue?
Those scarlet pillars, peppered round the town –
What do they do but advertise the Crown?
If there must be such objects in the street,
The colour, surely, should be more discreet –
Waiting-room brown, perhaps, demure and matt:
It may not catch the eye – but what of that?
We're not important. Will they care a pin
If we put letters in the litter-bin,
Or cannot tell an egg-shop from an inn?
Look, Planners, now, beyond the tavern, do;
There is a spire that advertises too!
O Lord, I rave. I've got 'em on the brain.
Planners, fly hence! Sweet Chaos, come again!

At the Royal Academy banquet on 30 April 1953 he replied on
behalf of the guests with a ringing call for the exemption of all the

arts from the penalties of taxation. 'No tax on thought! No levy on laughter! No duty on beauty!' He spoke about the current political obsession with full employment. 'What a cry! All this boasting about "Full Employment"! After two thousand years of Christianity, and Socialism, and science, is that the finest carrot we can set before the toiling asses – that all should be able to *work* – *all the time*? Anyone can work – we all like work – and we are rightly taxed for this indulgence. But when we have done, when we go forth to enjoy the finest things that man can make or do, the things that distinguish us from the savage and the sheep, whether it be fine writing or painting, fine music or singing, or fine riding on a fine horse, then it is barbarous to tax us as if we were enjoying some dangerous narcotic or intoxicant. No, "Full Enjoyment" is the cry. And that is the policy of all the parties, all the arts, all the guests for whom I speak tonight . . .'

He had recently cast into rhyme some thoughts on the custom of after-dinner oratory, transcribed on a postcard. His rhyming reflections deserve the permanence of the printed page, at the risk of copyright infringement by speakers with nothing to say.

> The dog, considered a sagacious beast,
> Does not give tongue when he has had a feast.
> Nor does the cow go mooing round the mead
> To tell the world that she's enjoyed her feed.
> Not even lions, I imagine, roar
> After a meal – unless they want some more.
> All Nature has agreed that it is best,
> When fully fed to ruminate and rest.
> The Ancient Romans, flushed with food and wine,
> Decided it was wiser to recline.
> The cannibal, when he has had his fun,
> Does not propose the health of anyone.
> But Modern Man, by some malignant fate,
> When he has eaten, simply must orate:
> And those who don't, though eager for repose,
> Must strain their ears for quantities of prose.
> If toasts and speeches have effective force
> Our land should be as healthy as a horse.
> If wishful drinking rings a magic bell
> Our Trade, our Industry, should do quite well.
> This quaint old custom could be understood
> If all the speeches were extremely good.

But it is not a very easy trade:
And more than half of them were best not made.
Oh, what a wise and comfortable thing
If all the toasts were silent – like 'The King'!
Oh, may I live to hear the Chairman say:
'Friends, you are welcome to our feast today.
Enjoy yourselves! Good company – good cheer!
And that's the only speech that you will hear!'

NOTES ON CHAPTER 21

1 Apparently a reference to *The Ivory Tower*, a play based on the tragedy of Czechoslovakia. Cochran produced it as a mark of esteem for Jan Masaryk.
2 Letter, 18 June 1973.

22

'*I am Increasingly Worried*'

He had recoiled from the terrors of war into the role of crusading humorist. Ever since, he had been in recoil from the inference that he was handicapped intellectually by his reputation as a professional 'funny man'. Exhorting him *sotto voce* in Parliament: 'Say it in *Punch!*' Chamberlain, as Prime Minister, had touched a nerve in APH that became more sensitive as the years went by, especially after his forced withdrawal from Westminster. He certainly had no wish to be 'taken seriously' in the dourly enervating sense of the term. Too often, in seeking to refute the implication that in mental calibre he was a lightweight, he subverted his own worth by dispersing his energies in eccentric enterprises and ill-timed flippancies.

His voluntary labours in a medley of causes helped to buttress his defences against that uncomfortable insinuation. 'I am very much obliged to you for adding yet one more chapter to your record of public service. I am afraid it has been a tedious and burdensome task.' The Lord Chancellor was writing 'very sincere thanks' (5 June 1953) to him as a member of the long-sitting committee on legal procedures and costs which was about to publish its report. Protesting that 'I keep on stumbling into committees, boards, councils, and even presidencies', he accepted an invitation that year to serve on the Council of the Society of Authors. It was the beginning of yet another of the extra-mural activities that were causing concern in his domestic circle.

A recurring disappointment since Cochran's death was that 'not one manager has come to Vivian Ellis and me and said: "Let's do a British musical together".' When 'a leading impresario' showed no interest in the musical play possibilities of *The Water Gipsies*, APH went boldly to work on a libretto for it 'on spec', and persuaded Vivian Ellis to provide the music.

Soon he was involved in public disputation about the marriage of divorcees in church, his appetite for controversy stimulated by ecclesiastical recalcitrance. He brought the conflicting views together in a little book, *The Right to Marry* (1954), an able piece of pamphlet-eering from which there cannot have proceeded much pecuniary good. An encouraging word came from the Warden of New College: 'I do very much admire the excellent temper in which you conduct the argument.' It was recognition of one of APH's best qualities, his classical, humanist approach to dialectic with its concomitant of civility to dissenters.

He was more despondent than usual about his health. He had not lost his faith in the vitamin cult, and was having supplies of pills and tablets sent to him regularly by the Organic Vitamin Company, of Berkhamsted. He was still 'cultivating the abdomen' in accordance with the Hornibrook principles; still 'massaging the liver' by his self-devised method of 'posterior exercises'; still going into the garden 'the last thing at night' to take a hundred deep breaths. Pertaining to a current medical controversy, he diverted his *Punch* public with some advice on living longer:

> Attend. I do not often sing to you
> To make you healthier, but now I do.
> The word coronary does not come down
> From *cor*, the heart, but from *corona*, crown:
> And I, for one, pronounce it in this way
> Whatever medical young men may say.
> Thus can the poet get the modern curse,
> *Coronary thrombosis*, into verse.
>
> . . . .
>
> Tycoon or Clerk, accept this diagnosis –
> You're heading for *coronary thrombosis*.
> Be your own caddy; be afraid of chairs;
> Ignore that lift and saunter up the stairs.
> Do not by jet whizz over to Quebec;
> But go by ship and march about the deck.
> And no retiring to 'a life of ease',
> For here's the certainty of heart disease.
> It will be best not only for your soul
> To weed the garden and bring in the coal.
> And pray each evening for a transport strike –
> Thus you may live as long as you would like.

His elaborate therapies were proving inadequate against disabling pain in the right shoulder and right arm, which he fancied was caused by 'congestion at the base of the neck'. If he associated it with the nursery accident of long ago he did not say so in the notes he made about his symptoms. He believed that the so-called congestion 'hinders the flow of blood to the brain'. He paid 'many visits' to an osteopath but abandoned them as being 'too expensive and not effective enough'. He wrote that he 'seemed to have lost the will to "get down to" a new big work. It has never deserted me before. I easily fall to the temptation to turn to smaller jobs'; for example, he was supplying an advertising agency with lyrics about washing machines and other kitchen equipment. *When I enjoy a cooling drink In some Sumatran crater, I thankfully recline and think Of the Refrigerator* . . . Orthodox medical opinion assured him that his trouble was 'a tired heart'. He was ordered to 'avoid all overstrain'.

Taking the diagnosis seriously, he decided, ruefully, to sell *Water Gipsy*, from his ownership of which so much of his life's contentment had been derived. Cranking her coupled Thorneycroft engines was becoming too obviously a test of his physical vigour. Nor was she even sentimentally attractive to a new Herbert generation, darting about the river in their dinghies and acquiring skills that were to outclass his. Not that he faced deprivation of the freemasonries of the river. He was the active president of the London Corinthian Sailing Club. He was still a member of the Thames Conservancy. He was on the best of terms with the Port of London Authority. He had good friends in the river police service, always welcomed aboard their launches.

Eric Norris, well known in the bookselling world, was with him at Hammersmith on the September day in 1955 when *Water Gipsy* was handed over to her new owner. He remembers APH standing silently by the river wall in the garden, watching her moving up river and out of sight.' He was very subdued.'[1]

Tax problems bore heavily on him. 'I am increasingly worried', he wrote, 'at the prospect of trying to maintain a sufficient income (after tax) to keep myself and my wife for the years to follow. It is not clear to me what steps I should take to relieve myself of some of the anxiety of planning the financial return from my work in order to leave myself sufficient energy, time and enthusiasm to continue to earn my living by writing.' His sons-in-law Anthony Lousada and

Christopher Clarke were solicitors. 'They were aware of my anxiety and fully shared it. Naturally, I turned to them for advice.'

A company called Haddock Productions Limited[2] was formed to take over his copyrights and his future literary output. 'I was to become an employee of the company for all literary purposes and would merely be paid a salary (after deduction of tax). I was not at all happy at the thought of putting myself under a contract of this type since I realised in doing so that I would be giving up my position as an independent author.'[3]

The new arrangement, given effect from 1 May 1954, was designed to ensure him £2,000 a year after tax. Its clear implication was that henceforth he would devote his time and energies to profitable work on behalf of the company. His fellow-directors may not have exchanged glances of surprise when it was announced that he was writing a prologue for Dame Edith Evans to declaim at Her Majesty's Theatre on the occasion of the Royal Academy of Dramatic Art's fiftieth anniversary on 31 May.

. . . . . .

From this Academy we do not spread
Some cult like archery, which should be dead.
Of all the arts, we think, that make a show
The one that matters is the one we know.
The scene-designer may deserve a shout:
But we must tell them what the play's about.
The author, bless him, has to have his fling:
But, privately, the player is the thing.
Let Science frolic with its valves and screens;
But flesh and blood must nourish the machines.
They will be dust when bombers misbehave;
But we shall still play Hamlet – in a cave.
Let them perfect their pictures as they wish,
Till we can smell the flowers – and the fish.
Somehow the taste, the hunger, will survive –
For first-hand feelings, and for legs alive.
There will still be some magic in a band:
There will be virtue in a voice not canned.
Somehow the ancient wonder will befall
And everything be ready after all.
The leading lady will consent to play,
And Chaos yield to Order 'on the day' . . .

Come, children, come, and write another page
In the eternal story of the stage.

. . . . . .

He revisited Australia for recuperative purposes in the winter of
1954/55. It was an occasion also for renewing the friendship that
he had begun in London with Robert Menzies, the Prime Minister,
their bond the law rather than politics. Beverley Nichols, also
visiting the Dominion, recalled an evening when he and Bob
Menzies were dinner-party guests at a house in a suburb of Sydney.
Their hostess mentioned that APH had written a poem called
Australia. A copy was produced, and the Prime Minister was
persuaded to read it aloud:

> . . . Blue hills, green gardens, and the golden plain,
> The birds, the herds, the gum trees and the grain.
> But then, the drought that makes men hate the sun;
> The fire that flies as fast as horse can run –
> Nature at war with all that Man has won –
> Australia! . . .

As described by Beverley Nichols, it was an emotional interlude
of misty eyes and faltering speech in a setting of 'mellow candle-light',
with gleaming silver, and 'the song of crickets from the garden'.
Apparently overcome, Menzies asked Nichols to read the final
stanza:

> Here is no place for sluggard or for slave:
> The mouth is merry and the breast is brave.
> Honour today the Fathers of the State
> Who found a wilderness and made it great,
> Believed in Providence but fought with Fate –
> Australia!

On his subsequent missions as a figure in world politics, Bob
Menzies never failed to let APH know when his itinerary took in
London. APH liked to mark those occasions by inviting half a
dozen of his friends, myself among them, to meet Menzies at lunch.
Menzies was the best of good company, and the jollity was usually
extended well on into the afternoon. When it came to settling the
bill, APH tended to behave as if he had rendered an important

service to Commonwealth harmony for which he could not reasonably be expected to pay.

Back from his Antipodean holiday early in 1955, he took time off from finishing the *Water Gipsies*' libretto to pose as the castaway in the BBC's perennially popular *Desert Island Discs* programme, compered by Roy Plomley, who remembers him claiming Handel's *Largo* as his 'signature tune'. His musical taste, as displayed to the listening public, could be equated with that of a last night at the Proms in Sir Henry Wood's time; inevitably the *Largo* (on the organ); Dennis Noble singing 'Song of Liberty', APH's words set to the music of Elgar's 'Pomp and Circumstance' No. 4; Chorale, 'Sleepers Awake' from the Bach cantata No. 140; Musetta's Waltz Song from *La Bohème*; selections from Offenbach's music for *La Belle Hélène*; 'vocal gems' from *Big Ben*; and Malcolm Sargent's arrangement of *Rule, Britannia*. For the 'one luxury' permitted the castaway, he chose 'a pair of binoculars for looking at the stars'.

A demand from the Inland Revenue for £828 2s. 6d. surtax had arrived during his absence in Australia. It was followed by a threat of legal proceedings. 'I suppose this is intended for me', he wrote '(though my name is not on it), and refers to income earned by me two years ago. Since then my circumstances have changed for the worse.' He thought it necessary to explain to the Special Commissioners that he was earning 'hardly anything' from *Punch*, and that the current newspaper strike had 'damaged and diminished' his income. 'There are prospects, however, of a musical play of mine, to be produced within a year, and that, I hope, will improve matters.' He enclosed a cheque for £100, 'not to show good will, for I bitterly resent the unjust taxation of authors, of which we have been complaining for years, but as an admission of legal liability. Perhaps some belated act of justice to my profession in the Budget will help me.' By way of final protest: 'I do not like receiving threatening printed notices in red. Such communications worry me so much that they injure my capacity for work, and make me feel like stopping work altogether. At the age of nearly 65 I think I deserve to, but that would not assist you much.' He asked that 'any further such communications' should be sent to his accountant, 'who will at least address me with politeness and consideration' (14 April 1955). A letter in the post to him from Villa Politi, Syracuse, Sicily, was exemplary in both respects. It addressed him as 'My dear Alan', and thanked him for 'kind remarks' that have evaded later research.

It was subscribed: 'Every good wish from your old friend, Winston S. Churchill' (15 April 1955).

In his dealings with the 'tax people' the humour that was his hallmark as a writer seemingly evaporated. What, too, of the once pervasive logic? The Special Commissioners can hardly have been impressed. The repeated exasperation may have been symptomatic of more than a sense of injustice; possibly, of deepening doubts about his professional future.

No longer was he being borne along on a flowing tide of fortune. In Bouverie Street he was regarded by the younger editorial men as an 'old square' who was obviously uneasy at the shifts in policy towards more liberalism or whatever, and whose arrival at the Wednesday luncheons was politely, rather than delightedly, welcomed. The death of Cochran had snapped his strongest link with the theatre. In the book world, since the publication of his parliamentary reminiscences in *Independent Member* (1950), and his fictional version of a phase of Napoleonic history, *Why Waterloo?* (1952), his reputation was being sustained largely by reprints.

His fellow directors of Haddock Productions Limited were waiting to hear of his embarking on 'a major new work', a play or a novel that would justify the company's existence. They were not particularly happy to see his name recurring in the correspondence columns of *The Times*, or with his casual article-writing; still less with his latest dedication of energy and time to the chairmanship of an Authors' and Publishers' Committee on obscene publications.

Nor had he reorganized his working day as a company employee. He was as slack as ever in dealing with a correspondence that was certainly more varied than that of most writers. Random contemporary sample: appeal from the controller of an Admiralty division for his help in naming a large array of new auxiliary vessels; Nevil Shute, aeronautics engineer turned novelist, giving reasons for his decision to emigrate to Australia; doggerel verse, thirteen stanzas, from Sir Waldron Smithers MP (Conservative, Orpington): *Dear Alan, May I thank you for all you have done, To give the British Public, A lead, as well as fun* . . . the Archbishop of Canterbury, Dr Fisher, clarifying a point of Church law about which APH had 'expressed amazement'. Successive secretaries tried in vain to stem the tide of procrastination, to be told time and again: 'Let's leave it till tomorrow.' Latterly, he would say with a dismissive gesture as if the mere act of putting his signature to a letter bored him: 'Answer it by telephone.' In his thesaurus, efficiency was a synonym for bondage.

Sir Alan Herbert to the Special Commissioners of Income Tax:

> 12 Hammersmith Terrace
> London, W.6.
> 8 June 1955

Sirs,   I thank you for the courtesy of your letter of 12th May, and for your consideration, which I should have acknowledged before but for the railway strike and the Government's injunction to avoid unnecessary letters.

I cannot accept your airy view of my financial position but will not waste time with further argument now. At this difficult time, I know, we must all do what we can to keep the social services going for strikers, though once again they are damaging nearly all my professional sources of income – books, newspapers and theatres; so here is a cheque for £728 2s. 6d. in settlement of this iniquitous tax.

> Yours faithfully,
> A. P. HERBERT

He and Vivian Ellis completed their 'musical' version of *The Water Gipsies* and waited hopefully to hear that a well-known management would produce it. The prospect faded; the script came back, and lay unheeded on APH's desk. A chance meeting with Peter Saunders at the Black Lion, Hammersmith, changed the scene. Saunders, a former press agent, was the man behind *The Mousetrap*, Agatha Christie's great play success. He had worked on Basil Dean's film of *The Water Gipsies* twenty years before. A hint from APH that the 'musical' was available at once alerted his interest. 'I was enchanted with the whole idea. It was a new world for me, and a most exciting one.' He undertook to produce the show. Casting and rehearsals began soon after. 'About a hundred' young women arrived for an audition at which it was hoped to discover some new musical-comedy voices. Saunders wrote that if APH had had his way, 'we would have had a chorus of a couple of hundred. Every time a pretty girl sang, he would walk down from the back of the stalls and say, "She's rather nice, isn't she? Can't we use her?" '[4]

After a preliminary and encouraging month in the Midlands, *The Water Gipsies* opened at the Winter Garden Theatre – 'the wrong end of Drury Lane' – in August 1955. A song of APH's written for an opening number, 'got the play off to a terrific start'. By the end of the first act Saunders thought that he had 'a smash-hit' on his hands. After the first interval, the mood of the audience changed. When, at the fall of the curtain, the leading lady, Dora Bryan, was pushed forward to take a call, someone shouted from the gallery: 'You saved the show!' It was the voice of doom, quoted in too many otherwise favourable newspaper notices. Peter Saunders had no doubt that 'it did more damage than anything that might have been said by the press. It did enormous harm at the box office.'

APH 'never tired' of listening to the comic exchanges he wrote for Dora Bryan and Pamela Charles, the two sisters in *The Water Gipsies* 'musical'. He dwelt on his 'nagging doubts' as a writer of humour for the stage. 'You think a line is funny when you scribble it down. It makes the company laugh when they hear it at the first rehearsal. When it has been said ten or twenty times nobody laughs any more, and you begin to wonder whether it is funny after all. Then, on the first night, if all those strangers open their friendly faces and throats in a loud, long laugh it is for the author a moment of triumph. If on all the other nights more thousands roar their irresistible laughter at exactly the same point of time the pleasure, the sense of power, does not diminish. This may be thought a rather shameful confession, but I make it gladly. Did not my song say: "I want to see the people happy"?'[5]

On the 150th night he was asked by 'a lady in the bar' what he thought of the show. 'I happen to be the author', he said. 'Oh – Mr Priestley?' she enquired, beaming with pleasure. The end came after seven months. APH assumed that for the producer it meant a loss of 'several thousands'. For himself, the final curtain had fallen on his career in the theatre. Not that he was yet ready to believe it. He had ideas 'for two more musicals, at least. After all,' he told an interviewer from Fleet Street, 'I do know something about this musical comedy business. I can still write a pretty good lyric. And I don't rhyme "Chartreuse" with "furs".'

NOTES ON CHAPTER 22

1 What became of *Water Gipsy* is not known. She might have been a popular attraction at the National Maritime Museum.
2 Haddock – a name familiar to readers of *Misleading Cases;* and later to a television public.
3 A. P. Herbert: Private notes.
4 Peter Saunders: *The Mousetrap Man* (1972).
5 *APH: His Life and Times.*

23

'I Object!'

He told *World's Press News* in January 1956: 'It is my boast that I can put any leading article into ten couplets or less.' When the Government under Harold Macmillan sanctioned the issue of Premium Bonds, he submitted to *The Times* 'a fourth leader in verse'. It appeared in the paper on 4 May 1956.

SOMETHING FOR NOTHING

See how the State, all-powerful and wise,
Walks in the wake of private enterprise.
Enlists a folly to avert defeat,
And brings the lottery to Lombard Street!
The citizen, uncertain of the end,
Insists on spending what he has to spend:
For why, says he, should anybody save
When what is left is pilfered from the grave?
And why invest, in these suspicious times,
When dividends are practically crimes?
Likewise, he cries: 'Two bloody wars I've won,
And I deserve some long-belated fun.'
So H. Macmillan, in the Silver Ring,
Puts naughty Britain on a goodish thing.
'A wager with a difference', he coos,
'It's heads you win – and tails you cannot lose.'
But there are mutters in the Church and Kirk:
'Something for nothing' – 'Wealth divorced from
       work'.
Strange – for the moralist will throw no stone
If we invest in industry or loan.
There money grows, like something in the soil:
But do we owe our taking to our toil?
Nay, though we earned the money we invest,

'Unearned', by statute, is the interest.
The Church itself is very wide awake,
Exists on money which it does not make.
And, I am told, not very long ago,
Bought better stocks – and made a profit so.
So in the scale of morals we should set
Higher, perhaps, the citizens who bet,
Brave souls who stake their money on their skill
With no smug certainty of losing nil.
'Something for nothing' is an empty slur,
For who works harder than the wagerer?
What anxious study of the horse, or hound,
Before the fateful animal is found!
We learn his pedigree, we probe his past,
And all the reasons why he finished last,
We read the pundits, or we use a pin,
And, either way, are wonders if we win.
Mark, too, the slaves who struggle in the pools
With permutation and relentless rules,
Pore over 'form' in microscopic print
And fill the tiny squares until they squint,
Though well aware, when all the labour's done,
The odds are many millions to one.
'Something for nothing?' Oh, that so much care
Were used by every worker everywhere!
And will the saints be very much more fond
Of those who rush to buy a betting bond?
'Something for nothing'? What about the State,
Grown fat on riches that it can't create,
Which, risking nothing to produce a play,
Takes tribute from the cash-box every day,
And does not care one tiny little toss
If it has robbed a profit or a loss?
Is not the Socialist's supreme concern
That men should have what other people earn?
In such low company, of Right or Red,
No honest gambler need hang his head.

What seemed like ticker-tape facility was not without its
accompaniment of background agitation. He told me: 'How often
I've been stuck after about eight lines!' He tended to particularize
less about rhyme than about sense. His weekly verse commentary
on the passing show that had been appearing regularly in the

Sunday Graphic for sixteen years, was becoming too often reminiscent of the fairy queen pointing in admonitory lines the moral of the pantomime. Sometimes he caught a popular feeling with apposite wit, as when, in December 1956, the United Nations Assembly passed a critical vote on the Anglo-French affair at Suez.

> YEMEN's against us! I shall die of shame.
> CAMBODIA and LAOS said the same.
> But these three 'nations', though of high renown,
> Could all be fitted into London Town.
> Then there was LEBANON (and SALVADOR
> Of whom I bet you never heard before).
> In this Assembly, to secure a vote,
> You need three palms, two camels and a goat.
> The STATES have one, but so has the UKRAINE:
> RUSSIA and Co. can count on eight or nine.
> Of those, observe, who hit us on the head,
> A half, at least, were brown or black – or Red.
> It's an injustice I can hardly bear,
> That MONACO's not represented there.
> EIRE opposes us with all her might,
> Which makes me fancy that we may be right;
> And, God forgive him, Eisenhower votes:
> Give aid to RUSSIA, and the UNITED GOATS.

Composing such pieces as 'Something for Nothing', a title with comfortless implications for Haddock Productions, probably cost him more in mental effort than he would have admitted. His co-directors thought it politic to let him know that they had observed 'that you have been as busy as ever of late in various directions, including some excellent letters to *The Times* – unpaid!' They may have had in mind, too, his recent appointment to the board of the Savoy Hotel Limited, a nominal directorship that was a compliment to his name and fame and largely justified by his quotably witty speeches at the annual general meetings. They suggested that he should now 'settle down to a long-term work' likely to be of 'solid benefit' to Haddock Productions. A resolution was minuted: 'That Sir Alan Herbert be directed to plan his activities' in compliance with the objects of the company.

'Yes,' he pencilled on a letter dated 21 May 1957. It was from his good friend John Astor of *The Times*, inviting him to deliver the

opening speech on the freedom of the press at the forthcoming annual
conference in London of the Commonwealth Press Union. 'Please
forgive me for worrying you. – John.' Two decades have not
devalued what he had to say on that occasion. He quoted, 'with a
glow of gratitude and pride', the opinion of Lord Chief Justice
Cockburn on 'the liberty of public writers' stated in a case involving
The Times in 1888: 'Who can doubt that, though injustice may often
be done, and though public men may often have to smart under
the keen sense of wrong inflicted by hostile criticism, the nation
profits by public opinion being thus freely brought to bear on the
discharge of public duties?' APH told the conference:

'When I speak of the freedom of the press I mean the freedom of
the writer – and the editor – to express and instruct the mind of
Man, not the freedom to exhibit the bosom and behind of Woman.'
He did not doubt, he said, that if John Milton 'had imagined some
of today's news sheets, if he had realised that he, with things to say
in his splendid way, would have to fight for space in a jungle of
busts and bikinis, babies in iron lungs, ladies in bubble baths,
corpses in woods . . . he would not have bothered to jot down the
Areopagitica at all.'

He sub-titled his new book, *No Fine on Fun, The Comical History
of the Entertainment Duty* (1957), and showed in it that he was as
superbly capable as ever of making light reading out of heavy
subjects; in this instance, the tax first imposed as an emergency
measure in the old war (1916) and crassly retained on the Statute
Book ever since to the profit of the Exchequer and the detriment of
enterprise elsewhere, especially in the theatre and the cinema. No
one realized more completely the nature of the problem, with its
central difficulty of finding a satisfactory definition of entertainment.
No one could have unravelled the tangled skeins of controversy
more skilfully or made out the case for abolition more persuasively
or, in the result, more influentially.

In a taxi he asked his wife: 'What are we going to the O'Bryens
for?' She reminded him that 1957 was their friends' silver wedding
year. 'They're having a celebration.' Before paying off the cab in
Knightsbridge he had written out as a salute (his word) on a
post-card:

Silver Bill and Silver Liz,
How strange and comforting it is –
Two such happy, healthy dears
After five-and-twenty years!
Oh, sweet pair! If you persist,
All the weddings on the list–
Aluminium – Platinum -
Hydrogen and Strontium,
Shall be yours to have and hold
Till you get to good old Gold.
Poor old Alan, poor old Gwen,
May not be about by then.
But a heavenly glass we'll fill,
To Diamond Liz and Diamond Bill.

He could not share the sense of wonder that gripped the minds of men at the prospect of the first of the 'lunar probes' being competitively organized in the USA and USSR. 'Lunatic probes' he called them. 'What good had it done to a single soul, that photograph of the backside of the moon?' The whole 'childish experiment' incited him to denounce the space scientists in an outburst of invective:

. . . The atom, which was nice and small,
You've made the monarch of you all.
You draw explosives from the air,
And alcohol from anywhere.
There's nothing that you can't pervert
To din, destruction, death, and dirt . . .[1]

As for the 'artificial satellites':

Lord, what a mess the firmament will be
When every nation boasts of two or three!

He received, in that controversial context, an attribution that rarely came his way. Commenting on the activities of the Committee on Contamination by Extra-Terrestrial Exploration, *The Times Educational Supplement* stated: 'It will be seen that CETEX's reasons for not bombarding the planets are not precisely those of the poet Herbert; but for once science and sentiment are pointing in the same direction.'

From the top table, at the great centenary dinner of the Savage

Club in December that year, he declaimed lines that may be memorably recited to Savages of a later generation assembling at the summons of their famous tocsin drum. *'Brother Savages, and Guests – and Ghosts; I answer, shyly, for the scribbling hosts . . .'* Alluding to some of the newer by-products of the professional pen – films, radio, television: *'At low advertisements we looked askance. Today we write them, if we get the chance.'*

He himself could no longer afford to 'look askance' at advertisement writing, a well-paid sideline, though a recent experience had not been happy. 'I am very disappointed', he wrote to the agency manager who had commissioned him to write the 'copy' for 'a run of 11 inch triple columns in *The Times*', and with whom he had to bargain uncomfortably when the series was summarily abandoned. Another commission, from Shell-Mex, required him to produce 'a poem' in which every line was to contain nouns beginning with S. 'Is S the letter richest in delight? It stands for Sense, and Scent and Sound and Sight . . .' on to a climactic fanfare for Super-Shell. When he allowed himself to be named a member of a football pools' panel given the task of deciding the probable winning teams after a spate of postponed matches, his editor in Bouverie Street, Malcolm Muggeridge, privately considered it 'a mistake'; good for his pocket, no doubt, otherwise diminishing.

Muggeridge admired and revived *Misleading Cases* as a pillar of the *Punch* literary edifice, eclipsed in durability only by *The Diary of a Nobody* (1892). He valued APH's skill as a librettist of the human comedy who could take a *pronunciamento* from the Treasury in London, or the State Department in Washington, and transmute it effortlessly, it seemed, into lilting light verse that often read as if it was meant to be sung. Recalling APH's 'attractive personal qualities', Malcolm Muggeridge remains firm in his belief that 'at heart he was a melancholy man'.

In earlier years that diagnosis would have been belied by a buoyancy of temper that was singularly impervious to deflation. His was hardly the tragedy of the artist who is aware of his limitations and fatuously defies them. More probably, reaching his sixties, he suffered the vexation of spirit that French rhetoric has postulated as 'the agony of the older generation in watching the rise of the younger'. To the hurt of rejections from *Punch* was often added that of the elaborately courteous regrets of other editors to whom he offered the unplaced articles.

In 1957 a new editor of *Punch*, Bernard Hollowood, took over from Malcolm Muggeridge, who left the job 'with infinite relief' at finding himself no longer 'under the professional necessity of trying to be funny'.[2] A contributor from the Second World War years, Hollowood was as radical in outlook as the earliest of his predecessors in the editorial chair who thumbed Mr Punch's nose at royalty and much else of the established order. He had come neither to jeer nor sneer but to reform. (He tried, and failed, to abolish the *Punch* title and image.) He recognized that APH retained the loyalty of a large body of readers, though they were not of the generation that was being looked to for new circulation. 'We disagreed politically but not seriously. He tended to harp on battles long ago. Of course he wrote like a dream when in form. I was always vastly impressed by his energy and readiness to "have a go". He was a good companion; a marvellous mixer.'[3]

APH complained of 'disturbing sensations after a spell of hard, concentrated mental work'. They were often a sequel to 'any job involving figures and calculations', which he 'always enjoyed', especially those arising from 'taking sights of sun and stars'. He thought it necessary to tell his fellow directors of Haddock Productions: 'I am not putting on an act. It is all rather worrying.' He assured them: 'I am only despondent when I think of those unjust and impossible taxes.' He had 'great faith' in a 'new doctor', Guy Beauchamp, in Harley Street, and was sure that 'the trouble can be put right'. His memorandum to the directors reverted to the tax problem. 'I feel I deserve some special consideration from the Commissioners.' Pointing out that he had 'not had much luck with film rights, etc., as some other authors had, he suggested that he had 'some potentially large literary assets unexhausted; e.g. film rights of *Bless the Bride*, and other works', and asked hopefully: 'Would it be possible to borrow money on the security of such properties (or my share in them) from some rich person who wouldn't expect his money back at once? Or get someone to buy them on spec.?'

He was working meanwhile on a didactic new novel, *Made for Man*, its theme developed from the rigid attitude of the Church of England to the remarriage of divorced persons in church. Somewhat surprisingly, his contract for it included publication in the USA, by the well-known Doubleday firm. They had published *The Water Gipsies* in 1930, and other books of his in the years between.

He gave no sign of lowered tone at the party held at the Savoy Hotel in April 1958 to celebrate the record-breaking success, so far, of Agatha Christie's play, *The Mousetrap*. He was asked to speak 'on behalf of Literature'. Gazing over his glasses at the closely packed standing throng of a thousand guests, he bade them: 'Ladies and gentlemen – pray be seated'. It was the laugh of the evening.

The occasion provided an opportunity for him to speak his mind once again about Entertainment Tax, and he made the most of it for a full half hour. Enthusiastic applause greeted his declaration: 'No tax on thought, no duty on beauty, no levy on laughter, no fine on fun.'

He was in even better form at the Christ Church gaudy at Oxford two months later, after the Encaenia at which he received an honorary degree (Doctor of Civil Law) in the company of the Prime Minister (Macmillan); the Leader of the Opposition (Gaitskell); Lord Beveridge; Sir Owen Dixon, Chief Justice of Australia; the musicians Poulenc and Shostakovich; and Tiselius, the bio-chemist from Upsala. On a day loud with oratory in the classical mode, his speech in rhyming couplets passed with acclamation into the annals of the university:

> We thank you, Sir, for all the flowered jests
> With which you crowned your glad and grateful guests;
> And for a feast with such a grace and glow
> As we poor Londoners can never know -
> Where wit and wisdom match the mellow wine,
> And men, by women undisturbed, can shine.
> Bacchus in conference with Socrates,
> Lucullus chattering with Thucydides –
> Can there be better company than these?
> And you have added Cicero. But no -
> For I was not so fond of Cicero.
> It's an Augustus you have heard tonight,
> Who knows as well the forum and the fight,
> Who, strong in storm and positive in plan,
> Seems to forget he's a Balliol man.
>
> . . . .
>
> Boy Beveridge you duly decorate,
> The Archimedes of the Farewell State,
> Who did so well distributing the gravy
> That poor Britannia can't afford a Navy.

Sir Owen Solon I regard with awe:
For here we have a Bradman of the Law;
And let them contemplate, the friends of schism,
This proud example of 'Dominionism'.
   Then there's an Orpheus – two – more moving far,
But less upsetting than their statesmen are.
And one of them, we hope, may now contrive
An Oxford Symphony – and stay alive.
   We hail Tilesius, for Sweden's sake,
Though most of science is a big mistake.
I wake at dawn each day and mutter 'Drat 'em!'
Those careless Cambridge men who split the atom.
I've seen no Sputniks, and I shall not try,
I don't approve of litter in the sky.
I hate the idiots who threaten soon
To fire a missile at the common Moon,
And mean to mutilate the only face
That is beloved by all the human race . . .

.   .   .   .

Oxford! In all the catalogues of worth
There is no name like Oxford on the Earth –
The only name, they say, that sounds as clear
As Coco Cola in the cosmic ear:
A name of love on all the nation's lips,
As 'Greenwich' still is mistress of the ships.
Set sail, brave boys, Frustration left ashore,
The flag of Oxford flying at the fore:
And let us whisper, as we put to sea,
'I'll give the world what Oxford gave to me'.

'It had an important place in the pattern of freedom, and literature, and public morals.' He was referring to the Obscene Publications Bill, on which he had been active as chairman of the Society of Authors' committee set up to promote it four years before. He had wanted it to be called 'The Protection of Literature Bill'. 'Its prime purpose is the protection of literature, of honest authors and publishers, from the uncertainty and injustice of the old Victorian law.' Under that law, authors and publishers, 'whose only offence may have been an error of taste or judgment', could be put in the dock. The Bill was not designed 'to give new licence to the lewd'; on the contrary, 'it gives new powers to the authorities in the pursuit and punishment of the merchants of pornography'.

He had 'no great interest in obscene publications. Most of them bore me'. His quarry, always, was folly, not vice; but, as he said, he had 'taken on the job' and intended 'sticking to it till it was done'.

In November 1958 Roy Jenkins, MP, 'able champion of authors and publishers' (APH), obtained leave to present the Bill to Parliament. His introductory speech drew cries of 'I object', which meant that 'it was blocked again, perhaps for another year'. Persuading himself that there had been 'dirty work' by the Government whips to prevent the Bill going through the Private Members' procedures, APH was 'pretty enraged'. In a letter to *The Times* (2 December), he disclosed that he was 'thinking of standing as an Independent at the East Harrow by-election. The great parties no doubt will laugh heartily at this information. They laughed heartily, I remember, in 1935.'

Within the next few days he received through the post cheques to the value of over a thousand pounds from well-wishers, many of whom appeared to be more concerned to see him back in Parliament than with obscene publications. He wrote to one of his supporters: 'There seems to be such pleasure about my standing.'

At the age of 68, he said, 'I did not really, for my own sake, want to go back to the Commons. Nor had I the wish to damage the Conservatives', who feared that his intervention would have that result. 'A gentleman called Heath,[4] I was told was in a great state about it. I can't think why. I did not flatter myself that I had the slightest chance.' He had been made 'fighting mad', he said, 'by this latest and worst example of the contemptuous Whitehall attitude to Private Members' rights that I had been complaining about for years. Also, it was an insult to our profession as authors.'

At the risk of being tagged 'the dirty books candidate', he appointed an agent, designed a rosette for himself and his supporters – 'heart of Oxford blue surrounded by a ring of Cambridge' – and composed a letter to the Electors of East Harrow bearing the title: *I Object*. It was an even more quotable polemic than his much talked-of election address in 1935; for example: 'I feel that Man, through Science, is Getting Too Big For His Boots – the old Greek *hubris*. The respectful use of Nature is one thing; cosmic tampering with Nature, the assault of heavenly bodies, is another. Nothing like this should be done except with the consent of Man – the United Nations.' Ten thousand copies were printed and published for him by The Bodley Head, price one shilling. He guaranteed £200 towards the costs. Two hundred and fifty copies, 'specially bound and signed by the author', were put on sale at a guinea each. 'Unusual, I agree. I blushed and demurred but I had no Party behind me and I might have needed the money.' A political correspondent pronounced it 'the election address of the century'. Lord Birkett, who had appeared in *The Well of Loneliness* case thirty years earlier, thought it worthy of Burke. APH reckoned it one of his 'best bits of writing', the more so because 'it worked'. There were no objecting cries when the Bill came up for its Second Reading after the Christmas recess. At that stage, he stood down, only to be accused of 'not being serious', a charge that he promptly repudiated as 'quite untrue'. His withdrawal may or may not have been strategic. Certainly there was no clear sign that the electors of East Harrow would rally to his side in decisive numbers on the day. The Obscene Publications Bill, much amended, became law in 1959. 'Rightly or wrongly, our five years of fussing saved that boring book *Lady Chatterley's Lover* – and a good many others.'

'No more committees – damn committees!' He was determined to 'stay in the study', to finish his long-postponed novel about the Thames sailing bargemen, his only major project in hand. For income he was dependent on his Sunday paper contract, on intermittent performing-right royalties, on acceptances from *Punch*. 'No – a thousand times!' he told Kilham Roberts, general secretary of the Society of Authors, who was pressing him to take command of what was to become the Public Lending Right campaign.

He was campaigning, meanwhile, on behalf of Roberts himself, and Elizabeth Barber, to secure recognition of their dedicated services to the Society of Authors in a forthcoming Honours' List. Heartily concurring, John Masefield wrote to him: 'I think you have a lucky way with you, and feel sure that you will succeed.'[5] (28 October 1958). Somerset Maugham, responding to APH's request for his support, thought it relevant to mention in his letter that 'a certain editor' sent a collection of Anthony Powell's novels to a post-war Prime Minister, 'who was so charmed with them (not having read anything but minutes before), that "within a month" the donor received the CBE' (1 November 1958).

APH's thousand-times-no rejection of the idea that he should 'tackle the libraries affair' on behalf of his fellow authors was

modified by persuasion to an understanding that he would conduct
'a preliminary survey' under the aegis of the Society of Authors,
with the help of J. Alan White, chairman of Methuen, the publishers,
and Stephen Tumim, a barrister neighbour of the Herberts at
Hammersmith. Between them they produced what was known as the
Herbert Memorandum. Published in March 1960, it covered all
the problems likely to be met in promoting Public Lending Right, a
term devised by APH and White over lunch at the Garrick Club.
From then on PLR became a public issue.

Insisting that it was to be his 'last political effort', APH undertook
the chairmanship of a joint committee of the Society of Authors' and
the Publishers' Association to further the creation of a public
lending right for books comparable with the well-established
performing right for music. His colleague, Alan White, estimated
that as his contribution APH wrote 'fully 50,000 words in exposition
of the authors' and publishers' case'.[6] From his account,[7] and from
the facts set out in the Society of Authors' bulletin Number 3, the
deduction may fairly be made that in the light of his declining
personal fortunes APH was too generous of his time and strength
in advancing the cause of PLR in those years, the more so as his
efforts were hampered by the apathy of all but a minority of his
fellow craftsmen. As Shaw had complained in 1932: 'What a
heartbreaking job it is trying to combine authors for their own
protection!' Once again APH invoked the spirit of Tennyson's
Ulysses. 'Nothing will make me give up.'

His first public engagement in 1959 (27 January) was to speak at
the 200th anniversary dinner of the Dumfries Burns Club. He
introduced himself as 'a poor timorous English beastie of Irish
extraction'. (A little later, in a written reference to Trinity College,
Dublin, he pronounced himself 'an Irishman by birth'.) He told
the clubmen of Dumfries: 'There is, they say, a lump of metal
going round the sun. It cannot be seen and, thank God, it cannot
be heard. But I am willing to believe it, for it is the kind of crazy
thing that Man thinks it good and clever to do. I heard the other
day some solemn ass describe the despatch of this lump of metal to
the regions of the sun as "the supreme intellectual achievement of
man".' The Burns' Club could make a grander claim. 'Long before
these modern marvels of communication were conceived, your poet
put a girdle round the earth with a single song,[8] owing nothing to

electricity or science, his only instrument the hearts and tongues of men.'

Over breakfast on a spring day that year he read the news that 'the business tycoon', Charles Clore, was planning to take over the Watney brewery interests. Momentarily *The Times* was as a red rag inflaming him to instant protest. Arming himself for combat with 20 shares in the threatened company, and in anticipation of an offer for them from 'the king of all the Cuckoos', he informed Clore by letter that, in effect, there was 'nothing doing', and proceeded to state his objection to the take-over system in general, and his resentment of any move likely to destroy or modify 'the infinite variety of the public house' in particular. He was concerned about the fate of his 'local', the Black Lion. 'It has a large garden near to the river which seems to me to be likely to catch the eye of any Cuckoo with an itch to build blocks of flats or offices in the wrong place.' His feelings overflowed into far from stately quatrains:

> Fly away, Mr Mighty!
>   There are bigger things to do.
> Why not buy the churches?
>   They're undervalued too.
>
> You're slipping, Mr Cuckoo!
>   Make an offer for St Paul's:
> There'd be room for lots of flats,
>   Or a dozen dancing halls.
>
> Fly away, Mr Wizard;
>   Start something on your own.
> Build a few more theatres,
>   But leave the pubs alone.

Clore, he said, 'replied most courteously' to his letter of protest. There had been no intention of making 'sweeping changes' in the character of the public house and certainly not of creating a uniformity that would be generally unacceptable. APH's views, publicized in the London evening newspapers, were not everywhere favourably received. He was accused in the City columns and in letters of 'sentimentalising the English pub', which was often 'grim and drab'; he was hindering 'much needed reforms'; and so on.

He spoke afterwards of having had 'a feeling of quiet satisfaction' at Clore's withdrawal from the fray. His stand at the time may not have directly influenced that result. What cannot be doubted is that he voiced a substantial hardening of public opinion against the take-over type of 'big business' operation. Once again it was unremunerative effort, even less so than that for which he received as payment from *Liberal News*, '1 Bot. Gordon's Gin, for edit. contribs.'

Haddock Productions Limited could look for no benefit from his pursuit of a new theme for Letters to the Editor: *Is It Cricket?* in which he derided 'the inelegant and laughable rubbing of the ball on shirts and trousers by bowlers and fielders to maintain the "shine" (*The Times*, 27 August 1959). 'I hope you will get your teeth into this matter', a reader, D. Y. Perkins, of Clevedon, Somerset, wrote to him, 'for I know that once your teeth are in they are not very easily dislodged!!!' Discussing 'this matter' in its technical and aesthetic aspects, APH concluded that 'the spectacle of a fast bowler rubbing his way into the television screen is one of the funniest things in modern entertainment'.

> . . . *And when you rub your buttocks, or your belly,*
> *Remember what it looks like on the telly,*

he wrote as part of a 'salute' in verse to Test cricketers being entertained by the British Sportsmen's Club in London. His muse never failed to oblige on those occasions, as Humphrey Ellis remembers from his *Punch* years. 'He would ring me and, without preamble, would ask: "I say, who is this chap Cheetham?" or "What do you know of Umrigar – does he rhyme with "vigour"?" He had always liked cricket, his devotion stopping short of recognizing it 'as a branch of religion'. He told members of the Surrey County Cricket Club: 'I cannot accept that it is the nurse of noble character. It is a tough, rough, unscrupulous and ruthless game.'

Elsewhere, he deplored the fact that one of the more sinister of contemporary social trends was polluting cricket reporting, and that a new and frenzied vocabulary was being resorted to by the commentators. 'Where in my day wickets "fell", the language of violence now tells us that they "collapse" or are "shattered".' Soon, he expected to read or hear of them "disintegrating" or even "exploding". 'Teams now "storm" to victory or are "slaughtered". As for the pronouncement that a team is "skittled out", it is absurd, because it suggests that all ten wickets fell at the same time.'

No great self-disciplinary effort was needed to disengage him from the allurements of a holiday in Cornwall (August 1960) to expound his views on D. H. Lawrence's notorious novel, *Lady Chatterley's Lover*. A case under the new Obscene Publications Act, arising out of the reissue of the book by Allen Lane and Penguin Books, was coming before the courts. As a prominent protagonist of the Act, APH was asked if he would be a witness for the defence. 'I am not sure that I could be helpful', he wrote to Michael Rubinstein, of the well-known Grays Inn law firm (28 August 1960). 'I have no pretension to be a literary critic.' He had previously made 'some unconsidered remarks about the book' to the Select Committee three years ago. At that time he had only 'dipped into' the novel. Now, on holiday, he had 'read it carefully, every word', and the author's own defence of it too. 'It explains his purpose much more clearly than the novel does.' He wished that Penguin had printed extracts from Lawrence's expository essay, *À Propos of Lady Chatterley's Lover* (1930).

Having read the novel more thoroughly, 'I still find it boring. I feel no interest in the principal characters; all are unreal and unattractive. Except in the way of duty, I don't think I would have finished the book. As a novel, I don't think it is important.' As a social document, 'it certainly is important and I accept most of the author's defence of it – not all. It is the work of a preacher, not a pornographer, and that is why, perhaps, I do not find it really entertaining. If I had to defend it I should say that it is an honest attempt in novel form to give healthy sex instruction. Lawrence himself thought it would be good for the young. The young today seem to know almost everything but often in the wrong way. He may be right.' Summing up:

'Any work by this writer must have some "literary merit". I am often maddened by his style. But there is some fine writing in the book, some good descriptions of nature and the industrial North, some eloquent passages on the domination of Money and the Machine and the dwindling of Man. And though my perhaps finicky taste is offended by the four-letter words, or the excess of them, I must admit some merit to the sexual passages in general. The law, I know, even under this Act, pays no attention to "intent". But any "expert" who is asked about "literary merit" in such an affair is entitled to consider "intent", for there cannot be true literary merit without honesty of purpose. Here, I am satisfied, there is complete honesty of purpose; that is, there is no "dirt for dirt's sake". That is not to say that *Lady Chatterley's Lover* has great merit as a novel.'

He was a principal speaker at the Oxford Union on 17 November 1970, debating the motion that 'This House has no Desire to Launch out into Space'. Englishmen, he claimed, have no apologies to make concerning the study of Space. 'I expect I know as much about Space and the Heavenly Bodies as many men here – and when I say Space I mean real Space, the unimaginably distant regions in which those fiery furnaces the stars reside, not this wretched little solar system of ours, with its pox of planets, lightless and phoney, visible only, like the University of Cambridge, by the reflected light of an authentic luminary.'

He stood before the House as 'the only Briton since the Venerable Bede who has renamed the stars – two hundred and eighty of them– and published his conclusions in a book. Even today', he asserted, 'I could pick out for you most of the sixty principal stars employed in navigation, north and south of the Equator – which is more than most of the Space fans can do.' With the aid of instruments and calculations, he could tell the House that 'at this moment Orion is rising due East of us, and the great star Capella above him has an altitude of 40 degrees; that at 12.30 the senior star Sirius should be visible south-east of this city, and at 3.20 will be standing on the meridian over Folly Bridge.'

He could make those 'frantic boasts' because of 'the labours of Englishmen' through the centuries. 'A million rockets to the moon will not put England any lower in the Space class.' He disapproved of 'litter in the sky', and could imagine a future in which sputniks and satellites would be used for aggressive broadcasting purposes –

> And monsters, motionless above the town,
> Will bellow threats and propaganda down.

He demanded of his Oxford Union audience: 'The sun in the morning and the moon at night – who is Man to interfere with them?' He commended to the House the 'wise words' of the Advisory Council on Scientific Policy, 1958–59, 'that we should concentrate on strengthening our economic position and improving the living standards in the poorer countries of the Commonwealth, and that it would be the grossest folly to leave those needs unsatisfied for the sake of space exploration'. He did not carry the day.

NOTES ON CHAPTER 23

1   *Sunday Graphic*, 6 October 1957.
2   Malcolm Muggeridge: *Tread Softly for you Tread on my Jokes* (1966).
3   Letter, 17 September 1975.
4   Edward Heath, then Tory Chief Whip.
5   He did.
6   *Performing Right Society Journal*, April 1966.
7   *A.P.H.: His Life and Times.*
8   *Auld Lang Syne.*

24

An Invitation from the Poet Laureate

'I should not like to confess exactly how much I owe to Methuen's by way of "advances" unearned. I mention this dismal fact only to throw a good word to all the wicked publishers. Your agent persuades them to pay you a generous "advance" on account of royalties; but if the royalties earned by the author fall short, far short sometimes, of the "advance" they do not expect you to return the difference. What other trade, I wonder, behaves so well?'

That confessional passage occurs early in APH's autobiography, as if it was imperative that he rid himself of what Thackeray would have called 'a thorn in the cushion' of his writing life. Whatever his rating at the sales counter, his publishers would no doubt have been reluctant to see his name pass from their list. Their hopes of another best selling novel from him, in succession to *The Water Gipsies* (1930) and *Holy Deadlock* (1934), remained unfulfilled. Other books by him had sold well; for instance, *Misleading Cases*; his *Topsy* series; and his volumes of verse.

The publication in 1960 of *Look Back and Laugh* was not simply an act of homage on his seventieth birthday; coincidentally, it was his seventieth book and marked also his fiftieth year as a contributor to *Punch*. It epitomized his most characteristic thought and writing through half a century, and above all confirmed his splendid constancy in wielding humour as the sword of common sense, a Meredithian phrase of which he was our most notable exemplar during those five decades. In effect the book was a *résumé* of the intellectual life of the Calverley-inspired schoolboy who, as if by a process of literary parthenogenesis, developed into the many-sided man of letters – poet, humourist, satirist, novelist, dramatist, librettist, propagandist, pamphleteer – and, if not strictly in the Shelleyan sense, an acknowledged legislator of the British part of mankind.

Faced by the incontestable logic of a letter (3 February 1961) from the tax authorities in which they suggested that 'provision to meet your surtax should have been made as and when the income arose', he wrote to them: 'I have read with care and attention your little homily, some of which was familiar. All of it was appropriate enough for ordinary income tax, but none of it, if I may say so, to this immoral surtax. I had an unexpected job last week, unexpectedly well rewarded (that is the way of our strange occupation), and I now enclose a cheque for £85' (9 February). His cheque was made out on 12 Hammersmith Terrace notepaper, 'duly stamped and crossed "Inland Revenue A/C", to be presented for clearance at his bank, National and Grindlay's, Parliament Street. The words in capitals were typed in red.[1]

> Dear Bankers, PAY the undermentioned hounds
> The shameful sum of FIVE-AND-EIGHTY POUNDS.
> By 'hounds', of course, by custom, one refers
> To SPECIAL INCOME TAX COMMISSIONERS:
> And these progenitors of woe and worry
> You'll find at LYNWOOD ROAD, THAMES DITTON, SURREY.
>
> This is the *second* lot of tax, you know,
> On money that I earned two years ago.
> (The shark, they say, by no means Nature's knight,
> Will rest contented with a single bite:
> The barracuda who's a fish more fell,
> Comes back and takes the other leg as well.)
>
> Two years ago. But things have changed since then.
> I've reached the age of three-score years and ten.
> My earnings dwindle; and the kindly State
> Gives me a tiny pension – with my mate.
> You'd think the State would generously roar
> 'At least, he shan't pay SURTAX any more'.
> Instead, by this un-Christian attack
> They get two-thirds of my poor pension back.
>   Oh, very well. No doubt it's for the best;
> At all events, pray do as I request;
> And let the good old custom be enforced –
> Don't cash this cheque, unless it is endorsed.

With no conspicuous success, a Lord Chief Justice, Winston Churchill, the head of the North Thames Gas Board, and several lesser mortals, had been prompted over the years to respond 'in kind' to APH's nimble poetizing. His rhyming cheque having been cashed, he was more than casually surprised to receive the following acknowledgment from The Office for the Special Commissioners for Income Tax:

> S.T.H. 31097/40.
>
> Dear Sir,
> It is with pleasure that I thank
> You for your letter, and the order to your bank
> To pay the sum of five and eighty pounds
> To those here whom you designate as hounds.
> Their appetite is satisfied. In fact,
> You paid too much and I am forced to act,
> Not to repay you, as perchance you dream,
> Though such a course is easy, it would seem.
> Your liability for later years
> Is giving your accountants many tears:
> And till such time as they and we can come
> To amicable settlement on the sum
> That represents your taxbill to the State
> I'll leave the overpayment to its fate.
> I do not think this step will make you frown:
> The sum involved is only half-a-crown.
> 　　　　　　　　　　　　　Yours faithfully,
> 　　　　　　　　　　　　　A. L. Grove.

To which he made reply:

> Your ref. S.T.H. 31097/40.
>
> I thank you, Sir, but am afraid
> Of such a rival in my trade:
> One never should encourage those –
> In future I shall pay in prose.

Hammersmith rateable values were another of his current vexations. The scale of them seemed to him disproportionate in relation to 'those old houses'. Numbers 12 and 13 in the Terrace had recently been declared 'of special architectural or historic interest' under the Town and County Planning Act 1947. He had 'spent two days grubbing about in old cheque books and bills', to establish that he had paid out over £2,000 'to the foul tribe of builders', called in to deal with 'fungoid floors, falling ceilings, tottering chimneys, pointing, etc.'. In consequence, 'refinements like painting have been beyond me'. One of the builders was made bankrupt, others were 'bad hats'. Confessing that he did not understand 'these things', the computation of rateable values, he wrote: 'My researches have been alarming but instructive in other ways. The way my Gas, Electricity, and Telephone bills have gone up in recent years . . .! God help us all!'

He was 'enraged by the contemptuous treatment that authors and publishers have had from this Parliament', *vide* the Libraries Bill debate in the House in December 1960. 'They certainly do not deserve to get free books from anybody.' Angrily, he demanded the return of works of his that he had presented from time to time to the House of Commons' library. 'A gracious letter' from the Speaker, Sir Harry Hylton-Foster, had a calming effect – 'it softened me'. The books were returned to the library. 'Splendid', the Speaker commented in writing. He hoped that APH would not allow his 'distaste for things said by some Honourable Members to become a distaste for the House of Commons, which is so much greater than them all' (21 April 1961).

APH's presence that month at a function organized by The Pedestrians' Association for Road Safety was reaffirmation of his long-held esteem for the aims and work of that body, founded in 1929. The proprietors of *Punch*, and Seaman, the then editor, were keen supporters of the Association from the beginning – APH a willing recruit. He wrote articles on road safety, and road accidents provided the theme of more than one of his *Misleading Cases*. Seniors of the Association, among them T. C. Foley, its secretary for many years, can still recite lines called *Go Slow* that he wrote during the war. They were reprinted and distributed to a public that never saw *Punch*.

> Go slow, you raving ass, go slow!
>   For there's a citizen ahead
>   Who will not help the nation, dead.
> It is a nuisance, I allow,
> That he should think of crossing now;
>   But he is late, as well as you,
>   And thinks he is important, too . . .

He pointed out inadequacies of the existing compensation laws, 'arguing, with others, that the introduction on a public highway of a means of automatic locomotion was potentially dangerous, and that the user of a car must accept responsibility for any injury thereby caused to a road user. This led to the introduction of third party insurance.'[2]

The announcement that he was to speak at a meeting arranged by the Pedestrians' Association in a Hammersmith hall resulted in a full house. In fact, his pulling power locally had been underestimated. The hall had to be closed 'on a crowd of angry people left outside, some of whom banged and kicked the doors in their frustration' (T. C. Foley).

In September 1961 he was asked, and agreed, to read the Lesson at the funeral service of an old friend, Michael Shepley, well-known actor. Shortly before the appointed hour he appeared at the sacristy of St Nicolas' Church, Chiswick, to tell the vicar, Prebendary Lewis Lloyd: 'I can't possibly read this Lesson. It says: "And there shall be no more sea". That's not my idea of Heaven.' Nor was he to be persuaded. The Lesson was read by Bernard Miles.

It is clear from his private records, and from the account rendered in his autobiography, that he devoted an inordinate amount of his working time in the sixties to the Public Lending Right campaign. A Libraries (Public Lending Right) Bill had been unsuccessfully presented to the House of Commons by Woodrow Wyatt, MP. An amended version, sponsored in the House by William Teeling, MP, met a similar fate. For a motion urging the Government to 'look sympathetically' at the authors' and publishers' case, David James, MP, secured the signatures of 140 of his fellow Members of all parties.

'Everybody is now conscious of our grievances', APH wrote. 'The term "Lending Right" has even got into the index of Whitaker's *Almanac*.' Otherwise, 'except in the minds of the public, we seem to have got nowhere'. He led deputations, wrote articles and letters to editors, noting that 'the *Daily Telegraph* has been a good friend to us' and did 'three weeks of logarithms', working out figures relevant to a new Libraries Bill that was being prepared.

Hardest to take was the opposition to PLR of the Library Association, which he was disinclined to believe represented the views of the full membership. Letters that he received suggested that it did not. But no hand had been raised in protest against the Association's policy at its recent annual general meeting, attended by 600 members. 'We regarded the librarians as our natural friends and allies', he wrote. 'They live by books (which is more than most authors do).' He was highly indignant, indeed 'appalled, ashamed', when the Library Association circulated a printed statement to MPs stating the librarians' objection to PLR. He and his colleagues among the authors and publishers 'could not believe that the librarians, serious bookmen, had composed this document'. He surmised that it was the work of the Association's secretary, H. D. Barry, a barrister, who had 'recently been professional adviser to the dentists', and who, he presumed, 'did not know much about books or copyright'.

APH's correspondence confirmed that 'we have friends in the library world'. To Raymond Moss, BA, FLA, then of St Helens, Lancashire, he wrote: 'What a brave man you are!' Moss had written to the Secretary of the Library Association: 'Our work is completely dependent on the efforts of authors and we owe to them our quite congenial jobs. It is quite a large debt. I do not think the authors are asking very much in return' (18 November 1962). APH had ample proof of goodwill in other quarters of the public libraries' service.

Determined to counter official indifference, which he decided was maddeningly embodied in the bland and portly presence of the Minister of Education, Sir Edward Boyle, he set forth the case for the authors, publishers, and librarians in an Institute of Economics' pamphlet, *Libraries: Free for All?* His stoical power of attention was obviously unimpaired: the missing element was his genial readability.

The long protracted controversy in and out of Parliament occasionally provoked him to extremes of impatience. In the contract for a children's book, *Silver Stream* (1962), he had a clause inserted to preclude its sale to the public libraries. An atmosphere heavily charged with dullness hung over a conference in 1962 of representatives of the authors and publishers and members of the Library Association Council. As an implacable foe of human dreariness, APH was a suffering man. A document fluttered to the floor from the table at which the secretary of the Library Association presided. APH immediately dropped to the all-fours position, crawled across the open centre of the circle of tables, seized the document in his mouth and deposited it in the secretary's place; as an eye-witness recalls, 'like a dog retrieving a bone'. By what was afterwards described as 'a good bit of clowning' he broke the oppressive spell.

Reviewing his labours at that time, the inconclusiveness of 'endless speeches, lectures, meetings, bouts of correspondence', he wrote: 'One does not despair. I am not bitter – but I am bloody angry', and resolved not to present a copy of his next book to the House of Commons' library.

In 1962 it seemed that the whole libraries' nexus was, for him, a matter of botheration. Not only was Public Lending Right still in abeyance. Under the Copyright Act of 1911, publishers were required to deposit copies of every newly published book at the British Museum and other national libraries. A letter to *The Times* raised the question whether 'the privileges at present enjoyed by the six Copyright Libraries could not be extended to the newer libraries', meaning those of the new universities. Reading it, APH told himself: 'This is my cue for public service.'[3]

A quick calculation showed him that the additional cost to the the publishers, at 1962 prices, would be 'at least £700,000'; and the resultant loss of royalties to authors, about £70,000. He sent a letter by hand to *The Times*: 'The whole principle should be killed, as the Royal Commission of 1878 demanded. Why on earth should a single trade be made responsible for equipping the nation's universities? The just and obvious course is to repeal Section 15 of the Copyright Act 1911 and start again. Let the Minister of Education draw up a list of institutions which ought to have free books, and let the Treasury provide.' His letter was 'spurned by return post on the grounds of "extreme pressure of space" '. He was put out. 'My letter was but 300 words or so. Extreme pressure? The correspondence was continued for another 8 days.' He rewrote the letter at greater length, sent it by hand to the *Daily Telegraph*. 'They printed it' (17 August 1962).

'An important new point' occurred to him; developed in a further letter to *The Times*. 'Let us be practical. Far better an annual grant (from the Treasury), which each library could use to buy the books it really wanted, six of one book, if required, none of many.' It was acknowledged but not printed. 'You covered too much of the same ground in the *Daily Telegraph*.' He retorted in a private note to the assistant editor: 'Does it mean that all readers of *The Times* read the *Daily Telegraph*? This is a new admission for your proud paper. The Top people, I understood, have never *heard* of the *Daily Telegraph*.' He set out, in a cheerfully pertinacious article intended for *Punch*, his objections to the statutory privilege granted to the

British Museum, the Bodleian, Cambridge University Library, the Library of the Faculty of Advocates (Edinburgh), the National Library of Wales, and Trinity College Library, Dublin, at the expense of publishers and authors. The article was amiably declined.

Rejections from *Punch* were falling like autumn leaves on his desk. In 1961–63 thirty-five of his articles came back to him, who once could have counted on all of them being used. In one accompanying letter he was told: 'Every square has a right to his squareness but isn't it rather kicking against the pricks to try and put it over to the public as a virtue?' Rejections were tempered by compliments. 'Very elegant – but I don't get it.' He had to bow the head to the rebuke: 'We can't go on saying that nothing new is any good when we are trying to lure new young readers.' His hardening prejudices against the changing scene of the sixties evoked the chilling editorial comment that his views tended to give *Punch* 'a reputation for being old-fashioned – something it's been fighting against ever since it *was* old-fashioned, decades ago'. By the mid-sixties his income from *Punch* had fallen to a point lower than at any time in forty years.

'The shame of dividends, the guilt of capital gain', was the text of his speech at the annual general meeting of the Savoy Hotel Ltd. in 1962. The shareholders around him were entertained by a digression in metric form.

> Save, save, they say, and put away
> What you would like to spend today.
> Don't drink – or smoke – or go abroad,
> And all the parties will applaud.
> But when the money's in your banks
> Expect no more the nation's thanks.
> Your earnings now have changed their name:
> They're CAPITAL, a cause for shame.
> While any yield that they may bring
> Is DIVIDEND, a filthy thing.
> And what may make the saver sore,
> It's UNEARNED INCOME, which pays more.
> But selling won't remove the stain:
> You make a beastly CAPITAL GAIN.
> You should be like the State, you fool,
> And make a CAPITAL LOSS the rule.
> Give some away to poorer men?

Oh, no, you're DODGING TAXES then.
In short, the patriots who save
Remain in error till the grave.
So die as quickly as you can,
And pay DEATH DUTIES like a man.

A letter from the Poet Laureate was written at the behest of the
Keeper of the Privy Purse. 'He desires me to ask whether your
engagements permit you to become a member of the Committee
judging for the Queen's Medal for Poetry.' To one who humbly
conceded that his verse had not even 'a small appeal to Apollo', it
was a high compliment to be invited to keep company with
Masefield himself, Siegfried Sassoon, C. Day Lewis and others.
APH's critical sensibilities were hardly to be put against theirs,
particularly in coming to conclusions about the new generation of
poets, whose work he had satirized in *Punch*. 'NO', is pencilled
boldly and probably wisely on the letter of gracious invitation.
'Alas, I feared it might be so', Masefield wrote in reply to the
request to be excused. He was constant in his regard for APH. He
wrote in August 1962 to a Canadian friend of APH and himself,
Leonard Brockington, QC: 'He never fails to hit his nail upon the
head, as he does again in an inimitable letter to *The Times* about
"shooting the moon".'

His critics had a point to make when they said that his view of
space exploration was suffused by an excess of sentiment. For
instance, he made much of a letter of mine published in *The Times*
that month in which I quoted the protest made to me by a shepherd
of the South Downs who was upset by reading about moon rocketry.
'I do hope they won't do it,' he said. 'At lambing time up here,
she's all I've got.' 'The poet Herbert' cited the letter in articles,
mentioned it in a speech, included it in his sobering cosmic anthology
Watch This Space (1964).

He was considerably exercised by difficulties arising from the
arrangement that he and Vivian Ellis had entered into more than a
decade earlier whereby, 'for compassionate reasons', they informally
assigned to Cochran the 'small performing rights' – excerpts from
words and music, television, amateur broadcasting, stock repertory,
etc. – in *Bless the Bride* and other 'musicals'. Cochran had spoken
of it as his 'little pension', the financial outlook for him in his ailing
old age being bleak. 'It was a personal gift', APH insisted again

and again. There had been no agreement that the 'said rights' should pass to anyone beyond Cochran. Neither APH nor Vivian Ellis objected when, after Cochran's death, his widow received benefits from the rights, it being understood that she had little if any other income.

After his death. Cochran's production company passed into other hands. The new owners believed that the small performing rights in question came under their control. In 1962 APH entered into a protracted argument by correspondence centred in the real ownership of the rights in dispute. In the course of it he was informed that Lady Cochran's financial position had been misrepresented, and that she was by no means 'destitute', as another of her benefactors had been told. APH concluded that there was 'a lack of frankness about Cochran's circumstances'.

In one of his letters pertaining to the rights problem he wrote to solicitors: 'After a life of service to the public, and especially the theatre (e.g. my 27 years campaign against the Entertainment Tax), my financial position is far from satisfactory. I at least am in no position to employ expensive solicitors and must conduct this tiresome correspondence myself. But since it has been, and perhaps will be, a serious distraction from remunerative work, I must warn you that every letter you force me to write will go into the bill of costs; and the time of a creative writer is much more valuable than the time, with respect, of the best of solicitors.'

Possibly with a lawsuit in prospect, perhaps to clear the air of cant, he wrote a detailed account of the affair from its beginning in a simple if imprudent gesture of goodwill to its development into a jigsaw-puzzle of misunderstandings. The temper he brought to his self-imposed task was certainly not that of a professionally serious man like the attorney in *Pendennis*. He might have been writing a *Misleading Case*. His 10,000 words of 'Comment on the Lamentable Dispute' between the parties involved were at least proof of the vigour and clarity of his mind at 72.

A resolute effort to complete the novel about the Thames bargemen that had run aground years before was subject to periods of intense preoccupation with problems proliferating from the new motorway extension of the Great West Road that had become 'an uncrossable speed track' isolating the residents of Hammersmith Terrace from the shopping and other local amenities. King Street was only 'three or four hundred yards away', yet he and his neighbours were now obliged to make a detour of 'a couple of miles' to reach it. The subject of rateable values had also come forward again as a major annoyance. He prepared a draft treatise apparently intended for submission to the District Valuer.

'This is a nice place to live – in the summertime; and I hope to die here. But the Clapham Junction of the air is just over there, and most of the big jets go right over us. They wake me twice at night. Helicopters too. We can't cross the Great West Road on foot or wheel. We are cut off from the shops and public transport, and many old friends are no longer seen this side. You must drive a mile or two in the opposite direction before you can start your journey into London, wasting a lot of time and petrol. The Road itself is now a terror to travel on, and what's more, we have to maintain this through-speedway out of the rates.' Concerning the isolation of Hammersmith Terrace, a remark of his was circulated locally on both sides of the motorway: 'If we are to survive, it looks as if we shall have to go in for incest.'

He delved into the rateable values of neighbourhood properties of note, among them six on Chiswick Mall, 'which may fairly be described as mansions'. He found discrepancies that were 'manifestly absurd and unjust'. Tabulating his findings, he proposed that 'the Hammersmith Valuer should think again'. Then, back to Chapter XIII of the novel and his description of a Thames barge race:

The barges which had been holding anxiously towards the wind went to starboard, and all sixteen, like racehorses released, bore down on the line, all on the port tack, all heeling gently, a splendid show of silent strength. There must have been, I thought, 50,000 square feet of coloured canvas pulling and thrusting, horsepower incalculable, but not a sound. There were names among them, *Sara, Veronica, Cambria, Sirdar*, as fair and famous on the water as the favourites of Epsom or Ascot . . .

NOTES ON CHAPTER 24

1   In 1974 National and Grindlay's Bank issued a display advertisement illustrated by a cheque for £2 10s. drawn by APH on the label of a bottle of Veuve Clicquot. The advertisement stated: 'The late (and sadly missed) A. P. Herbert liked keeping us on our toes. Hence the decidedly eccentric cheques he presented from time to time – written on wine bottles, on napkins, on eggs, or even in verse. We never failed him. . . .'
2   T. C. Foley, OBE, letter, 1 September 1975.   (See illustration).
3   A. P. Herbert: Private notes.

25

So Miscellaneous a Life

For TERESA[1]

8 February 1963

Attend, I beg, while Abraham describes
Yet one more triumph of the best of tribes!
One turns one's back, and miracles are done:
Teresa tells me she is twenty-one!
Is this the tiny creature I recall .
Not 'so high', no – she had no height at all.
That wicked winter in her cot she lay
Like some brave crocus in the snow today.
This is a sister winter: but behold
A splendid sapling conquering the cold!
For this young tree has met the cruel stroke
Of frost and fortune like an ancient oak.
The Stoic virtues of the old are sung:
How much more admirable in the young!
'A rose by any name . . .?' The poet errs.
What matters most is what the rose prefers.
Now, she commands, this blossom come of age,
'Tessa' no more, Teresa takes the stage.
Well done! I wish that other folk forgot
The crude abbreviations of the cot.
Farewell, then, Tessa dear. The play's begun –
Enter TERESA – and a record run!

In his first year in Parliament he had induced the King's Printer
to abolish superfluous stops in official publications, including the
Orders of the Day papers of the House of Commons, on economy
grounds. Doing so, he believed he had 'saved the taxpayer thousands
of pounds'. Now, thirty years later, he drew attention again to 'this
black spot plague' that was infecting the printed page everywhere.

His peculiar vigilance may have had an impact on typography beyond the bounds of Her Majesty's Stationery Office: he claimed to have purged the *Observer* of 'redundant punctuation'. He even carried the argument into the boardroom of the Savoy Hotel Ltd., criticizing the company's 'otherwise elegant' printed report for 1962.

His Savoy Hotel directorship apparently gave him a taste for ostentatious cigar smoking that seemed oddly out of character and suggested to some ancient members of the Savage Club that he was impersonating Phil May, the once celebrated *Punch* artist. A Strand bookseller said: 'We always knew when APH had come in – his cigars had a super-aroma.' The Savoy Grill was given full marks for its amenities in the Thames novel he was trying to finish; for him pre-eminently a focal point of the civilized life. In the sixties he shared his preference for it with the adjacent restaurant, dominated by the *svelte* personality of Luigi, who is named in the novel. He lunched there regularly with Frederic Lloyd, general manager of the Savoy Theatre, and Malcolm Sargent, who always studied the menu with care to avoid any dish requiring mastication likely to impede his conversational flow. At one of the lunches Sargent denounced the introduction of artificial insemination into human affairs. APH went home and wrote a poetic protest inscribed 'With acknowledgments to Sir Malcolm Sargent':

> It's not adultery, the lawyers say,
> For wives to have a baby in this way.
> Well then can there be reasonable blame
> If those who have no husbands do the same?
> Let spinsters too enjoy the matron's blisses,
> And by deed poll assume the rank of 'Mrs'
> There is no name they may not employ –
> 'Churchill' or 'Sargent' – 'yes, it was his boy'.
> And all the world will say 'A bonny baby.
> 'She claims it's So-and-so's. Of course, it may be'.
> Thus shall we multiply through all the Earth
> The Christian wonder of the Virgin Birth;
> And pagan multitudes will see the light,
> At last confessing that the Bible's right;
> While naughty maidens who have made a boob
> Will answer glibly 'No, it was the Tube'.
> Science, another big success, we own,
> But is there nothing you can leave alone?

'It is sad that we get older but there it is.' That *tempus fugit* memorandum to APH in February 1964 was signed 'Harold', i.e. Harold Macmillan, the Prime Minister, who was soon to retire from active politics for health reasons. More poignant intimations of the change and decay motif were impressed on APH that year. Old friends haunted his memory; no longer the old familiar places: Norman Birkett, Cedric Hardwicke, James Gunn, Trefor Jones, R. C. Robertson-Glasgow. APH attended memorial services, now and then as panegyrist, occasions 'not for mourning but for a salute'.[2] He rarely if ever disclosed his feelings in terms of personal loss.

Neither was it an invigorating year professionally. His royalty statements for the six months to June showed that his return from twenty-eight books in print was just over £40. Through the ever-watchful Performing Right Society he received £528. 'Don't put your daughter into literature, Mrs Worthington', he advised in a post-prandial speech. 'Put her into song writing.'

'You do know how to get something done.' The acknowledgment was from J. Alan White, then chairman of Methuen. He and APH had worked in close harmony as PLR campaigners. The 'something' that APH had accomplished in 1964 was a change of heart at the Arts Council of Great Britain, which bestowed patronage to the extent of about £1,500,000 a year on opera and ballet, music and the drama. Literature was not explicitly provided for in the Council's Charter (1946). APH objected to the omission, which he considered anomalous, and in 1957 he made it the subject of a *Misleading Case* in *Punch*, *Haddock* v *The Arts Council of Great Britain*. 'No one took the slightest notice' – a sure and certain incentive to him 'not to let go'.

In 1962 a House of Commons committee under the Conservative Government recommended the incorporation of Literature in the Charter. Again the point was not taken. When APH found that in the previous year the Council had made 'grants and awards' amounting to £215 for 'Poetry and Literature', he insisted that its action was *ultra vires*, and declared that if necessary he would challenge its legality in the courts. Correspondence between him, the Arts Council, and Whitehall in 1964 was a model of epistolary civility. It had been initiated by him, writing to the London *Evening Standard*: 'Mr Abercrombie [secretary-general, the Arts Council] says he is spending more money on poetry. Good – but I don't think he's entitled to spend any.' When he asked the general secretary: 'Could I see a copy of the entire Charter – or is it a mile long?' he was sent a copy: 'It is not much over three furlongs.'

At the core of the exchanges was the need for an acceptable definition of 'fine arts', to which the Council's terms of reference were confined. APH drafted a statement of the case for amending the Charter for submission to the Chancellor of the Exchequer, Reginald Maudling. It was an elaborate document, witness to his indomitable perseverance. He examined as many authoritative definitions of the fine arts as he could find, quoting extensively; e.g. from the views of a Slade Professor of Fine Art, and from Collingwood's *Outlines of the Philosophy of Art*. To those he added the *obiter dicta* of High Court judges.

At first sight of the document the Chancellor may have fancied that he had been presented with a parody of a *Misleading Case*. 'You have given me something to think about!' he wrote (18 March 1964). Having thought about it, he could not agree that there was 'a strong case for amending the Charter'. It was for the Arts Council 'to decide how to spend their money'. APH was 'astonished'. Having apparently thought again, the Chancellor wrote to the chairman of the Arts and Amenities Committee that he did not regard the Charter 'as preventing the Arts Council from devoting part of their resources to the literary arts'.

Remarkable, APH reflected, that no one at the Arts Council or the Treasury had seen fit to 'reveal this verdict earlier. It remained for the interfering Mr Haddock to extract the truth.' The results have since been made evident in grants to poets, novelists, and other writers. It was a leading member of the Publishers' Association who expressed in a letter to APH his colleagues' 'gratitude for your splendid solo effort'.

Literature and the State was the timely and congenial theme of his lecture to the Royal Society of Literature in December 1964. It was an opportunity for him to patch threadbare propaganda for PLR, and to survey bureaucratic attitudes generally to the contemporary literary scene. His enlivening and often witty dissertation constituted a polemic worthy of the permanence given to it in Vol. xxxiv of *Essays in Divers Hands*, published for the Society by Oxford University Press.

The Public Libraries and Museums Bill had come on to the

Statute Book that year with no provision in it for Public Lending Right, for all the strenuous and sustained effort by the Society of Authors, including four deputations to Whitehall. In the last five years APH had supplied stimulating leadership – 'years of unrewarded toil for the authors who, I sometimes feel, deserve everything that comes to them, they give you so little support'. It seemed to him that he was becoming too exclusively identified with PLR in the public mind. 'Feeling tired', he resigned the chairmanship of the Authors' and Publishers' Lending Right Association, while remaining 'still in battle order'.

It was a good year for the Savoy Hotel shareholders (he insisted that they be called investors). Congratulating them at the annual general meeting in April 1965, he remarked that the favourable results had been achieved 'without the aid of those European imports, Professor Balder and Dr Dasch'. The sly allusion was mirthfully received by those present who had no love for the Treasury, his *bête noir* since 1940 and Kingsley Wood's book tax. 'I can buy a lunch for my American publisher, eligible for tax relief, but not for my London publisher, though I am trying to sell the same book to him at the same time.' He thought it sad that 'a great department of State should descend to such niggling measures'. They could only have been conceived 'by mean and malignant minds'.

Approaching his seventy-fifth birthday (24 September 1965), he could say that he 'still enjoyed life, warmly and gratefully', as well he might, writing from the Astors' yacht in the Mediterranean in June. Apparently under the impression that *Punch* was still interested in the journalism of anniversaries, he made notes for a possible article. 'Every night I thank God in wonder that so far I have escaped the cruel blows that have hit so many better men'. He supposed that at last he would be 'confined to bed or a wheeled chair, or totter, step by step, if nothing worse befalls me'. His 'one fear' was not death 'but the daunting preliminaries'. He was not, he confessed all over again, 'a very religious man – say, a non-playing member of the Church of England'. In the sense that he was 'constantly thankful for good health and reasonable fortune', he felt that his life had become 'one long religious experience'.

As for 'sage advice', he could only suggest: *Never give up*. 'It comes nearly first with me – temerity being my principal vice. I go on fighting for causes that to all others seem lost.' Summing up, 'few ordinary citizens, without excursions into crime, or exploration, can have led so miscellaneous a life. What an idiot! What a warning to others! Ruin is the reward of the Jack-of-all-trades. My finances now are frailer than they ever were. Never mind. I would do it all again,' fortified by 'those words from Tennyson's *Ulysses*', which he had long had by heart:

> Old age hath still his honour and his toil,
> Death closes all, but something ere the end,
> Some work of noble note may yet be done . . .

His long enjoyed regular income from the *Sunday Graphic* had disappeared, like the paper itself, a casualty of proprietorial upheaval. Working for it week by week for more than twenty years, with no break except during his wartime journey to Newfoundland, he set up some kind of Fleet Street record. Another sign of changing circumstances was the winding-up of Haddock Productions. The young directors saw 'no valid reason for keeping the company alive'.

Work in hand consisted of the unfinished novel, and a book about the Thames, 'a new look at it from source to sea'. Concurrently, he was making notes about sundials, a subject that had long engrossed him, historically and technically. He had now persuaded his publishers that there was 'a book in it'.[3] One of his objects in writing it, he said, was to refute Belloc's denigrating couplet:

> I am a Sundial, and I make a botch
> Of what is done much better by a watch.

He was delighted by my sundial story, which concerned the setting up in our garden at Rodmell of an engraved leaden sundial dated 1671. A village neighbour, Percy Thompsett, who worked for the Ouse River Authority, offered to cement the stone pedestal. 'You needn't go to too much trouble', I remarked, not wanting to hinder his Sunday morning gardening. Slow in replying, he said: 'I suppose you'd agree that the old fellow who made this dial all those years ago took a lot of trouble over it?' I nodded yes. 'Well, then, don't you think that out of respect for his memory we ought to do the same?' APH blinked in a moment's silence; obviously moved and trying not to show it. Then he drawled in an exaggerated ex-parliamentary fashion: ' 'ear, 'ear – 'ear, 'ear!'

His old *Punch* colleague and friend, H. F. Ellis, recalls from 1965:

'I rashly told him that my sundial down here in Somerset lost about two hours a day. He pursued me with telephoned enquiries about the angle of its gnomon, informed me (when I gave him the angle) that my sundial might command a good price in Trebizond but was useless near Taunton, and sent me a home-made hardboard sundial with correct gnomon (cut from a school protractor) hinged to it, and the inscription: "A.P.H. *fecit* for 51° 15' N".'

With the gift of the sundial Ellis received a letter of two closely typed quarto pages that reads like a not too serious but acutely informed treatise.' Your longitude, I gather, is 3°7' West. This means that the Sun will always pass over you 12 minutes and 28 seconds after it has passed over Greenwich. So on Christmas Day when the shadow falls on 12 the Taunton pubs will have been open for twelve minutes and a bit, and when the shadow says 1 you will have missed the 1 o'clock news.'

'The first seventy-five years are the worst', Neville Cardus[4] wrote to him on 24 September 1965, and enquired: 'Where can I get hold of *Holy Deadlock*? I've read it some dozen times with joy; but now somebody has pinched my copy. What a gorgeous book!'

In December 1965 APH opened the prestigious international chess congress at Hastings. 'He was the only man ever to be asked back to open it a second time since the event was founded in 1920.'[5] He spoke on that second occasion at Hastings as 'a spectator on the fringes of chess for many years'. He shared his wife's veneration for the game but not her recondite knowledge of it. With her he met some of the great masters: Botvinnik, Gligoric, Petrosian, and the woman world champion, 'that small dynamo', Nona Gaprindashvill. He asked in his speech why there was no British champion, and thought he had the answer, a lack of encouragement in 'high places'. Chess was 'the most companionable form of intellectual exercise that existed'. In his estimation it had 'most of the merits of art, science, and sport, and none of their notorious disadvantages – incertitude, arrogance, pugnacity.' As for the Hastings congress, he regarded it as 'one of the finest of human fellowships'.

He had resigned from the chairmanship of the authors' and publishers' group formed to promote PLR as if he was casting off a heavy burden. Within weeks he took on the chairmanship of the internationally influential British Copyright Council, consisting of delegates from twenty different organizations involved in the assertion and protection of the copyright of authors, publishers, composers, musicians, artists, photographers, 'and all that sort of thing'. Copyright in its many ramifications tested even his exceptional powers of comprehension. 'Never can a Chairman have presided over so many discussions so little of which he really understood.' The widening use of tape recorders, copying machines, computers, amplified the copyright complexities, and increased the need for stricter respect for the principles and practice of the Copyright Act. APH gave thanks in print to the secretary of the British Copyright Council, Reynell Wreford, 'who understands everything', and who continues to think of him in superlatives: 'unique, brilliant, lovable'. Another congenial and indispensable guide and counsellor in that highly specialized context was Royce Whale, then general manager of the Performing Right Society, who did much to consolidate the foundations of the British Copyright Council. The APH characteristic that remains strongest in his recollection was 'his infinite good nature'.

He made copyright infringement of a particularly glaring kind an excuse for threatening to withhold income tax payments due in 1966 on the ground that the Government was showing untoward tolerance of 'illegal radio pirates' operating in the Thames estuary. 'For nearly two years they have been robbing or damaging writers, composers, musicians and others', a grievance vigorously renewed in letters to *The Times*. From his mood of defiance he lapsed into a sentimental reminder to the Inland Revenue Authorities that he was 'now an old man of $75\frac{1}{2}$, still trying to keep going in a precarious profession'. Instead of sending him 'blackmailing letters in RED INK' (his capitals), he suggested that 'a polite inquiry' about his present circumstances would have been more seemly. 'Like you, I do not always receive money when it is due' (21 February 1966).

The Rhodesian crisis provoked him to condemn the Labour Government's policy towards that country as 'bombastic, brutal *colonialism*', a case of 'the big fellow saying to the little fellow: "We know better how to run your country than you do." ' That, he maintained, was 'the essence of colonialism' (*Evening Standard*, 22 February 1966). 'You have in a long life seldom written anything better', Sir John Masterman wrote to him from Oxford. 'Lots of folk can take a commonsense view. Very few can express that view in a manner which will convince the doubtful. You can. We hardly ever meet – and that is my loss' (19 February 1966).

He was elected vice-president of the Performing Right Society, whose president, Sir Arthur Bliss, Master of the Queen's Musick, told him by letter: 'At our Council meeting yesterday an unanimous wish was expressed to pay some tribute to you for all that you have done for authors' rights' (11 March 1966). On 1 June he delivered an ode that he had written to mark the installation of the Society's new computer.

Welcome, you wonderful, unnatural toy,
To this august Society's employ!
Without your like, it seems, this Age can't act:
No Bank can add – though they can still subtract.
Our minds are still as mighty, rather more,
But everything's more muddled than before,
And we present our lives to a machine
Simply to ask it what the Hell they mean.
Yet, lest Conceit exceed its proper span,
Always remember you were made by Man.

. . . . .

Most of your kin are vulgarly content
To serve mere Business – or the Government:
But you were destined for a nobler part,
To mother Music and the Metric Art.
Who else could calculate how much is written,
How much is won, by Beatle or by Britten?
Or reckon justly what the earnings are
Of (A) an organ, (B) a group guitar?
The poets too will pester you as well
Who write the songs the music-makers sell.
Nor, like your brothers, will you sit and smile
At the conundrums of a single isle.
All round the globe, wherever people play
A Song, a Symphony, a Suite in A,
You'll open wide the ear that never shuts,
The sound will penetrate those cunning guts,
And you will whisper – or perhaps you'll whinny –
That APH, in Spain, has earned a guinea;
Or you will click 'Let twenty shillings go
To Tikorak the Top Pop Eskimo'.
All round our coasts, on fort or frigate, still
The Pirates use our work without our will,
And you, reluctantly, will have to treat
The Conscience Money some of them secrete.
But pray remind them, as you count the pence,
That these do not diminish their offence . . .

In a speech at Islington he casually remarked that if he had his just dues as an author he would be earning 'as much as the Beatles'. He was rattled when a Guildford chief librarian replied in the *Daily Telegraph* that, 'excellent as they may be', his novels 'belong to a past age'. It was the librarian's experience that when they were withdrawn from the shelves 'no one asks for them'. Dismissing 'the petty personal insult', APH replied: 'I love the picture of a Chief Librarian solemnly removing some of my works from his shelves in order to prove that I am not so popular as the Beatles. The point is conceded. Now he can put them back' (March 1966).

'So, my dear 75 year old friend, I think it better if we don't take your advice', Bernard Hollowood, editor of *Punch*, wrote returning an article that APH had submitted on the new Selective Employment Tax (16 August 1966). Another unsuccessful article brought the comment: 'I'm afraid I don't like this one very much. Oh, dear . . . .' (21 August). Yet another came back because 'it doesn't seem to hang together' (22 September).

Two days later the post brought him handsome acknowledgments of unpaid services rendered to the Performing Right Society and the British Copyright Council. His presence in the chair of the Society was 'a constant joy' to his colleagues: so wrote the general manager, Royce Whale. 'We are all very proud to have you as our Vice-President.' For the British Copyright Council, the secretary, Reynell Wreford, wished 'to record our deep and sincere gratitude for your admirable and very successful direction of our affairs' (23 September 1966).

His pleasure in writing *The Thames*, published in October 1966, sparkled through many of its pages like sunlight on water. Love and lore suffused them; a rich harvest of the forty and more years since he bought his first sailing dinghy at Gamages. Not that the book was a dragnet for the recovery of past joys or that its focus was his presidency of the London Corinthian Sailing Club, an office to which he was more proudly attached than to some others. Sentiment and romance were ballasted by practical wisdom distilled from what can only have been intensive study of the problem of 'taming the tide'. His advocacy of a Thames barrage to prevent what could still be overwhelming disaster was carried over into *The Times* correspondence columns in the following months. If the existing plan to build a barrage in the lower reaches by 1980 becomes a reality of the river, his personal propaganda for the scheme in general cannot in justice be overlooked.[6] Incidentally, it brought him yet another vice-presidency, that of the Thames Barrage Association, founded in 1935.

His book did not receive the attention that he may reasonably have thought it merited. Reviewers seemed to be in league against him as a superannuated author. He may have been a shade less than delighted to hear of the success of an amateur writing talent. His old friend 'Monty', the retired field marshal, had written to say that he was at work on a history of warfare, for which his publishers had received advance orders for 250,000 copies; also: 'My memoirs have sold a million.'

APH to the editor of The *Daily Telegraph*:

> Sir, A Minister, you report, hopes that somebody 'will accept this step as a necessary prerequisite for improving staffing standards'.
>
> I have never understood what 'pre' adds to 'requisite' (can there be a 'postrequisite'?). A 'necessary prerequisite' is surely an example of presuperfluity. But if the Minister must rub it in, would 'a prenecessary prerequisite' help? Or perhaps just 'necessary'.
>
> The Minister is the Minister of *Education*.
>
> Yours respectfully,
A. P. HERBERT

18 January 1967

The advent of a new word 'psychedelic' in the popular vocabulary impelled him to compose an ironic piece on the dead languages. He gave it the heading 'De Mortuis' and sent it to *Punch*. It was gracefully and firmly declined. 'We disapprove in a very solemn fashion of everything you are trying to say. Otherwise, of course, our admiration for you and all your works remains undimmed' (1 March 1967).

. . . those poor dead languages [he wrote], Latin and Greek, have seldom been deader. Even Oxford, Winchester and Eton are flinging the last fragments to the wolves. Yet here is this new dead word flourishing in most unlikely soil. It may have been invented by a learned '*psychiatrist*' but it is part of the joyous chatter of coffee bars, pharmacophils, and parakmetes (new word for beatniks – *parakme* means decay) . . . . Why, for that matter, the absurd word discotheque? This is pure Greek, Ancient Greek, deceased Greek and, I suggest, rather painfully *derrière-garde*. I laugh heartily every day as I watch the dead languages bursting out, like June, all over.

No doubt his *Punch* friends were as pleased as he was to see the article given prominence in the *Guardian*, where it was reprinted five years later as an example of 'the style and verbal wit which made him famous'. Posthumous smiles are raised as one reads: 'Our rulers and solemn leader writers talk happily about the optimum level of prices. No member has yet cried "Mr Speaker, this is the pessimum policy", but that may come.'

His performance at the Savoy Hotel company's annual general meeting in April 1967 amply warranted the chairman's earlier inference that 'the circulation of *The Times* increases on the day Sir Alan's speech is published', i.e. as an adjunct of the company report. It was his tenth year as a spokesman in that place, and what he had to say has not staled since.

Brother investors, I am choosing my language carefully. As I have remarked before, we are all urged to invest in industry for our country's good, but we become contemptible 'shareholders' if we do. As 'shareholders' is now a term of abuse in certain important quarters, so 'profit' is a name of shame; and I am surprised, Sir, that you allowed that ugly word to creep into your otherwise excellent speech. Indeed, I question whether we are wise to publish a document called a *'Profit and Loss Account'*. Surely a simple *'Loss'* account would be more acceptable to many of our thinkers, workers, and rulers today.

If by some accident or bungling a profit does emerge it should not be distributed boastfully as a *'dividend'* (another odious word). This should be called a *Penalty* or *Fine*, to be paid by the company, with apologies, for their bad behaviour in permitting such an anti-social phenomenon as a *'profit'* to occur. The aim should be for every company to finish the year all square – as, with the aid of the taxes, many individuals do. This may mean that it is impossible to increase the staff or repair the machinery; but what does that matter?

The word *'wages'* too has now acquired an element of personal gain which makes it inappropriate to the times. A demand for a rise in wages is hard to distinguish from that disgraceful impetus the *'profit motive'*. We should speak rather of a *'personal existence allowance'*, for that, after all, is all that, under the doctrines of today, any man is entitled to receive. Anything above that, anything that enables him to buy a television set, is evidently 'profit' of the grossest kind, and no modern thinker can be content with that sort of thing.

He wrote a personal letter headed 'Not for Publication' to William Rees-Mogg, editor of *The Times*, on the subject of 'the superfluous full-stop – an old cause of mine', which had been successful in the thirties 'when I got it removed from Parliamentary papers and saved the tax-payer a mass of money'. He now asked: 'I wonder if you realize where *The Times* offends', and set out instances in his letter. He hoped that 'one day *The Times* will be stopless', like the *Daily Telegraph*, and 'all the weeklies'.

Another internal matter in which he thought fit to involve himself was *The Times* practice of prefixing 'Mr' to the names of persons referred to in court reports. Querying it, he was editorially informed that to deprive such persons of the prefix 'seemed, in effect, to be prejudging the cases'. In considering the question, 'we have run into a whole thicket of problems of usage' (7 April 1967).

He entered the Common Market controversy in May 1967 with an article arguing that 'tinkering about with GMT and BST' – the latter, 'Beastly Summer Time' to him – 'to suit Europeans and certain harassed business men is a waste of time'. His *persona grata* status in Printing House Square was never more flatteringly honoured. His unrepentant opinions were 'splashed' across four columns and given the bold type heading of an event. In the accompanying photographic reproduction he looked like a well-pensioned pirate in a striped vest posing beside the prow of an old Thames hulk. 'Leave the clocks alone,' he demanded. 'If western Europe want uniformity let them come *back* to Greenwich time, the time appointed for them by the nations in 1884. Then in most of the Common Market (if we go in)[7] land, sea and air will tick together. If we feebly go over to western European time there will still be an hour's difference between the trains in the Channel Tunnel and the ships and aircraft above it, between Big Ben and the Boeing, Paris and the Queen Elizabeth. How very unbusinesslike! How contrary to Common Market principles.'

Although APH's obsessions were always artfully controlled, the editor of *The Times* may have doubted it as the recipient of two excessively long letters from him on Summer Time (27 and 30 June 1967). Either letter would have filled more than half a *Times*' column; rash presumption, considering the lavish treatment recently accorded to his views. Weighty with calculation and observation, the unpublished letters read now as if they were written under a compulsive necessity that was not of the intellect; a self-persecuting drive that had its own peculiar satisfaction; a tragic dominant of his psychic life.

He accepted the presidency of the Society of Authors with no more than a token protest against assuming any new office. In fact, it was one of the proud days of his life when he was elected unanimously to a succession that included Tennyson, Meredith, Hardy, Barrie and Masefield. The chorus of approbation was led by Compton Mackenzie: 'I really am delighted. You are the right – indeed, the only – man for the job' (25 July 1967). 'There is only one author who doesn't realise what all of us – let alone the public – owe to you, and that is APH.' The commendation was from Sir Arthur Bryant, the historian (25 August 1967). Later came the testimony: 'The Society of Authors never had a more fitting or a more dynamic President' (*The Author*, Winter 1971).

It would have been a sign almost of senility if APH had left unremarked the announcement that *The Times* had commissioned a sundial from Henry Moore, the sculptor. His response was to improvise a model from 'a grandson's hoop, string, screws, a wooden garden table, and a whisky crate'. In a letter printed in the PHS Diary (16 October 1967) he reported that 'though imperfectly constructed, it is working well', and suggested means by which the same might be said for the sculptor's version, one of them involving bringing in engineers to provide a turntable. As for the talk of it being a 'symbolical' sundial, what would be thought of a grand-scale 'symbolical' clock that did not tell the time?

He returned to the subject in another personal letter to the editor. 'Tomorrow, I reckon, *The Times* sundial will be wrong by 46 minutes, on 1 June by 1 hour and two minutes, on 1 November by 1 hour and 16 minutes. My own model, rotated a little, will be telling Summer Time or Greenwich Time at will. It is a great pity that they did not take my advice, published in your Diary, put the thing on a turntable and make it do the job. Then it could have been the last stronghold of GMT or up to date with BST, and either way a good example of modern 'technology' applied to ancient art. As it is it will, except for its appearance, which is fine, be a meaningless mess' (19 February 1968).

NOTES ON CHAPTER 25

1 Teresa Pudney had battled through a long illness. Other granddaughters, coming of age (old style), received similar tributes from the head of the family.
2 From his address at the memorial service to Jack Hylton, February 1965.
3 A. P. Herbert: *Sundials – Old and New* (1976).
4 Sir Neville Cardus, CBE (1889–1974) distinguished music critic of the *Guardian*, and writer on cricket.
5 Frank Rhoden, honorary director, Hastings Chess Congress: letter, 6 June 1973.
6 For evidence of the time and energy he gave to that cause see Chapter 5 in his book, *The Thames*.
7 'I do not want to enter it on any terms'. – APH in 1961.

26

'Nothing is Wasted, Nothing is in Vain'

His New Year mail brought him a letter from Hammond Innes, the novelist: 'Thank you for keeping the flag of my case flying' (5 January 1968). The case involved what APH had roundly condemned as 'a shameful persecution' by the Inland Revenue. 'In good faith', the novelist had made over one of his books to his father who took the proceeds and presumably paid tax on them. The Revenue then demanded tax on 'notional income' – the amount the author would have received if he had not assigned the book. APH was scathing. 'The vultures forced him up to the Appeal Court. His costs might have been £8,000', if the Court had not ruled in his favour. It was a victory also for the Society of Authors under its new president He ensured that the case was well and truly publicized. 'We are not a society for reading literary papers but for getting things done.' Whatever the presidency may have meant to such of his predecessors as Tennyson and Hardy, APH gave to it more than his name.

Yielding to exuberant back-slapping persuasion at an 'Authors of the Year' party, he agreed to write his autobiography, 'a good chunk' of which, he pointed out, had already appeared in *Independent Member* (1950). Subsequent negotiations through his agents, A. P. Watt & Son, brought him a contract for a book of 'not less than 80,000 words', with an advance of £2,000. The book was to be delivered in time for publication on or near his eightieth birthday, 24 September 1970. It meant that he had about twenty months in which to complete the work.

He showed no keenness to make a start with it. His more immediate concern was to establish relations with the new regime at *Punch*, which had passed under the control of United Newspapers. His attempts to do so were largely wasted effort. When he received the ominous intimation with a rejected article: 'We seem to have read this before', he riposted with a deft but almost, it seemed, desperate elaboration of a letter that had caught his eye in *The Times*' business pages. The writer of the letter, E. J. Beaven, a Leicestershire mining engineer, forecast a disastrous run-down of 'our chemical and industrial civilisation' in the next decade or so as a consequence of the exhaustion of mercury-bearing ore supplies and of the indispensable quicksilver derived from them. 'There are no known alternatives.'

Punch thought it 'rather an odd subject', and returned the article because 'you don't make your own concern with it come alive'. APH thereupon sent it to *The Guardian*, where it appeared under the title *Whither Quicksilver?* on 20 April 1968. 'I take you very seriously', he told Mr Beavan. 'As the article was originally intended for *Punch*, I had to write rather lightly', while obviously hoping that he had not written in vain.

The new policy-makers at *Punch* had drastically dissociated it from the past that APH knew. While his personal links with the office had become tenuous, he had the countervailing satisfaction of identification with a medium more compulsively expressive of the spirit of the age. BBC television screened his *Misleading Cases*, expanding their appeal into areas in which previously the law was a subject for entertainment only in terms of crime and detection and dramas in court. 'They had a surprisingly wide appeal' he wrote of the programmes, gladly reporting the refutation of his doubts about the feasibility of adapting the *Cases* for visual purposes. 'The simple folk in Hammersmith shops were as enthusiastic as " my learned friends" ', thanks in no small measure to the performances of Alistair Sim as Mr Justice Swallow and Roy Dotrice as Albert Haddock.[1]

Few viewers beyond the metropolitan pale, and not many within it, were aware that *Misleading Cases* had more than literary distinction. They had acquired prophetic significance in legal circles and, like his first election address (1935), had contributed to the formation of attitudes favourable to law revision and possible reform; for example, in the Administration of Justice Bill, 1968.

Impressive in another and less gratifying if flattering sense was the attention given to certain of APH's fictional judgments by lawyers in the United States. 'A serious American work', *The Lawyers*, solemnly cited one of the *Misleading Cases* to make the point that no such judgment could prevail in an American court. Another of the *Cases*, in which Haddock was charged with unseemly behaviour as a passenger in an Underground train seated opposite a girl in a mini-skirt, was reported as authentic news in French and Italian newspapers. 'Such episodes disturb me', APH wrote. 'I never set out to be really misleading.'

The Singing Swan, that was to have been a seagoing version of *The Water Gipsies*, was published in June 1968, more than thirty years after its first chapters were drafted. Not many novels by established writers that season can have received less attention from the reviewers: probably a more dispiriting experience for APH than anyone was allowed to know. Reading *The Singing Swan* now, one can agree that it had little claim to critical respect. Too obviously his heart was not in it. The book has an almost poignant lack of zest. Its pages glow only when he is describing the lower Thames, its reaches, tides, sunsets, ships, navigators. An evasive and difficult to define undercurrent of impatience occasionally breaks the surface, as if from a final realization that he was a novelist *manqué*.

His ability to function more effectively in the real world than in the realms of fantasy was made manifest again when in April 1969 he wrote to *The Times* about parliamentary discipline, with particular reference to the suspension of four Labour Party members who abstained from voting in a division, during the debates on the Labour Party's abortive attempts to bring in an incomes policy. Here he was, standing up once more for the constitutional right of the individual 'to vote and speak according to his judgment and conscience'. Nor was his letter a mere rhetorical flourish. With his customary exactitude, he had consulted the authorities from far back in the history of Parliament. 'In 1621 the Commons declared', etc.; 'In 1695 the House resolved', etc. And there was Standing Order 30 which put the matter beyond all doubt. 'A Member is not obliged to vote.' He hoped that 'some indignant victim will complain to the Speaker. If this puts a brake on the Party system some of us will be delighted: for it is the unreasonable practice of the Party system that has ruined Parliament' (25 April 1969).

Sir Alan Herbert to the editor of *The Times*:

12 Hammersmith Terrace,
W.6.

1 May 1969.

Sir,　On Monday, April 28, you kindly printed a letter in which I denounced as unconstitutional the 'disciplinary' methods of the Labour Party Whips. On the following day the Chief Labour Whip was removed from his office.[2] On Wednesday his successor withdrew the four sentences of 'suspension' which I had in mind. Sir, we could hardly ask for a more rapid and drastic response to a brief letter in *The Times* – and we must be fully grateful to all concerned.

I am, Sir, Yours respectfully,

A. P. HERBERT

To be praised too heartily for an achievement of the distant past is not necessarily exhilarating for a writer who believes his powers to be undiminished. Elizabeth Bowen's esteem for *The Secret Battle*, expressed in a letter to APH in July 1969, may have been for him an uncomfortable tribute to lost excellence. 'Its awe-inspiringness and greatness as a novel stand out even more as I read it again. My husband, Alan Cameron, held *The Secret Battle* to be not only the truest war novel but one of the grandest novels of his time. How wonderful the Gallipoli part is. One feels implicated in everything that is going on. And the beauty, in spite of everything, of the land and sea . . .'

A little later in the year there came another intimidating reminder of the widening gulf of time. 'Do try to get to Grillion's this session', Sir Arthur Bryant wrote to him. 'You are now our oldest member' (23 October 1969), Not long before, a voice had echoed across the river at Hammersmith: 'That's the residence of Sir A. P. Herbert. He's a famous novelist – or was.'

Time in a less formidable aspect became a major concern of his that summer with the announcement of the Government's intention to give permanence to British Standard Time. The presidents respectively of the Royal Institute of Chartered Surveyors, The Institute of Navigation ,The Royal Geographical Society, The Royal Astronomical Society, had written to *The Times* urging 'most strongly' that there should be no departure from 'the unique status' of Greenwich Mean Time or of the Greenwich Meridian. 'We concur in the arguments so brilliantly adduced by Sir Alan Herbert.'

It was important reinforcement of his case. Putting aside work on the opening chapters of his autobiography, he proceeded to relate the history of British Summer Time, and to attack its extension into the winter months, in thirty thousand words for paperback publication under the title, *In the Dark*,[3] a masterly pamphleteering exercise.

He was no less readily diverted from contractual obligations when he read the assertion by a newspaper yachting correspondent that 'feet and fathoms, nautical miles and knots, are all on the way out'. It was irresistible provocation to launch yet another correspondence in *The Times*. In the course of it he clashed with 'a gallant Captain' of the United States Navy 'who was not very polite'; guilty, in fact, of the ultimate affront of suggesting that APH was 'trying to be funny' in objecting to the displacement of the time-honoured fathom by the metre.

He was still conducting his campaigns in and out of print with a force of conviction suggesting that it was his life's prime purpose to create enclaves of common sense in a disorganized universe. His faculty for preserving the single-minded approach to any problem or cause amid a variety of other interests was always remarkable. He was now stating the case for the 'fathom lovers' in *The Times*, and simultaneously denouncing the abandonment of Fahrenheit for Centigrade in the *Daily Telegraph*. 'In these battles I am well aware that I was "sticking my neck out", but no one has successfully twisted it. What saddens me is that more people, with better title and resources, do not stick their necks out.'[4]

The humbug of much of the contemporary clamour against the visit of the Springboks from South Africa stung him into poetic rejoinder. Once again the rhyming couplet was the perfect instrument for his satire.

> . . . Russians come to Wimbledon and play,
> But no high thinker has a word to say.
> Chess masters come from Russia here in hordes,
> But no idealist upsets their boards . . .
> Young Russians played some Soccer here last week;
> No one was shocked - I did not hear a shriek.
> I do not cry 'Go home, you godless blighters!
> What are you doing to my fellow writers?'[5]

The Thames-side stroll that he had taken with the author of *Vice Versa* nearly sixty years ago led him to an impressive local climax on 17 November 1969, when he appeared before a civic assembly in the council chamber at Hammersmith Town Hall to receive the honorary freedom of the borough. 'In recognition', the citation went, 'of his distinguished record as author, playwright, poet and parliamentarian, and in particular of his affectionate and active concern for the borough of Hammersmith during a residence of more than half a century.' He signed the freeman's roll 'amid a standing ovation' (Official report).

The prospect that had pleased him during the walk with F. Anstey was doubtless in his mind when he told the burgesses in his speech: 'The curving coasts of Chiswick and Hammersmith provide, I maintain, the most beautiful view in riverside London.' Looking ancestral, he continued: 'My wife and I have lived beside this great river of ours for nearly four and fifty. years. It must be a healthy neighbourhood, for we have four fine children, fourteen grand-children, and five great-grandchildren. How all this happened, by the way, without any assistance or instruction from the BBC I cannot explain.'

Confessing that he was not 'absolutely clear' about the practical value of becoming a freeman of Hammersmith, he recited some of the wider freedoms he would wish to enjoy with his fellow citizens generally – 'freedom from British Standard Time in the cold black mornings of winter; freedom from Whitehall fads and follies like Centigrade; freedom from the metric system; freedom to drink beer by the pint and not the litre; freedom from all the unnecessary novelties that year by year are thrust into our daily lives without our asking'. At 79, he was still in good voice. 'So they've made you a freeman of Hammersmith', was a fellow member's greeting on his next appearance at the Savage Club. 'You won't believe it', he replied, 'but only a few weeks ago they were dunning me for the rates!'

Recognition of his services to the larger comity was being considered. Influentially backed, his name had gone forward for a life peerage. As he was no Party man, his place in the queue of possible new peers may have been disgracefully low. Meanwhile, he was made a Companion of Honour. 'In action faithful and in honour clear.' He went to Buckingham Palace in February 1970 to be invested by the Queen. The Companions' motto was the subject of a letter to APH from the assistant private secretary, who informed him that Her Majesty was 'most grateful' to him for sending 'the lines by Pope on Addison' from which the motto was taken (9 February 1970).

His earlier dawdling approach to the task of writing his auto-biography was compelling him to exertions that were more taxing than he knew. He was 'working overtime to get the damn' thing finished' for the birthday date, handing sheet after sheet of pencilled manuscript to the latest of his secretaries, who, like her predecessors, was required to type to the music of Wagner, now 'mostly *Tristan*'.

Forcing himself to prodigious effort, he delivered a typescript extravagantly exceeding the stipulated length. He was put to the disagreeable necessity of cutting 'about 30,000 words'. Page proofs arrived with admirable dispatch. His perfunctory attention to them was all too obvious in the finally printed work. His exertions had brought on a recurrence of the nerve prostration that had been part of his medical history down the years. One morning he stumbled in from the riverside garden murmuring apprehensively: 'I think I'm all right', and half collapsed in the nearest chair. The medical verdict was that he had suffered an 'arterial spasm'.

Most of that spring and early summer he spent in the posture of a semi-invalid, not merely watching but affectionately observing the terrapins emerge from their winter sloth in the garden pool; the green increase of bud and bulb; the antics of the water birds on the river: a long overdue obeisance from one who had never shown more than a passing interest in the beauty and mystery of the natural scene.

'I will do my memory exercise', he would tell over-solicitous visitors to his bedside. He would then recite a sentence seventy words long as reassurance of unimpaired faculties. Given to reflection, not intro-spection, he regretted during that parenthetical phase never having written 'the great novel'. He wished also that he had 'made more of an impression' in the theatre. He sent in his resignation from the Thames Conservancy, the governing body of the river from Tedding-ton Weir to its Cotswold cradle and, according to him, of 'thousands of miles of tributary streams as well'. He had been dutiful and happy in his attendance at the monthly meetings, a proud unpaid servitor of the Board for thirty years, always on his up river trips proud to don his yachting cap with its Conservancy badge. Official acknowledgment of his services followed on Ministerial foolscap. 'No one could have done more to foster interest in the amenity value of the Thames.'

It was a matter of particular concern to Victor Bonham-Carter, general secretary of the Society of Authors, and his organizing committee, that by midsummer 1970 APH had recovered much of his old form. They had chosen the river as the setting for a spectacular celebration of his eightieth year. On the evening of 23 July, with his family and a host of friends and admirers, he went on board the chartered Thames steamer *Queen Elizabeth* for what was to be more than a pre-dated birthday party. Escorted by two vessels of the Royal Naval Reserve, the steamer moved down river from Cadogan Pier, Chelsea, on a stately progress to Greenwich.

At the House of Commons members waved greetings from their Terrace. Officers and crew of HMS *President* lined the deck at her Embankment mooring. There were salutes from passing tugboats. Down river, *Cutty Sark* was 'dressed overall' in his honour. At Greenwich, APH was welcomed by the Admiral President of the Royal Naval College, who conducted him to the Painted Hall, where he received enthusiastic laudations from his fellow authors. It was a splendidly successful occasion; for many of us memorable still.

Taking a cue from the recently televised series of *Misleading Cases*, *Punch* devised its own APH anniversary; his sixtieth year as a contributor. In the last week of August foreign tourists lingering in the precincts of St Paul's Cathedral stared in wonderment at a cow being led into the nearby branch of Barclay's Bank. 'Pay A. P. Herbert £5' was writ large on its left flank, with the signature of the editor of *Punch*. APH was present to cash the negotiable cow. It was honoured by the bank, whose spokesman hoped 'not to see the practice extended'.

APH's prominently displayed article in *The Times* on obscenity in the theatre (26 August 1970) was proof enough that his polemical powers were intact. 'Truly admirable', Compton Mackenzie wrote. 'I wish people would realise as the Romans did that manners and morals are interlocked. The founder of your school must have realised it.' That fellow octogenarian of his added:[6] 'I like to think that both of us have always fought the good fight. God bless you, dear Alan.' What was to be APH's last article in *Punch* appeared that week, a retrospective sketch recalling his apprentice years under Seaman and Knox.

He was one of the 'select few', as Roy Plomley recalls, to make a second appearance in the BBC's evergreen *Desert Island Discs* programme, another of the year's compliments. He made somewhat self-indulgent use of the opportunity, choosing songs from his own musical shows but also Walford Davies's *Solemn Melody*; Walter Widdop singing his heart out in The Prize Song from *The Master-singers*; and Malcolm Sargent's rearrangement of *Rule, Britannia*, which APH was amused to remember set a prominent man of the left, Aneurin Bevan, 'clapping like a Churchill' at 'the Proms'. For his castaway reading, he thought that 'two or three Dickens novels, bound together', would suffice.

Exceptional publishing speed ensured the appearance of his autobiography a few days ahead of his eightieth birthday, 24 September 1970. In spite of the lamentably lax proof reading, which suggested to his old friend of Oxford days, Harry Strauss (Lord Conesford, QC), that the printers had 'gone mad', *APH: His Life and Times* was widely and generously noticed, ridding him of any fear he may have had of renewed neglect. As a metropolitan author, he had good reason for satisfaction also in the recognition given him in the provincial press, where his initials were not the familiar insignia that they had been for so long in London. Unanimity of inference that he well and truly embodied Burke's injunction: 'Live pleasant', was complete. Above all, there was concerted acknowledgment of his tireless championship of the transcendent twentieth century human cause, the sanctity of the individual.

The autobiography was by no means wilful self-testimony to its author's own exceptional individuality. True, there were negations of the genuine humility that was part of the texture of his mind; for example, quoting the full marks given him for this and that achievement: the liberty could be allowed an eighty-year-old who in his prime had something to boast about and who rarely if ever did so. To be appreciated, relished even, by Chesterton and Kipling, Wells and Bennett, Galsworthy and Belloc, can be held to excuse a mild touch of vainglory.

The book amply endorsed the absence of the manic element from APH's temperament. Its equability, with or without the reinforcement of vitamins, deep breathing, and the eccentric sphincterial discipline, may have added to his length of days. He provided all too few clues to the growth of his mind or to his emotional development, prompting the significant reminder that his best book, *The Secret Battle*, re-issued that year, was written in circumstances of deep psychic distress. Never afterwards did he reach affinity with the great company of neurotics from whose torments most master-pieces have come.

APH: His Life and Times is neither confiding nor confessional. Chronicling his adventures on the slopes of the twin summits of Parnassus, it tells us that he never subscribed to the vulgar interpretation of success as getting rather than giving; that he placed integrity first among the social virtues, and regarded taking oneself too seriously as the prime human error. It also leaves us in no doubt of his answer to the oldest of metaphysical questions: Is life worth living?

A birthday eulogy of APH from Sir Robert Menzies appeared in *The Times* on 3 December 1970. 'He has enriched our lives and even the Statute Book. He more than any other writer of our time has perceived and expressed the fundamental capacity of our race to laugh at difficulties.' That good friend of his had written to *The Times*, he afterwards confided, 'with a twinge of conscience'. APH had referred 'most generously' to him in the autobiography, whereas in his own memoirs, which were about to be published, Sir Robert had not mentioned APH, 'feeling that it might be thought to have obituary significance'.

The year ended for APH in a crescendo of public and private celebrations. He received 'a standing ovation' at a banquet of publishers' representatives. BBC radio interviewed him, and broadcast nightly instalments of his novel *The House by the River*. He was seen to be in full enjoyment of an evening 'in the chair' at a Savage Club dinner. He had aged in appearance, in manner hardly at all. The look in his eyes was still that of one who had command of reserves of humour and tolerance and of formidable determination. He did not carry himself as if he had written his last article for *Punch*, his last book, or his last letter but one to *The Times*.

In the last days of 1970 he was taken to Middlesex Hospital for care after a seizure that affected his left side and arm. It did not deprive him of his capacity to fend off despondency. Inflicting the nurses with requests in French was one of the outlets for his natural buoyancy of spirit. Within six weeks he was home again, supported by pillows that ensured him a constant view of the Thames.

He had hoped in print to be spared 'a protracted ending'. Fate had it otherwise. His physical powers waned, with occasional waxings, through many months. In August 1971 he wrote his last letter to *The Times*, an appeal for parliamentary good manners in refraining from 'witty derision of the literary exertions of Mr Harold Wilson', whose political memoirs had just been published, and of the 'marine activities' of the Prime Minister, Edward Heath, leader of the British team competing successfully for the Admiral's Cup.

By then he was describing himself as 'a recumbent nuisance'. When a Chiswick neighbour, Lady Davidson, called to see him he extemporized the lines:

> There was an old man who said 'Damn!
> What the hell of a nuisance I am.
> The girls are so kind,
> They don't seem to mind.
> But - what the *hell* of a nuisance I am!'

His death on 11 November 1971 was marked by the rare personal mark of respect of a leading article in *The Times*, supplementing an obituary notice that sent him down to posterity as having done 'more than any man of his day to add to the gaiety of the nation'. The brief, boldly displayed obituary notice in *Punch* was illustrated by a photograph of him waving a benign farewell. For the memorial service on 6 December the church of St Martin-in-the-Fields was crowded to overflowing. APH had provided the epilogue, sung to Vivian Ellis's music, in the lines:

> This is not the end; this is but a beginning:
> When the fight is lost, there's a fight worth winning.
> Nothing is wasted, nothing is in vain:
> The seas roll over but the rocks remain.
> They can break man's happiness but not man's will:
> Little lamps of liberty will smoulder still,
> Till the trumpet sounds and we break the chain
> And the wings of the spirit ride the free air again.[6]

On 7 December the *Congressional Record* of the United States House of Representatives appeared with four pages of memorial tributes paid to APH by congressmen from Ohio, Missouri, West Virginia and Wisconsin. Included in their speeches were long excerpts from *Misleading Cases* popular among American lawyers. The 'gentleman from Missouri' (Mr Hungate) observed that though 'Sir Alan P. Herbert, the man, is gone, his legacy to mankind lives on. His style, his humour will continue to give us the tremendous opportunity to look at ourselves, our laws, and our civilization, and not to be afraid to laugh at ourselves.' The 'gentleman from West Virginia' (Mr Hechler) referred to APH as 'a sight of London, like St Paul's, though he wears his dome at the side. He has written verse not equalled since Praed. He has graven his name into English law. He wanted only a Sullivan and a bad temper to beat Gilbert at his own game.' The 'gentleman from Wisconsin' (Mr Reuss) recalled that 'one of the characters in Herbert's musical *Bless the Bride* is provoked to exclaim in song: "If I'd only done the things I thought of doing, What a lot of splendid things I should have done". No such qualms for A. P. Herbert. He did the things he thought of doing.' Another of the speakers, Mr Monaghan, expressed as a summarizing sentiment: 'A. P. Herbert has left us after brightening our lives for far longer than the span allotted the average man. We shall not read his pieces any more but he passes on leaving behind a notable record of legal, political, legislative, and literary achievement.'

Robert H. Land, Chief of the Reference Department, General Reference and Bibliography Division, The Library of Congress, has written: 'Neither the Clerk of the *Congressional Record* nor the Research Department of the *Congressional Quarterly* has any record or recollection of a similar tribute to another English writer in the proceedings of Congress' (Letter, 19 August 1974).

NOTES ON CHAPTER 26

1 Three series of *Misleading Cases* were televised, in 1967, 1968, and 1971.
2 On 30 April 1969 *The Times* announced that John Silkin had been replaced by Robert Mellish.
3 The Bodley Head (1970), 'price 6s'.
4 *APH: His Life and Times.*
5 *The Times*, 4 November 1969.
6 From *Tough at the Top* (1949).

Index

In order to avoid a large entry under A. P. Herbert references have been made to a particular subject wherever possible. The first paragraph of entries under his name refers to items about him which do not fit easily into the sub-headings which follow it. In other sub-headings throughout the index A. P. Herbert is abbreviated to APH.